News Frames and National Security
Covering Big Brother

Did media coverage contribute to Americans' tendency to favor national security over civil liberties following the 9/11 attacks? How did news framing of terrorist threats support the expanding surveillance state revealed by Edward Snowden? Douglas M. McLeod and Dhavan V. Shah explore the power of news coverage to render targeted groups suspicious and to spur support for government surveillance. They argue that the tendency of journalists to frame stories around individual targets of surveillance – personifying the domestic threat – shapes citizens' judgments about tolerance and participation, leading them to limit the civil liberties of a range of groups under scrutiny and to support "Big Brother."

Douglas M. McLeod is the Evjue Centennial Professor in the School of Journalism and Mass Communication at the University of Wisconsin–Madison. His research centers on communication content and effects, particularly in political contexts, focusing on social conflicts and the mass media as well as framing and priming effects on attitudes and behaviors.

Dhavan V. Shah is the Louis A. & Mary E. Maier-Bascom Professor at the University of Wisconsin–Madison, where he is Director of the Mass Communication Research Center. His work focuses on framing effects on social judgments, digital media influence on civic and political engagement, and the impact of health information and communication technologies.

Communication, Society and Politics

Editors
W. Lance Bennett, *University of Washington*
Robert M. Entman, *The George Washington University*

Politics and relations among individuals in societies across the world are being transformed by new technologies for targeting individuals and sophisticated methods for shaping personalized messages. The new technologies challenge boundaries of many kinds – between news, information, entertainment, and advertising; between media, with the arrival of the World Wide Web; and even between nations. Communication, Society and Politics probes the political and social impacts of these new communication systems in national, comparative, and global perspective.

Other Books in the Series

(*continued after the Index*)

News Frames and National Security

Covering Big Brother

DOUGLAS M. McLEOD
University of Wisconsin–Madison

DHAVAN V. SHAH
University of Wisconsin–Madison

CAMBRIDGE
UNIVERSITY PRESS

32 Avenue of the Americas, New York, NY 10013-2473, USA

Cambridge University Press is part of the University of Cambridge.

It furthers the University's mission by disseminating knowledge in the pursuit of education, learning, and research at the highest international levels of excellence.

www.cambridge.org
Information on this title: www.cambridge.org/9780521130554

© Douglas M. McLeod and Dhavan V. Shah 2015

First published 2015

Printed in the United States of America

A catalog record for this publication is available from the British Library.

Library of Congress Cataloging in Publication Data
McLeod, Douglas Malcolm.
News frames and national security : covering big brother / Douglas M. McLeod, University of Wisconsin, Madison; Dhavan V. Shah, University of Wisconsin, Madison.
    pages cm. – (Communication, society and politics)
Includes bibliographical references and index.
ISBN 978-0-521-11359-5 (hardback) – ISBN 978-0-521-13055-4 (paperback)
    1. Mass media – Political aspects – United States.   2. Mass media – Influence – Case studies.
3. Mass media policy – United States.   4. Communication in politics – United States.
5. National security – United States.   6. Terrorism – United States – Prevention.   7. Electronic surveillance – United States – Public opinion.   8. Privacy, Right of – Public opinion.   9. Civil rights – United States.   I. Shah, Dhavan V.   II. Title.
P95.82.U6M384   2014
302.230973 – dc23   2014017800

ISBN 978-0-521-11359-5 Hardback
ISBN 978-0-521-13055-4 Paperback

Contents

Preface and Acknowledgments

When this story began more than a decade ago in the early fall of 2001, we were relatively new professors at the University of Wisconsin. We were in the process of launching a research collaboration that has lasted to this day. We were on our way to work when a report came over the radio that a second plane had struck the World Trade Center. Within the hour, we were both at work watching CNN in a conference room along with other faculty, staff, and students. Like everyone else in the room – and so many others across the country – we sensed that the world was about to change.

What we didn't know was how profound this change would be, nor that we would spend the next decade writing this book that focuses on one particular aspect of this change, the War on Terror, how it was covered in the media, and the effects that this coverage had on the public. But we did know that the public opinion survey that we were planning was going to have to be redesigned to deal with public reactions to the 9/11 attacks. As the ensuing weeks unfolded, we read news reports about the federal government's reorganization of its various intelligence agencies, as well as proposed legislation that would allow them to fight terrorism more effectively. This legislation, dubbed the PATRIOT Act, was passed overwhelmingly by both the House and Senate and signed into law by President Bush on October 26, 2001, only 45 days after the 9/11 terrorist attacks.

Throughout the fall of 2001, we encountered the concerns of civil libertarians, who warned that the PATRIOT Act would violate the civil liberties of innocent Americans, particularly political activists and Arab-Americans. Alarmed at this prospect, and curious as to how this concern might be received by the public, we began planning a series of experimental studies in the summer of 2002, work that continued through the spring of 2004. These experiments collected the data that we analyzed for the framing studies reported in the later chapters of this book. At the time, we worried that our experimental stimuli, hypothetical news stories about how the government was using the PATRIOT Act to engage in the surveillance of peaceful groups, innocent of plotting or executing acts of terrorism, might be seen as far-fetched scenarios. But then, during this period, more to our dismay than relief, news reports began to trickle out that confirmed suspicions that the PATRIOT Act was being extended beyond investigating potential terrorists to conduct surveillance of Arab immigrants and citizens as well as political activists.

Initially, these revelations spurred our sense of urgency to develop the results of our research into what ultimately became this book. As we were doing so, reports indicating that the scope of surveillance might actually include a broader cross section of Americans, not just terrorism suspects, came out in 2006 and 2007. As we drafted and revised the book, we waited to see if President Obama would roll back the PATRIOT Act and government surveillance when he took office in 2008, as he had campaigned he would. When we spoke to reporter Eric Lichtblau prior to the election, he warned us that Obama would not cede the powers provided by the PATRIOT Act. And indeed, he did not. As we recast the book to consider a prolonged climate of fear and an ongoing War on Terror, other revelations shifted our thinking regarding the findings and the book. In 2010, the *Washington Post* had published a series of reports under the title of *Top Secret America,* which detailed just how massive the government's national security system had grown to be. These reports strengthened and supported the claims of our research, leading us to revise the book to include them. Yet we also felt a certain unease that there was more information to come. And there was. In 2013, Eric Snowden leaked documents to major news organizations detailing the true size and scope of the surveillance state. Big Brother was watching, and he was watching all of us. Shortly into 2014, even President Obama had to admit that the government surveillance had gone too far and was in need of greater oversight. With that decision, the arc of our story was sufficiently complete, with the surveillance state and its toll on civil liberties being questioned in earnest.

It is this fundamental tension between national security and civil liberties that is at the heart of this book. As we note in Chapter 2, external conflicts and domestic threats often push the pendulum of the national agenda, including government policy and public opinion, in the direction of national security. As time passes, and the conflict or threat subsides, the pendulum often swings back toward civil liberties. In the aftermath of 9/11, we expected the pendulum to swing back relatively quickly but were struck by how long it took this to occur. To be sure, the 9/11 attacks as well as the PATRIOT Act and its application have raised the stakes and complicated these processes unlike anything we have seen before in American history. What is starkly clear is that the news media played an important role in this story, both in terms of what they reported and how they reported it – how they "covered" the PATRIOT Act. The research that is the subject of this book represents an exploration into the role that the media play as an intermediary between the political actors and the larger public in understanding how this law has been applied.

We chose the subtitle for this book, *Covering Big Brother*, because the two alternative readings of the title reflect the two strokes of the pendulum in the tension between national security and civil liberties. First, we mean it in the sense that, particularly in the first decade after 9/11, the largely complacent mainstream media were essentially covering *for* Big Brother by allowing elites to frame the issue of terrorism around individual exemplars while the pendulum swung out toward national security. But more recently, with the help of key whistleblowers, elite journalists became more active in performing their watchdog function in covering Big Brother's activities and abuses as the pendulum began to swing back toward civil liberties.

As important as these insights regarding the swing of the pendulum between national security and civil liberties may be, we believe that an equally important contribution of this book arises from the various ways in which we reconceptualize framing theory to provide direction for future research on media effects. The conventional approach sees the news frame as a "story-level" concept, a characteristic of a news story as a whole, under which information and facts are assembled into a package that connotes a particular meaning and fosters certain cognitive, affective, and behavioral outcomes. This approach also raises certain complications for effects researchers; most notably, how do we identify and isolate the frame of the story for subsequent experimental effects testing?

Framing effects researchers have taken different approaches to answering this question. Some scholars advance specific frames that are narrowly tied to the story in question (e.g., a global warming frame), whereas others use transcendent frames, which are applicable across a wide variety of story contexts (e.g., an ethical frame). In addition, some work argues for an idealist conception of frames, manipulating the story frame in isolation while holding all other information constant, whereas other work advances a pragmatic conception of frames, in which accompanying features and facts strengthen and support the frame. While the goals of the former approach are laudable in terms of internal validity concerns, there are two limitations that impede their advancement. First, it may be impossible to identify exactly what content feature constitutes the frame, and thus, it may not be feasible to manipulate only the frame. Second, we realize that frames may derive their true power through their co-occurrence with the facts and other information that fit them.

The research presented in the middle section of the book that examines these issues was a product of the Mass Communication Research Center (MCRC) at the University of Wisconsin–Madison. Though literally hundreds of graduate students have been involved in MCRC projects since it was founded by Ralph Nafziger in 1959, very few outsiders, including many of our own colleagues, truly understand the MCRC, what it is, and what it does. To put it simply, the MCRC is more of a pedagogical philosophy than it is an institution, an organization, or even a place. The MCRC pedagogy is based on the premise that the best way to learn theory and research is to do it, and to do it collaboratively, in a open peer-learning environment.

Jack McLeod, who was brought into the MCRC by Percy Tannenbaum in the early 1960s, instilled this pedagogical philosophy. In 1966, McLeod took over the leadership of the MCRC and guided teams of graduate student researchers through the yearlong process of designing, executing, analyzing, and publishing research based on community surveys that were conducted each fall on an annual basis. These efforts yielded scores of influential publications in the field of political communication research. Perhaps even more important than that, these projects involved dozens and dozens of graduate (and undergraduate) students, training them in the finer points of social science research, and launching many successful careers in research and academia. Over the years, the MCRC developed the collaborative culture of which we were the beneficiaries when Jack McLeod retired at the end of 2000.

Our first turn as faculty mentors of the MCRC was in the fall of 2001. Indeed, it was only about a week into our stint that a group of terrorists set out to hijack four airplanes. This tragedy and its aftermath became the focal point of our political communication research and output for the next five years. During this time, we were blessed with a large of group of bright and dedicated graduate students, many of whom are co-authors on the research chapters of this book. Through these 9/11 data collections, we were able to witness the benefits of MCRC collaborations. We trained and learned from many outstanding scholars, almost all of whom are now rising stars in political communication. Those students honed their research skills working on this project. As graduate student collaborators, they learned about research through painstaking, and at times agonizing, deliberations over even the smallest of research details. We recall (admittedly somewhat fondly) several incidents in which the intensity of this work led to some heated debates and internal battles among the students. But the output of this process is high-quality research, proof that good graduate training and groundbreaking scholarship can go hand-in-hand. And we would be remiss if we did not acknowledge that students are not the only ones who learn from this collaboration. Very often, we learn just as much from the graduate students, who bring new techniques, the latest research, and fresh ideas to these collaborations.

To be sure, the MCRC was, and remains today, a vibrant laboratory for learning about the practice of research. Fueled by collaboration, sweat equity, and a desire for learning, the participants continue to do high-quality, multi-method, theoretically grounded research that is making important contributions to the field. While this is certainly not the fastest way to produce research, we personally feel it is the best way to both generate knowledge and mentor scholars.

Acknowledgments

Before we close this preface, we want to acknowledge those who have shaped the development of our respective careers and research programs. Sadly, we cannot identify all of them here, as the list is far too long. We apologize for any inadvertent omissions.

But before we do that, we must first thank the editors of the Communication, Society and Politics series, Lance Bennett and Robert Entman, for both their patience and their guidance. Thanks also to Lewis Bateman and Shaun Vigil of Cambridge University Press, who served as our principal editor and senior editorial assistant, respectively, and moved this volume from the proposal stage though the production process. We also thank Mark Mastromarino for his assistance with our manuscript indexing.

We are also grateful to the University of Wisconsin for various forms of support that made this research possible, including the Vilas Associates Award and the Journal Communications/Warren J. Heyse Faculty Excellence Award. Both of us were grateful recipients of each of these awards, which supported us during the research for this book. During the writing of this book, we were supported by our respective chaired professorships, the Evjue Centennial Professorship (Doug) and the Louis A. & Mary E. Maier-Bascom Professorship (Dhavan). Other sources of support, such as the College of Letters and Science Hamel Faculty Fellowship, were also critical to this undertaking.

We were the beneficiaries of the efforts of many individuals who contributed invaluable assistance to this book. First and foremost, we thank the graduate students who were members of the MCRC during the period when this research was conducted. Among them are the following scholars, whose names we are proud to list with us on the chapters in the Framing Effects Research section of this book because of the integral roles they played in the design, execution, and analysis of this research: Cory L. Armstrong, Lucy Atkinson, Michael P. Boyle, Jaeho Cho, Homero Gil de Zuniga, Hyunseo Hwang, Heejo Keum, Nam-Jin Lee, Seungahn Nah, Hernando Rojas, and Michael G. Schmierbach.

Three of the chapters in this section had their origination in articles published with our co-authors in *Communication Research* (Sage Publications), *Human Communication Research* (Wiley), and *Journal of Communication* (Wiley). Accordingly, we thank Sage and Wiley for granting us permission to reengage with that earlier work in this book. Chapter 4 draws and expands upon "Cue Convergence: Associative Effects on Social Intolerance," which was originally published in *Communication Research* in June 2006. Likewise, Chapter 6 further develops ideas initially engaged in "Personifying the Radical: How News Framing Polarizes Security Concerns and Tolerance Judgments," which appeared in the July 2005 issue of *Human Communication Research*. Finally, Chapter 7 extends work presented in "Expressive Responses to News Stories About Extremist Groups: A Framing Experiment," which was published by *Journal of Communication* in June 2006. Although our analyses and interpretations have changed, these pieces served as the starting points for this book.

We are also grateful for the involvement and feedback of Elliott Hillback, Tom Hove, Michael McCluskey, and Chris Long, who were also graduate students at UW-Madison during the time that this research was conducted.

We extend special gratitude to three of our former students: Melissa Gotlieb for her thorough proofreading of drafts, Porismitah Borah for her work on the manual content analysis, and Ben Sayre for his work on the computer content analysis. We also thank our colleagues, Jim Baughman, Jim Danky, Don Downs, and Bob Drechsel, for their valuable insights into the history of the tension between national security and civil liberties.

A special thank you goes out to our graduate school advisors at the University of Minnesota, Phil Tichenor and Dan Wackman, who prepared us well for our professional careers – as researchers, teachers, mentors, and colleagues. Since taking faculty positions, we have continued to receive excellent mentoring and guidance from numerous current and former colleagues. And, as we have assumed our own roles as mentors, we consider ourselves lucky to have been able to work with many wonderful graduate and undergraduate students, who have made what we do enjoyable. Our early collaborators on framing research, Ben Detenber, David Domke, David Fan, Jim Hertog, Amy Jasperson, Olga Malinkina, and Mark Watts, had a profound effect on our thinking.

The countless hours spent discussing the nature of communication influence with our colleagues at the UW – Michael Pfau, Robert Hawkins, Sharon Dunwoody, Lew Friedland, Hemant Shah, Zhongdang Pan, Al Gunther, Ken Goldstein, Barry Burden, Kathy Cramer, and Charles Franklin – have been invaluable for our thinking in this book and beyond. We are also grateful for the thoughts and perspectives of political communication scholars at other universities, especially Bruce Bimber, Joe Cappella, Robert Craig, Claes de Vreese, Jamie Druckman, Chip Eveland, Ron Faber, Rod Hart, Lance Holbert, Gerald M. Kosicki, Nojin Kwak, Jenny Lambe, Jörg Matthes, Elizabeth Perse, Jochen Peter, Vince Price, Steve Reese, Nancy Signorielli, David Tewksbury, and Younchul Yoon.

But ultimately, we couldn't have done this book without many good friends and family members who have stood by us over the years. We are deeply grateful to have been part of such wonderful families, who have provided daily support and inspiration over the years. Dhavan thanks his wife Christine, who has been his toughest critic and staunchest supporter, his wonderful kids Gabriel and Isabel, and his mother, Dharmishtha, and father, Vinod, who instilled in him a love of learning and a commitment to research. Doug thanks his partner Kathryn Otto, his sons Ethan, Dylan, Aidan, and J.J., his sister Katy, his cousin Johnny, his mother Donna, and certainly not least, his father Jack, to whom Dhavan owes a debt as well.

Finally, we would like to thank the heroes of this story. In an era when the institutions of journalism are being threatened by financial pressures that have imposed severe cutbacks on news organizations, including the dismantling of investigative units, a small cadre of reporters doggedly pursued the story of the expanding surveillance apparatus of the federal government. Particularly prominent were Eric Lichtblau and Charles Savage of *The New York Times*; Michael Isikoff of *Newsweek*; Dana Priest, William Arkin, and

Barton Gellman of the *Washington Post*; and Glenn Greenwald of *Salon.com* and *The Guardian*.

But, of course, this story did not come out through the efforts of investigative journalists alone. The journalists were fed information from sources, many of whom remain anonymous. Whistleblowers, such as William Binney and Edward Snowden, who observed what they felt was an egregious violation of civil liberties, exhibited extreme courage in standing up and sharing information and substantiating documents. They came forward at considerable professional and personal sacrifice. They were branded as traitors, lost their livelihoods, had their homes invaded, and, in the case of Snowden, had to leave his home country altogether.

Without the efforts of intrepid journalists and conscientious whistleblowers, most of what we know about the extent of domestic surveillance might still be buried. The stories about Big Brother's activities that were told through the media, even those that personalized surveillance by highlighting individual targets, eventually let the pendulum swing back far enough that the powerful individuals within the power structure began to take civil liberties infringements seriously. Without the pressure from that pendulum swing, President Obama might never have acknowledged that "high-tech surveillance poses a threat to civil liberties" in his announcement that he intends to impose greater oversight and restrictions on the NSA's domestic spying activities. Ultimately, these news reports lifted the veil on Big Brother's surveillance activities, doing what the news media are supposed to do in their role as the fourth estate, providing a check on the activities of government. In the process, they confirmed what we only feared was possible when we embarked on this research.

Introduction

News, National Security, and Civil Liberties

"After September the eleventh, I vowed to the American people that our government would do everything within the law to protect them against another terrorist attack. As part of this effort, I authorized the National Security Agency to intercept the international communications of people with known links to al Qaeda and related terrorist organizations. In other words, if al Qaeda or their associates are making calls into the United States or out of the United States, we want to know what they're saying."

– President George W. Bush
May 11, 2006

"Last December, the *Times* reported that the N.S.A. was listening in on calls between people in the United States and people in other countries, and a few weeks ago *USA Today* reported that the agency was collecting information on millions of private domestic calls.... The N.S.A. began, in some cases, to eavesdrop on callers (often using computers to listen for key words) or to investigate them using traditional police methods. A government consultant told me that tens of thousands of Americans had had their calls monitored in one way or the other."

– Seymour M. Hersh
The New Yorker
May 22, 2006

These opening statements reflect fundamental, yet opposing, concerns in what has been one of the most important postmillennial debates for American democracy, the tradeoff between protecting national security and defending civil liberties. Though this debate has been evident since the dawn of U.S. history, the terrorist attacks of September 11, 2001 raised its intensity to an unprecedented level, as the course of both foreign and domestic policy have been substantially altered. On the international front, these attacks led to protracted wars in Afghanistan and Iraq. On the home front, and central to the focus of this book, the Bush administration pushed the USA PATRIOT Act (officially titled the Uniting and Strengthening America by Providing Appropriate Tools Required to Intercept and Obstruct Terrorism Act) through Congress on October 25, 2001, substantially expanding the government's surveillance powers in ways that were unimagined at the time of its inception. Since that time, the law has been reauthorized twice, first in July 2005 and again in May 2011, with the key provisions now extended until June 2015. This law thrust the debate to the center of the American political stage, as policymakers, activists, and citizens considered the steps taken to prevent another terrorist attack.

The public visibility of this debate steadily gained intensity in the years that immediately followed the 9/11 attacks, but then began to subside toward the end of the decade. It is important to note that the declining visibility was not a function of a shift in policy accompanying the change in presidential administrations. In fact, the Obama administration "left the surveillance program intact [and] embraced the PATRIOT Act" (Baker, 2010). Though the public visibility of the debate was relatively dormant around the turn of the decade, prominent politicians from both parties expressed continued concern that the government was exceeding its authority in engaging in domestic surveillance. During the most recent debate over extending the PATRIOT Act in 2011, Senator Ron Wyden, Oregon Democrat and member of the Intelligence Committee, stated, "When the American people find out how their government has secretly interpreted the Patriot Act, they will be stunned and they will be angry" (Savage, 2011). Likewise, Senator Rand Paul, Kentucky Republican, argued, "We were so frightened after 9/11 that we readily gave up these freedoms. Not only would I let these expire, but I think we should sunset the entire PATRIOT Act" (Associated Press, 2011).

In 2013, two major news events catapulted the issue of domestic surveillance back into the public limelight. First, on April 15, two bombs exploded near the finish line of the Boston Marathon, killing three people and injuring another 264. Various security cameras captured the perpetrators in the vicinity, leading to the identification of the suspects and a massive manhunt. These bombings were the worst terrorist attack on U.S. soil since the events of September 11, 2001, reinvigorating calls for government surveillance powers in the name of protecting national security.

Two months later, major U.S. media organizations began breaking a series of stories based on leaked government documents, which indicated that the scope of the government's domestic surveillance programs went far beyond what was commonly believed, both in terms of the intrusiveness of their tactics and scope in terms of who and what was being scrutinized. At the heart of these leaks was former CIA employee and NSA contractor Edward Snowden. Snowden was vilified in some circles as a significant threat to domestic security and hailed in others as a champion of civil liberties (Klein, 2013).

The Boston bombings and the Snowden leaks raised additional debate over the appropriate extent and scope of antiterrorism measures. Among the persistent questions surrounding the PATRIOT Act are: What kinds of surveillance activities was the government pursuing, against what kinds of groups, and who would define the legal limits of these new powers? These queries have led to deeper questions about what kinds of surveillance techniques are acceptable for use in a democratic society, what the American citizenry will tolerate with regard to the reduction of civic liberties, and whether this would differ depending on what kinds of groups and individuals are being targeted.

Despite the high volume of stories about the government's domestic surveillance activities, only a minority of Americans expressed concern that the government has "gone too far in restricting the average person's civil liberties," with 46% of registered voters nationwide expressing this view in a July 29–31 Quinnipiac University Poll. Contrary to the belief that the public would grow angry when it learned about surveillance abuses, criticism of PATRIOT Act activities has been relatively muted. Indeed, more than half of those polled expressed support for federal surveillance programs, indicating they are necessary to "keep Americans safe" (Quinnipiac University Poll, July 29–31). Thus, even when the dragnet monitoring policies came to light, most people accepted these practices as an expected cost of life after the 9/11 attacks, likely as a result of how the threat of terrorism was presented to the public through the press.

As the epigraphs indicate, the press framed this debate in ways that only at times questioned the limits of government power, with journalists giving voice to the perspectives of the administration with comparatively less attention to their critics. It is the relationship between the press, politics, and public policy that is the focus of this book. The research reported herein looks at how the nature of news coverage of these surveillance efforts affects audience thoughts about the controversy, tolerance toward the targets of government action, and responses to government power. We contend that the way that journalists have chosen to cover the threat of terrorism seems to have contributed to public acceptance of the erosion of civil liberties.

With the passage of the PATRIOT Act, critics rallied in opposition, first decrying the erosion of civil liberties and more recently contending that the surveillance provisions have been misused. Indeed, news reports have revealed that the FBI, under the Bush administration, applied provisions of the PATRIOT Act to monitor civil rights, antiwar, environmental, and other progressive advocacy groups, maintaining thousands of pages of documents on these legal, mainstream organizations. Under the Obama administration, these same policies have been applied to conservative groups such as citizen militias, Christian activists, and the Tea Party (Priest and Arkin, 2010a), and now, according to the Snowden revelations, to journalists, political elites, and even to the general public. Prior to Snowden's leaks regarding the secret NSA surveillance programs, analysis by the Electronic Frontier Foundation indicates that the FBI may have committed more than 40,000 possible intelligence violations since being granted these new powers (Rumold, 2011, January 30). Since that time, it has become clear that government surveillance was far more extensive, touching nearly every American citizen. Given the extent of these monitoring activities, public response to these revelations has been surprisingly muted, which we believe can be explained by the patterns of news production and the effects of resultant news coverage. Specifically, the personification of threats (from Osama bin Laden to Khalid Sheikh Mohammed, from Julian Assange to Edward Snowden) has figured large in the framing of terrorism policy.

This book, then, explores the effects of the media in this domestic front of the War on Terror asking questions of central importance to the fields of communication, political science, psychology, and sociology in post-9/11 America: How does news coverage concerning government scrutiny of individuals and groups shape citizens' thoughts and actions concerning the tension between national security and civil liberties? Under what conditions is a citizenry that values liberty willing to sacrifice these basic freedoms in the name of security? Do the frames favored by journalists and editors reduce tolerance toward outgroups and constrain participation in defense of civil liberties? Does it matter who is presented as the targets of surveillance? Do singular targets, by accentuating fear and minimizing the scope of government surveillance and resulting media coverage, make it easier for the public to accept the erosion of civil liberties?

We explore a range of answers to these queries guided by two integrated models of communication framing. The first model, the Message Framing Model (MFM), connects communication framing to different levels of the message system – from the language cues used to label issues and groups, to the news frames used to organize press accounts. Our second model, the Message Processing Model (MPM), synthesizes concepts identified by past research into a comprehensive model of how messages are processed, and links these processes to effects on a wide range of thoughts, feelings, judgments, and actions. Together, these models clarify a media effects process that remains fractured and disparate with different definitions and theoretical explanations for what framing is and how it works. As such, they unify a variety of communication phenomena concerning message effects on individual responses, ranging from the micropsychological to the social-behavioral. These models, which we develop and then test through a series of experimental studies, are the central theoretical contribution of the book.

In applying these models to our research, we focus our attention on the journalistic practice of framing news stories around individual exemplars. That is, journalists tend to personalize news stories about social issues and problems by framing stories around specific cases for the purpose of illustration, which may shift emphasis away from the broader implications of the issue. We focus on this individual vs. collective framing distinction because we believe that it is particularly consequential for social tolerance and related democratic judgments. Personifying frames, as opposed to generalizing ones, are thought to shape attributional processes and alter the spread of activation through memory (Iyengar, 1991). As such, this work not only has relevance for scholars studying political culture, national security, and civil liberties after 9/11, but also broadly informs all explorations of citizen sensitivity to communication framing, and the conditions under which responsiveness to framing devices is most pronounced. The results of our efforts specifically add to our understanding of political communication, media psychology, news sociology, and democratic theory.

Our conclusions are based on a series of experimental studies that investigate how the construction of news stories, more specifically the framing of language in news texts, influences audience members' news processing, interpretations, attitudes, and behavioral intentions. This research yields a set of findings and implications relevant to a wide range of audiences, including policy makers, working journalists, academic researchers, and graduate and undergraduate students in a range of disciplines. It weaves together several of the most active areas of political communication, media psychology, and news sociology research, including the conditional nature of news framing and cueing effects, the political sophistication of citizens, the sources of social prejudice, and the nature of political participation, examining them in the context of this highly salient debate from contemporary American society. We use these findings to further revise and expand our theoretical models of communication influence.

Outline of Book

The book consists of eight chapters. Chapter 1 provides our theoretical overview and presents a new framework for understanding communication framing effects. It is here that we present and detail the two models, the Message Framing Model (MFM) and the Message Processing Model (MPM), that guide the research contained in this book. Chapter 2 discusses the context of this research and the implications of our models for a range of democratic outcomes related to the debate between national security and civil liberties. In particular, we focus on three core citizen competencies: the sophistication and integration of political cognitions, the nature of political tolerance judgments, and the degree of political engagement. Chapter 3 covers elements of our research design and concept explication for our experimental research on framing in the context of the domestic War on Terror.

The next four chapters present the results of our research. The research chapters are clustered around the potential consequences of media framing for the citizen competencies mentioned earlier: political sophistication, social tolerance, and political participation. Each of these chapters, which are co-authored by graduate students who worked on our research team (all of whom are now faculty members at other universities), explores the effects of communication framing – both the direct and conditional influences – in theory-driven yet innovative ways. Chapter 4 examines the interactive effects of frames and cues on indicators of the spread of activation through memory, specifically attitudinal consistency and response latency, as they relate to tolerance toward Arabs in the United States. Chapter 5 explores the impact of framing on the complexity of attitude formation regarding the national security/civil liberties conflict. Chapter 6 considers the interplay of framing and political predispositions on tolerance toward various activists groups, focusing on how individual framing polarizes tolerance judgments both in support of and in opposition to political groups. Chapter 7 investigates framing effects on willingness to take expressive political action in support of or in opposition to the targets of government surveillance, reflecting orientations toward national security and civil liberties.

The concluding chapter synthesizes our research findings and discusses their broader social and political implications. Ultimately, this book provides an organizing framework for examining framing effects, an important, yet fragmented, area of mass communication research. We illustrate this framework by contributing innovative, original research to the existing literature on framing effects conducted in the context of the defining political issue of our time, the tension between protecting national security and honoring civil liberties. At the same time, we believe this application of framing theory provides unique insights into public acceptance of the erosion of civil liberties in the wake of the 9/11 attacks, as the modes in which the news media presented the threat of domestic terrorism implicitly supported national security efforts.

PART I

CONCEPTUAL FRAMEWORK

Understanding Message Framing and Effects

"Ever since the 1970s, when Army intel agents were caught snooping on antiwar protesters, military intel agencies have operated under tight restrictions inside the United States. But the new provision (Senate Bill S.2386, Sec. 502), approved in closed session last month by the Senate Intelligence Committee, would eliminate one big restriction: that they comply with the Privacy Act, a Watergate-era law that requires government officials seeking information from a resident to disclose who they are and what they want the information for."

– Michael Isikoff
Newsweek Magazine
June 21, 2004

"Among the Americans who complain about the Patriot Act, Mohammad Junaid Babar probably dislikes it more than most. Absent that often-criticized federal statute, Babar still might stroll the sidewalks of New York, gathering money and equipment for al Qaeda. According to the unsealed transcript of his June 3 appearance before U.S. District Judge Victor Marrero, Babar pleaded guilty to five counts of furnishing 'material support or resources to a foreign terrorist organization.'"

– Deroy Murdock
The National Review
October 25, 2004

Both of these passages from magazine articles – the first from *Newsweek* and the second from the *National Review* – discuss the implications of domestic surveillance activities by U.S. government agencies. But this is where the similarity ends. These two excerpts represent two very different ways of telling a story about government surveillance. One obvious difference is that the first excerpt emphasizes the issue of civil liberties, while the second emphasizes the issue of national security. In addition, the stories illustrate two different common targets of government scrutiny: activist groups and Arab groups. But a more subtle difference is that the first story addresses the broader policy implications of surveillance in relation to large groups, while the second focuses on a single, potentially dangerous individual.

The differences in these stories raise a number of questions: Would audience members react differently depending on which of these stories they encountered about the debate over domestic security and civil liberties? How would the frame of the news story, whether it organized the issue around individuals or collectives, shape reactions of audience members? Are audience members more likely to favor national security over personal freedoms when seeing individuals or collectives targeted under the PATRIOT Act? This book shares insights from research designed to answer questions about the influence of such stories – news content concerning the surveillance of collectives or individuals, both domestic and international.

The answers to these questions are particularly important in a period when government surveillance of U.S. citizens has reached unprecedented levels. FBI agents have infiltrated groups of antiwar protesters to surveil their activities. The military has held over 500 suspected terrorists at Guantanamo Bay, including some who are U.S citizens. It was initially revealed that the NSA and other intelligence gathering units within the U.S. government were maintaining databases of over 300,000 individuals and tracking the phone calls of millions of others. Bank transactions and e-mail communications are also being monitored (Priest and Arkin, 2010a,b). More recently, leaks by Edward Snowden have made clear "the vast scope of the National Security Agency's reach into the lives of hundreds of millions of people in the United States and around the globe, as it collects information about their phone calls, their e-mail messages, their friends and contacts, how they spend their days, and where they spend their nights" (*New York Times*, 2014, January 1).

We contend that whether audience members respond with silence and support for these activities, or with outrage and opposition, is, in part, a function of how the news media frame this issue and the ways they depict implications of particular avenues of action. The research in this book explores these issues. Our research is based on two large experimental studies examining the effects of news stories about government surveillance of "terrorists" under the auspices of the USA PATRIOT Act. Certain features of the news stories, such as the story frame, were systematically altered so that we could examine how audiences would respond to different versions of the story. This research follows a tradition of inquiry that has been rather loosely organized under the label of framing effects research. This tradition of scholarship has long been fragmented, by some accounts "fractured" (Entman, 1993), and continues to require clarification and cohesion. In this chapter, we begin by providing an underlying theoretical structure to organize extant framing research and then use this structure to situate and guide this experimental research.

We begin by providing a typology that organizes and clarifies the different strands of framing research found in communication, psychology, sociology, and political science. We build on some recent efforts to codify frame distinctions, both extending and specifying this prior work (D'Angelo, 2010; de Vreese, 2005; Matthes, 2009; Shah et al., 2009). Beginning with Pan and Kosicki (1993), followed by Kinder and Sanders (1996), Shah et al. (1996), and a range of other scholars (see Druckman, 2001; Chong & Druckman, 2007b; Scheufele and Tewksbury, 2007) have highlighted the distinction between frames in communication texts and frames in thought. This distinction has often been crossed with other categorization schemes to generate typologies to organize research, including efforts to distinguish between "generic and issue-specific frames" (de Vreese, 2005) to examine "precision versus realism" on the framing continuum (Vraga et al., 2010).

These typologies exist beyond the numerous frame distinctions that have been offered by scholars over the last three decades: gain versus loss (Tversky and Kahneman, 1981), episodic versus thematic (Iyengar, 1991), ethical versus material (Shah et al., 1996), and strategy versus policy (Cappella and Jamieson, 1997; Lawrence, 2000), along with the dozens of frame categorizations that are particular to a certain issue or class of issues. Along these lines, existing definitions of what constitutes a frame are explored with research that represents common approaches to framing effects categorized into our conceptual framework. Ultimately, our review of this literature leads to the development of two new models that integrate the processes of framing and priming effects: the Message Framing Model (MFM) and the Message Processing Model (MPM). These models present our perspective on frame building (how frames become manifest in texts) and frame setting (how frames come to influence thought), identifying the factors that amplify and attenuate such processes and effects (de Vreese, 2005; Brewer and Gross, 2010). They provide the theoretical basis for our research, integrating a sizable body of currently fractured and unfocused work.

Message Framing and Framing Effects Research

The concept of framing can be found throughout the social sciences as a way of describing how messages, based on certain patterns of emphasis and exclusion, can structure the thinking of the people who encounter them. Sociologists such as Gregory Bateson (1972) used the term as an analogy to a picture frame, implying that any communication organizes the perceptions of audiences by suggesting that they should attend to what is within the frame and ignore what is outside it. Alternatively, psychologists Kathryn Bock and Helga Loebell (1990) apply the metaphor of the structure of a building, asserting that frames provide a skeleton that "shapes the process and products of construction," thereby providing certain "openings" from which the interior of the building can be viewed. In both analogies, the features of the object remain largely constant, but the act of framing alters what features observers attend to when they encounter them. As Matthes (2012, pp. 248–249) writes, frames "are a part of culture, they guide how the elite construct information, they affect journalists' information selection, they are manifest in media texts, and they influence cognitions and attitudes of audience members."

Few scholars, however, have attempted to merge a formal understanding of how frames become embedded in messages with a comprehension of how they influence the thinking of individuals. This lack of convergence is at least partly because framing has developed along two discrete disciplinary lines – one socio-logical, the other psychological – with scholars from these differing perspectives generating bounded conceptions of framing and favoring certain methodologies to examine their presence in messages and their effects on audiences. Further, theorizing about framing has often lacked attention to its conceptual moorings, especially the complex interplay of news construction and audience cognition (Pan and Kosicki, 1993), instead relying on the simple division between frames in texts and frames of thought (Scheufele, 1999).

Even within the narrower context of political communication research, the definition of what constitutes a frame varies from scholar to scholar, and from one "master discipline" to another. Researchers in political science and com-munication differ considerably in their assertions about who does the framing and how frames find their way into news. As Robert Entman (1993) asserted over two decades ago, "despite its omnipresence across the social sciences and the humanities, nowhere is there a general statement of framing theory that shows exactly how frames become embedded within and become manifest in a text, or how framing influences thinking" (p. 51). Although there has been a great deal of research on news framing and framing effects, an integrated view of framing still eludes us.

Within the fields of political science and communication, the concept of framing effects generally focuses on the manner in which the construction of communication texts, usually news content, influences individual thoughts and feelings by structuring press accounts around certain themes or labels (Entman, 1993; Pan and Kosicki, 1993). Some scholars favor treating framing as the sociological process of news construction that results from interactions with and dependency on elite sources (Bennett, 1990; Entman and Rojecki, 1993; Gamson, 1992; Lawrence, 2010; Snow and Benford, 1988), while others understand framing as the psychological dynamics of audience consumption and schema activation that results from the interaction between what is in the text and what is in memory (Fiske and Taylor, 1991; Price and Tewksbury, 1997; Zaller, 1992). In fact, we consider framing to involve both of these processes, one an outcome of press–source relations (Bennett, 1990) and the other an outcome of audience–text interactions (Price and Tewksbury, 1997).

Implicit to many of the sociological studies is the perspective that media frames order or organize audience perceptions by including and excluding cer-tain messages, turning "unrecognizable happenings or amorphous talk into a discernible event" (Tuchman, 1978, p. 192; also Gitlin, 1980; Goffman, 1974; Graber, 1988; Hall et al., 1978; Rachlin, 1988). As Ball-Rokeach and Rokeach (1987) argue, media do not merely serve an agenda-setting role in public discourse, but are crucial to establishing the range of criteria for constructing, debating, and resolving social issues.

Inspired by framing research, in its most recent formulation, agenda setting is thought to operate at different levels, with news coverage building salience and prominence of the topic among the public at the first level, and building an image for the issue based on the specific attributes that are made salient in that coverage at the second level (Wanta et al., 2004). As McCombs and Valenzuela (2007) contend, "which aspects of an issue are covered in the news, and the relative emphasis on these various aspects of an issue, makes a considerable difference in how people view that issue." From this perspective, the media and public agendas do not merely align in term of issue salience, but also around key attributes. Some have argued that the claims of a "second level" are merely an effort to subsume framing under the broader agenda-setting paradigm (see Jasperson et al., 1998). These scholars point to the theoretical efforts of Price and Tewksbury (1997), who understand agenda setting and framing as closely related forms of knowledge activation – accessibility of mental constructs for agenda setting and applicability of those activated constructs for framing.

Nonetheless, the extension of agenda-setting concepts into framing research has taken a number of forms (Scheufele, 2000). One is work on frame setting, which considers how news frames can make both the "story object, as well as the frame used in the story, more salient" (Aday, 2007, p. 768). How these frames become embedded in news texts and make their way to the public is a complex process that is shaped by forces operating at a variety of levels of analysis (see Entman, 2004). Shoemaker and Reese (1996) organize the vast literature on the factors that influence the content of news into those that operate at the levels of the individual journalist, the journalistic profession, the news organization, the news organization's position within the social system, and the culture/ideology. Entman takes this a step further, offering a model of cascading activation to explain this process. Entman's model asserts "how interpretive frames activate and spread from the top level of a stratified system (the White House) to the network of nonadministration elites, and on to news organizations, their texts, and the public – and how interpretations feed back from lower to higher levels" (p. 415).

It is not our intent to review the sizable literature on news sociology here, or to provide a detailed dissection of how frames make their way into the news, for other scholars have already done that work (see Bennett, 1990; Entman, 2003; Entman, 2004; Gitlin, 1980). This literature shows that the news, and indeed the frames that are used to construct the news, is the result of a complex interplay between the state and the press, with political elites working to get certain frames and issue labels adopted by journalists as a way to advance their policy agendas, while reporters rely on certain preferred frames as a way to simplify news production and package the news for audience consumption. This view also recognizes, as Neuman, Just, and Crigler (1992) contend, that individuals "do not slavishly follow the framing of issues presented in the mass media"; rather, people "actively filter, sort, and reorganize information in personally meaningful ways in constructing an understanding of public issues" (pp. 76–77; see also Gamson et al., 1992). Our interest lies with the influence of these frames on audiences, and the interplay of message and cognition that produces framing effects.

Organizing Research on Framing Effects

The existing research on framing effects has yielded contrasting approaches to conceptualizing message frames, reflecting Entman's (1991) conclusion that framing is a "fractured paradigm." We classify these approaches according to a 2 × 2 typology (Figure 1.1) that is based on two dimensions: a *purity* dimension that ranges from "idealistic" to "pragmatic" approaches and a *generalizability* dimension that ranges from "context-transcendent" to "context-specific" approaches to news framing. In this figure, we have located some of the more prominent framing effects studies using the two dimensions of this typology.

Frame Purity. The first dimension concerns the strictness of the approach that research takes to conceptualizing frames in order to observe framing effects. This continuum spans from narrow idealistic approaches to broader pragmatic approaches. This distinction is similar to what Iyengar (1991) refers to as a methodological tradeoff between "precision" and "realism." In a similar vein, Druckman (2001) distinguishes between conceptions of framing as a matter of "equivalency" and as a matter of "emphasis." The former investigates how different descriptions of a problem or an issue with "the use of different, but logically equivalent, words or phrases" (Druckman, 2001, p. 228) change opinions or preferences.

These idealistic approaches take the rather stringent view that in order to study framing effects, researchers must isolate the frame while all other features of the message are held constant. Typically, this approach lends itself to experimental studies that alternate frames across different conditions in strictly controlled settings. In doing so, this approach emphasizes that all other factual and stylistic elements of the message must be comparable so that researchers can observe the pure influence of the frame. That is, alternative messages must provide equivalent information and be of equal size and structure, varying only in the broad interpretive framework they provide (Vraga et al., 2010). The emphases of this approach are on the internal validity of experimental design and the insights into psychological processes.

The most widely cited example of this approach to conceptualizing message frames is provided by Tversky and Kahneman (1981), who demonstrate that

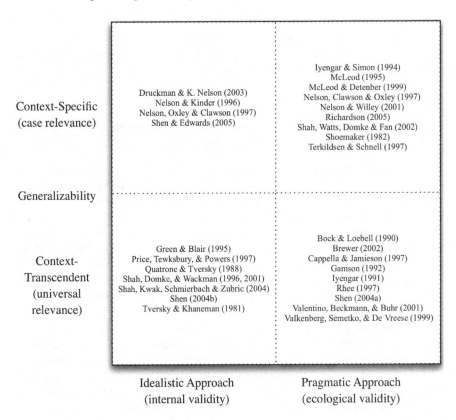

	Idealistic Approach (internal validity)	Pragmatic Approach (ecological validity)
Context-Specific (case relevance)	Druckman & K. Nelson (2003) Nelson & Kinder (1996) Nelson, Oxley & Clawson (1997) Shen & Edwards (2005)	Iyengar & Simon (1994) McLeod (1995) McLeod & Detenber (1999) Nelson, Clawson & Oxley (1997) Nelson & Willey (2001) Richardson (2005) Shah, Watts, Domke & Fan (2002) Shoemaker (1982) Terkildsen & Schnell (1997)
Context-Transcendent (universal relevance)	Green & Blair (1995) Price, Tewksbury, & Powers (1997) Quatrone & Tversky (1988) Shah, Domke, & Wackman (1996, 2001) Shah, Kwak, Schmierbach & Zubric (2004) Shen (2004b) Tversky & Khaneman (1981)	Bock & Loebell (1990) Brewer (2002) Cappella & Jamieson (1997) Gamson (1992) Iyengar (1991) Rhee (1997) Shen (2004a) Valentino, Beckmann, & Buhr (2001) Valkenberg, Semetko, & De Vreese (1999)

Generalizability (left axis); *Purity* (bottom axis)

FIGURE 1.1. A typology of existing framing effects research.

presenting solutions to a problem in terms of gains or losses, all the while maintaining the logical and numerical equivalence of the facts, can change individuals' aversion to risk. A particularly notable illustration of these classic prospect theory studies is the Asian disease experiment. In this study, respondents were randomly assigned to one of two differently framed, but probabilistically equal scenarios. Some participants encountered a scenario in which the decision alternatives were framed in terms of gains, while others encountered decision alternatives framed in terms of losses. Both scenarios asked respondents to react to the following problem:

Imagine that the United States is preparing for the outbreak of an unusual Asian disease, which is expected to kill 600 people. Two alternative programs to combat the disease have been proposed. Assume that the exact scientific estimates of the programs are as follows:

[Gain Scenario]
- If program A is adopted, 200 people will be saved.
- If program B is adopted, there is a 1/3 probability that 600 people will be saved, and a 2/3 probability that no people will be saved.

[Loss Scenario]
- If program A is adopted, 400 people will die.
- If program B is adopted, there is a 1/3 probability that nobody will die, and a 2/3 probability that 600 people will die.

In each condition, respondents were asked which decision alternative they favored, program A or program B. When the experimental subjects encountered the gain scenario, 72% favored program A, the risk-averse option. However, when they encountered the loss scenario, 78% favored program B, the risk-seeking option. Thus, a simple change in perspective, even with absolute numerical and probabilistic equivalence, resulted in a dramatic shift in willingness to opt for the risky alternative.

Other scholars have adopted this narrow conception of framing by shifting the perspective offered to understand a problem or an issue without any changes in factual information or stylistic features of the message. Although most of the studies that we categorize as "idealistic" try to isolate and systematically alter the frame, few have the purity of Tversky and Kahneman's ideal type. Instead, most fall on the idealistic end of the continuum between precision and realism. They make a strong effort to maintain factual and stylistic consistency, focusing on the essence of the frame shift, though often quotes or other minor features are altered to invoke particular frames. This approach to framing privileges an uncontaminated setting in which to test framing effects over the pragmatism of understanding more realistic frame shifts as they co-occur with changes in factual content of substantive stylistic alterations. Idealistic approaches accept the assumption that the frame can easily be separated from other message differences such as changes in factual information contained in a news story, for example, or structural features such as photographs or headlines that accompany the story. However, limiting the manipulation of frames to numerically equivalent, factually identical, and stylistically consistent alterations imposes limitations on the scope of message frames – and framing effects research – by creating a methodological challenge of how to isolate the frame and an empirical constraint by neutering the power of the frame when it is stripped of the fact packages that accompany it. This has led some researchers to adopt less constrained orientations toward frames, which we call pragmatic approaches.

In pragmatic approaches, which Druckman (2001) refers to as "emphasis" framing, researchers make an implicit argument that it is impossible to fully manipulate a frame without changing some of the basic facts that are presented. That is, different frames necessarily call for different sets of facts. Research in this tradition argues that it is impractical, if not impossible, to hold the facts constant when you shift across frames. For example, McLeod and Hertog (1999) describe two alternative frames for covering social protest, the debate frame and the riot frame. While the debate frame would focus on the protesters, the protested, and the positions of both sides of the debated issue, the riot frame would be more likely to focus on the police and elaborate on property damage and arrests. Facts covered by the reporter change with the frame.

Studies using the pragmatic approach (e.g., Iyengar, 1991; McLeod and Detenber, 1999) take a more relaxed view of internal validity, preferring instead to stress ecological validity by presenting more realistic variations in story manipulations, often using real stories from the news media as experimental stimuli. Although pragmatic approaches provide a more ecologically valid way of testing framing effects in that real world stories are not limited to differences in equivalencies, this type of research raises a critical problem of clearly distinguishing what is causing the framing effect, whether it is the result of the frame or other content differences. That is, experiments designed to assess the effects of pragmatic or emphasis-framing differences have a hard time creating different story frames while holding all other story characteristics constant.

The most prominent illustration of the pragmatic approach to framing effects is Iyengar's (1991) distinction between episodic and thematic frames. His research explores the tendency of reporters to construct social issues around specific instances and individuals, which he refers to as episodic framing, as opposed to journalists' less frequent emphasis on broader trends and social conditions, which he calls thematic framing. He tested the effects of such frames across a series of experimental studies. In one study, experimental stories focused on the issue of illegal drugs. The episodic story focused on two drug-dependent individuals, while the thematic story focused on systemic rates of drug abuse and the policies used to address the problem. Not only did the time frame and the social level of the story shift across these two instances – as would be required to narrowly shift from episodic to thematic framing – but so did the sources referenced in the report along with the facts used to construct the central assertions. Emphasis on episodic frames was found to shift experimental subjects' "attributions of responsibility both for the creation of problems or situations (causal responsibility) and for the resolution of these problems or situations (treatment responsibility)" to the people featured in press reports (Iyengar, 1991, p. 3).

We should again point out that our distinction between the idealistic and pragmatic approaches should really be seen as a continuum with studies such as Tversky and Kahneman (1981) at the idealistic end, and studies such as Iyengar (1991) at the pragmatic end. Research from along this continuum contributes to our knowledge in different ways. Studies at the idealistic end tell us more about the precise power of the frames themselves to induce effects, while studies at the pragmatic end tell use more about the true power of media messages. As such, we should resist the temptation to discount either approach to framing effects research. While the critics of the pragmatic approach are correct in asserting that such research should not make claims about the "effect of the story frame," they should probably stop short of claiming that pragmatic research is not "framing effects" research. Since different frames tend to dictate different sets of facts as journalists construct stories top down starting with the frame, it may be unrealistic to hold everything but the frame constant in most news story contexts. For example, when it comes to news stories about a protest, it is hard to imagine how one story could be framed as a debate and another as a riot using the exact same set of facts. While studies that adopt the pragmatic approach do not isolate the effect of the frame, they do test the differences between stories that are framed differently, and as such might be called framing effects studies.

Frame Generalizability. A second salient dimension of framing research is whether the framing distinction in question applies only to the specific issue featured in the message (*context-specific*), or is generalizable across a variety of situations (*context-transcendent*). Situation-specific frames are more narrowly constructed around a particular issue. For example, Richardson (2005) used situation-specific frames of promoting diversity and redressing inequities to study the effects of newspaper editorials about affirmative action. Nelson and Willey (2001) provide another example. In their study, the authors developed two news stories about the 1996 "pizza redlining" controversy in San Francisco in which pizza delivery services were accused of refusing to provide service to predominantly African-American neighborhoods. One news story used a "crime" frame; this story underscored the pizza delivery company's claim that the redlining policy was adopted to protect the safety of the delivery drivers. The other story used a "race" frame, which emphasized racial discrimination inherent in the policy.

One particularly notable example of this approach to framing effects research was conducted by Shah et al. (2002), who analyzed media content and then tested the effects of the news framing of sex scandals during the Clinton presidency. They found that three prominent frames existed and had differential effects: The Clinton behavior frame (i.e., accounts of his liaisons and evasions), the conservative attack frame (i.e., denouncements of Clinton's behavior), and the liberal response frame (i.e., questions of the conservatives' motives). These frame categories, which were found to work in tandem to explain Clinton's rising job approval ratings during the height of the Lewinsky scandal, were developed inductively by looking at media coverage, and were not presented as generalizable to other presidencies or political sex scandals. Rather, they were coded and tested in an effort to explain the opinion dynamics at the time. In this work, like the others, the frame categories were constructed narrowly to fit the study topic.

In contrast with these context-specific frames, context-transcendent frames are both more abstract and more generalizable to a wider variety of issues. Examples include episodic versus thematic frames (Iyengar, 1991), strategic versus issue frames (Cappella and Jamieson, 1997; Rhee, 1997), ethical versus material frames (Shah et al., 1996), issue versus character frames (Shen, 2004b), and loss versus gain frames (Tversky and Khaneman, 1981). For example, Cappella and Jamieson (1997) examine the effects of framing politics through sports and war metaphors (i.e., strategic framing) as opposed to the presentation of politics as a debate among divergent perspectives (i.e., issue framing). In a series of controlled experiments across two political contexts, the Philadelphia mayoral election and the health care reform debate, they found that framing influenced information recall and respondents' cynicism.

Likewise, Iyengar (1991) attempts to demonstrate the generalizability of his distinction between episodic versus thematic framing, placing him in the bottom-right quadrant of our typology. This quadrant of pragmatic and content-transcendent framing research contains some of the most prominent framing effects studies, including work by Cappella and Jamieson (1997), Gamson (1992), and Price et al. (1997). Iyengar's experimental studies concerning crime, poverty, and unemployment provide some support for the transcendent power of this pragmatic frame shift; however, many tests of the central hypothesis, while directionally consistent, fail to achieve statistical significance. These weak effects may result from the confounding of two distinct frame dimensions in the contrast between episodic and thematic coverage, one of the possible problems of a pragmatic approach. That is, episodic coverage as defined and tested not only favors specific instances over enduring problems (i.e., time span), it also emphasizes individual situations over societal conditions (i.e., social level). The framing distinction explored in this book – individual versus collective frames – isolates the social level dimension and opts for a more idealistic, yet nonetheless transcendent approach.

Applying the Framing Research Typology

Before explicating the individual and collective frame distinction that is at the center of this book, we turn to the conceptual value of our typology for clarifying extant work on framing effects and for advancing the study of message framing, writ large. We believe that this typology helps organize the tremendous diversity of framing research, and in doing so, begins to resolve the conceptual confusion that surrounds the concept. Although some argue that a particular cell of the typology represents the "true definition" of message framing, there is little agreement on which cell that should be. We contend that work on news framing and effects benefits from a conception of framing that encompasses all of the work covered in this typology, yet also recognizes the particular strengths and weaknesses of each approach.

We begin in the lower left quadrant (idealistic/transcendent) of the typology. Here we find research that emphasizes the transcendent quality of message frames – that is, their ability to cross issues and news categories – yet conceives of framing very narrowly, focusing only on the shift in the perspective provided to the audience by the journalist. For scholars who take this position, facts are supposed to remain identical across various frame categories so that the pure effect of the transcendent frame can be tested and isolated. Apart from the obvious advantages of this approach for purposes of internal validity and for testing the generalizability of frame power across multiple issues, it suffers from a number of serious limitations.

First, treating the definition of framing so narrowly often neuters the frame, removing the factual shifts and stylistic changes that often accompany changes in journalistic orientation. As a result, the full effects of shifts in perspective are not assessed because accompanying changes in the fact packages and reporting norms, such as quoting particular sources, are omitted, with the purity of the frame and the supposed transcendence of the frame category limiting assessment of its impact.

A second related problem stems from what might be called "the challenge of frame isolation." That is, how can researchers surgically manipulate the frame while holding the rest of the content constant? The frame is, according to many, not any particular element of the text, such as the headline or lead paragraph, but the perspective woven throughout the entire text. It is a Gestalt, derived from the story's entirety. Many idealistic studies settle for manipulating the headline or lead paragraph as a proxy for isolating the frame, then maintain the rest of the story across conditions as a constant set of facts. As such, not only may it be hard to argue that the frame has been truly isolated, but the resultant news stories may no longer reflect realistic variations of stories as they occur in actual day-to-day reporting.

In the upper left quadrant (idealistic/specific) of the typology, we find one effort to address this limitation by making the frame shift more specific to the issue at hand. Although internal validity is still stressed in this approach, the decision to conceive of the frame as issue-specific allows for greater realism when generating the framed messages, and may have some advantage with regard to external validity as well. As a result, the shift between different ways of narrowly framing a single issue tends to be more flexible to the demands of correctly representing the journalistic norms of preparing news around that topic. Unfortunately, this approach also comes with limitations.

The most important among these is the idiosyncratic nature of many of the frames, which often limits the relevance of the finding to the specific context of the study. In addition, the continued narrowness of the frame manipulation still removes much of what may provide the power of frames to activate thoughts, shape attitudes, and encourage behaviors.

The upper right quadrant (pragmatic/specific) of the typology sacrifices some internal validity in order to examine frames through a more pragmatic approach. Some of these studies examine framing effects outside the laboratory through survey analysis or longitudinal modeling. Even those that employ experimental designs do not strictly adhere to the logic of only manipulating the frame of the message while holding all other message elements constant. Instead, the research populating this quadrant operationalizes frames in terms of a shift in both perspective and the associated facts. Although not asserted explicitly in many cases, this work operationalizes frames as a package that combines the shift in perspective along with a corresponding shift in the accompanying facts, sources, and subjects. For example, the different frames of the Clinton-Lewinsky scandal explored by Shah et al. (2002), not only offered different vantage points from which to view the issue, but also referenced different story elements, quoted different sources, and referred to different historical moments. While this is more ecologically valid, it does come at the expense of narrowly crediting the shift in perspective with the observed effects.

The lower right quadrant (pragmatic/transcendent) is the location of much of the most widely cited framing work, with exemplars from Iyengar (1991) and Cappella and Jamieson (1997), among others. Research in this quadrant has been critiqued for confounding frame shifts with alterations in other substantive features of news content, sacrificing too much internal validity for the sake of ecological validity, especially when testing framing effects within an experimental design. Although those critiques may have some merit, they also miss the larger conceptual issue at stake here. The work in this quadrant attempts to test the effects of context-transcendent frames in their full ecological power. In this conceptualization, the power of the frame lies not only in the shift in perspective or definition of an issue, but also in the other changes that shift in perspective necessitates. From this perspective, to study the effects of frames, especially transcendent ones, the shift in frame perspective cannot be isolated from the associated changes. Of course this limits the ability of the researchers to claim framing effects in the narrow sense typically applied to experimental research, which attempts to isolate the specific feature of interest while holding all else constant. Nonetheless, many insights about framing can be gained from these studies.

Layering Frames and Cues

Organizing framing effects research in this way highlights the fact that work must balance the need for realism with the need for precision. Internal and ecological validity are both required to adequately test framing effects, particularly in experimental settings. We contend that this demands the *layering* of subtle manipulations that are invisible to the experiment participants, with one of these factors shifting the frame in the precise, idealistic sense of research on the left side of this typology, and other factors shifting accompanying elements such as story subjects, journalistic sources, or elite cues that often change along with the frame in research on the right side of the typology. By crossing these elements in an experimental design, the effects of the frames can be separated from the other story elements that have often been a source of concern. At the same time, it may be that the effects of framing are more dramatic when coupled with fact packages and news cues that reinforce and complement the frame (Shah et al., 2002; Shah et al., 2004).

Existing research draws a distinction between news story frames and cues. While the frame has traditionally been seen as a characteristic that provides structure to the news story as a whole, the term "cue" has often been used to describe specific objects within the news story (Kuklinski and Hurley, 1994; Mondak, 1993). In other words, cues may be thought of as the labels and descriptors that journalists use to represent elements within the story. Just as news frames help to bring meaning to the story as a whole, cues bring meaning to particular concepts within the story. In this sense, there is a parallel between frames and cues. We could think of cues as concepts that are framed in a particular way, an idea to which we will return.

Like frames, cues are the product of a variety of factors operating at different levels to shape the nature of news content (Shoemaker and Reese, 1996). However, some of these factors may be more influential in shaping the application of frames and others more important in determining journalists' choice of cues (Cho et al., 2006). Journalistic norms and conventions, as well as concerns for attracting audiences, may be particularly influential in shaping framing choices, while the selection of cues is more likely to be the product of the relative power of elite sources to assert their preferred labels (e.g., the use of "freedom fighter" as opposed to "insurgent rebel") into the news discourse (Bennett et al., 2006; Edelman, 1993; Entman, 2004; Gamson, 1992; Gans, 1980).

Frames and cues may operate similarly in terms of the way they affect audiences. They both are likely to interact with an individual's cognitive network to shape subsequent judgments (Price and Tewksbury, 1997). In terms of isolated effects, we might expect frames to have more influence than cues, as they bring meaning to the entire story rather than just a particular element of the story. However, in reality, frames and cues do not operate in isolation. In creating a coherent story, journalists may select frames and cues that fit together. If a journalist is writing up a story about welfare using an episodic frame, it is likely that the cues used to describe the actors and events will be consistent with that frame. In this case, if the story is framed as an exposé of welfare abuse as opposed to one about the safety net, cues such as "welfare cheat" are more likely to appear. As such, frames and cues can be expected to work together, thereby enhancing their power to influence audience judgments (Cho et al., 2006; Keum et al., 2005; Shah et al., 2004; Shah et al., 2010). Unfortunately, very few studies have attempted to look at the way that frames and cues work together, which should be expected in competitive, elite discourse-driven democracies (Chong and Druckman, 2007a,c). This book is designed to fill this void. Before doing so, we first articulate the research requisites and theoretical models that provide the basis for this research.

Research Requisites

Testing the interplay of frames and cues, as well as other story elements such as source attributions and story subjects, requires large participant pools to provide enough power to be able to cross various message dimensions into realistic media portrayals, while maintaining sufficient power to reveal the typically weak effects of one-shot framing experiments. We adopt this approach in our research in order to investigate the effects of message framing in the context of news stories about government surveillance of Arab and activist groups. Though our messages focus on the tension between civil liberties and national security that are raised by government activities associated with the USA PATRIOT Act, the frames that we chose to manipulate (individual vs. collective presentations of surveillance targets) are transcendent in the sense that these frames are found in news coverage across a variety of different contexts. In our stimulus messages, the individual versus collective framing distinction pertains to whether the news story about FBI surveillance of either an Arab group or an activist group presented a personalized account by focusing on a particular individual as the subject of the story.

In day-to-day news coverage, this distinction can be observed in stories on a variety of topics ranging from natural disasters (e.g., Hurricane Katrina) to government policy (e.g., the impact of welfare reform) to social problems (e.g., crime). For example, stories about illegal drug use will often be framed around an individual exemplar to illustrate problems associated with drug addiction. Alternatively, stories about drug abuse may be framed in epidemiological terms in order to illustrate the scope of the problem. Realistically, many stories on drug abuse (and other relevant topics) may involve a mix of individual and collective frames. It is a common journalistic practice (in television news, in newspapers, and especially in news magazines) to open stories with individual exemplars to add human interest and bring the story to life, and then back out to a more holistic perspective to discuss the impact on larger units of social organization such as groups, communities, and societies. For the purpose of experimentally isolating the impact of this type of framing, and to examine its interaction with other message features, the stimulus stories used in our research were constructed to represent pure forms of the frames.

More significantly, the research reported in this book strikes a balance between the idealistic and the pragmatic approaches to framing effects research. On one hand, our operationalization of the individual and collective frames maintains the vast majority of story content (including the structure, language, and basic facts) across experimental conditions. As such, we can isolate the main effects of the influence of the frame, upholding the idealistic approach's emphasis on experimental control. On the other hand, we cross the story frame condition with other factors that manipulate related yet distinct content elements (i.e., cues and source attributions). We do this in order to: (a) examine the interactive effects of story frames with these other elements; (b) provide a more accurate rendering of the true power of message construction, which may be underestimated by adherence to the idealistic restriction of holding everything constant but the frame; and (c) observe message effects as outcomes of broader content differences in accordance with the pragmatic approach's emphasis on ecological validity, especially in competitive environments in which elites compete over how issues are labeled (Chong and Druckman, 2007a,c; Shah et al., 2004; Shah et al., 2010).

Limited Effects of Framing

Several years ago, one luminary in the field of communication, Steven Chaffee (personal communication, August 7, 1998), remarked that most studies examining the impact of news frames have failed to find significant effects. To the extent that this was an accurate assessment of past research, we might expect that researchers would have become discouraged and lost interest in framing and framing effects. However, this has not been the case. Instead, framing research remains an active area in the fields of communication and political science. Part of this continued attention may stem from the realization that the theoretical and methodological limitations of many early studies may have led to the underestimation of framing effects.

First, most studies of framing effects have used single-exposure designs, in which researchers sought to examine whether exposure to an isolated message with a particular frame might have an impact on audience members. Effects of a single message may be small or short-lived. However, if the nature and application of frames is largely consistent, framing effects may cumulate to the point where they are more powerful and durable. For example, exposure to a single protest story that frames a particular protest group as being deviant may lead to a short-lived judgment about the group featured in the story but may not have a strong impact on attitudes toward protests and protest groups in general; however, if news stories about protests consistently frame protest groups as deviant, the media may have a powerful, long-term effect on attitudes toward protests as a form of democratic participation (McLeod and Detenber, 1999). Such effects, though potentially powerful, may be hard to observe using traditional experimental methodology. The rare examples of longitudinal modeling of framing effects lend support to this perspective, with such analyses explaining large shifts in public opinion over time (Shah et al., 2002).

Second, the effects of news story frames may interact with other story elements such as cues, sources, quotes, evidence, or other content features. The composition, consistency, and synergy of the content elements may influence the nature of the frame's effects. The idealistic approaches adopted by many experimental studies of framing effects attempt to isolate the effect of the frame by holding most story elements constant and manipulating only a small portion of the text that constitutes the "frame" in alternative experimental conditions. While satisfying concerns about internal validity in isolating the effect, this procedure may underestimate the effects of news stories as the frames interact with, and are reinforced by, other elements of the story. Likewise, pragmatic approaches sometimes confound two or more textual elements as they attempt to test the effects of alternative frames, possibly resulting in the effects of one dimension countervailing and suppressing the effects of other dimensions, thereby reducing the ability to discern influences.

Third, framing effects may be conditional, resulting from an interaction between the news frame and the predispositions of the individual who encounters it. That is, certain individuals are more susceptible to framing effects than others such that the effects of a frame on some individuals may be strong, while others are not affected at all. If predispositions are not taken into account, one might conclude that framing effects are weak, if they exist at all. Ideology, prior knowledge, political attitudes, and value orientations may each influence frame resonance.

Our examination of framing effects, grounded in an understanding of the breadth of framing research and situated within the typology we offer, attempts to address or account for all of these issues. We understand that framing effects may be quite small in single-exposure studies, and we therefore examine effects using large samples to generate enough statistical power to observe influence of this size. We recognize and embrace the idea that frames may interact with other story elements, and therefore create layered, factorial experimental designs that allow us to examine the interplay of these elements on relevant outcomes. Finally, we appreciate that framing effects are often conditional, and therefore attempt to account for how differences that individuals bring to the processing of media messages might amplify or attenuate these effects.

Message Framing Model

Our review of the literature on news frames and cues led to the development of our integrated Message Framing Model (MFM; see Figure 1.2). This model is based on the observation that news frames and cues have much in common, yet differ in terms of the level of the textual unit to which they are applied. Although cues tend to be directed at individual words and phrases, frames are conceived as covering contentions and accounts. As such, meaning can be embedded in any textual unit from single words (i.e., concept frames) to entire texts (i.e., story frames). When a journalist applies a label to represent a concept, the choice of labels implies a limited range of meanings to the audience. While this label may mean different things to different people, the range of decodable meanings is to some degree prescribed by the label choice. As such, the use of different cues would prescribe a different range of potential meanings. For instance, a journalist could label the leader of an activist group as an advocate or an agitator. This cueing (or concept framing) is likely to fundamentally alter the meaning for audience members.

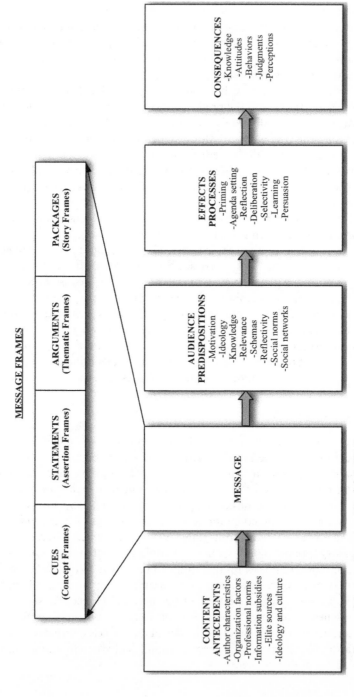

FIGURE 1.2. Message Framing Model (MFM).

26

Similarly, as the journalist compiles concept labels into a sentence, meaning is framed within the resultant statements (i.e., assertion frames). Sentences are then compiled into arguments, either explicit or implicit, about a perceived reality (i.e., thematic frames), which are then packaged into a holistic piece (i.e., story frames). While this bottom-up ordering of composition (from smaller units to larger units) follows the way that a journalist would actually write a story to create meaning, it is likely that the process in the mind of the journalist is both top down and bottom up. That is, before the journalist composes a news story, the construction is guided by the perceived norms for that story type, guided in much the same way as a builder following the blueprint for a house. That abstract blueprint for the news package is likely to convey a certain meaning for the whole (story frames). Of course, political and economic elites can influence the content of news through their rhetoric and information subsidies, particularly how journalists use certain cues to label issues. Thus, the indexing of elite opinions can shape the smaller textual units journalists employ, such as political idioms, shorthand acronyms, and terminology (concepts and assertions). All of these component parts, then, are likely to work to reinforce certain preferred meanings for the audience.

A more concrete illustration may help clarify some of the elements of this model. For example, McLeod and Hertog (1999) describe the characteristics of the "protest paradigm," a common pattern used in writing stories about social protest that tends to connote certain preferred meanings to the audience. One of the major preferred meanings that stems from the protest paradigm is the notion that protesters are deviant. This is conveyed through a number of textual elements. Derogatory labels (e.g., "extremists" or "militants") may be used as concept labels. Assertions may also be framed in such a way as to further communicate deviance (e.g., "police are concerned that these extremists may create problems in downtown Minneapolis"). Such assertions may be assembled into thematic structures embedded in a story that frame the protesters as lawbreakers, detailing the nature of their crimes and punishments. Ultimately, these concept labels, assertions, and themes are assembled into the broader story frame. In this case, the overarching frame of the story may be one of "protesters versus police" rather than "protesters versus the intended target of the protest," a crime story rather than political story.

These textual elements are at least partly a product of the message creator and news organizations that produce them, as well as the political elites who offer them up to journalists and editors. For example, elites and journalists prefer to evoke individual examples to illustrate issues, with news norms encouraging the personification of issues. Ideological and cultural factors can also work to naturalize certain modes of news construction and lead to certain frames being emphasized. Of course, the resonance of these frames on audience members is largely dependent on their personal predispositions and the nature of their cognitive networks.

The meaning embedded within any of these units (from concepts to stories) can interact with an individual's worldviews and cognitive schemas to produce differentiated outcomes. The different predispositions and schemas that individuals bring to the message lead to a range of decoded meanings, a notion referred to as "polysemy" (Hebdige, 1979). In the case of the protest example described earlier, audience members who are politically predisposed to oppose the protesters, or even those who have no prior opinion, are likely to reject the protesters and their message. On the other hand, audience members who are inclined to support the protesters may respond by reading between the lines and coming to a different conclusion about the protest: they may reject the mainstream media account of the protest as biased, or they may even seek alternative sources of information that might lead to a different conclusion regarding the merits of the protest – a set of responses that reflect "media dissociation" (Hwang et al., 2006). As this suggests, in addition to understanding how journalists choose to construct press accounts, we must also understand how audiences process the news.

Message Processing Model

Our approach to framing effects is guided by an integrated Message Processing Model (MPM) that we have derived from prior research (Higgins, 1996; Higgins and Brendl, 1995; Price and Tewksbury, 1997). This model is based on the notion that message frames – in all of their forms – interact with audience members' preexisting orientations and memory store, which are then used in the process of interpreting experiences and making subsequent judgments. Various cognitive processes identified by past research have been integrated to make this model applicable to framing and priming effects. The components of this model include availability, applicability, accessibility, activation, usability, recency, and chronicity (see Figure 1.3).

When an audience member encounters a media message, potential effects are influenced by the "availability" of relevant background information (organized in memory in the form of cognitive schemas) that is retrievable for use in message processing (Higgins, 1996; Tversky and Kahneman, 1973). Cognitions may be available in the memory store because they have been frequently or recently activated for other purposes and remain near the "top of the head." Of course, activation may also be a function of the goodness-of-fit between stored information and the content of the messages that individuals encounter, the "applicability" of existing schemas, from which cognitions may be sampled, to the task at hand (Bruner, 1957; Higgins, 1996). Not all of the cues, assertions, arguments, and packages that comprise message frames will have corresponding cognitions in each individual's memory store that are applicable for activation. These differences in applicability are often referred to as "frame resonance."

As the message is processed, relevant available schemas will be "activated" along with other available schemas (Anderson, 1983; Price and

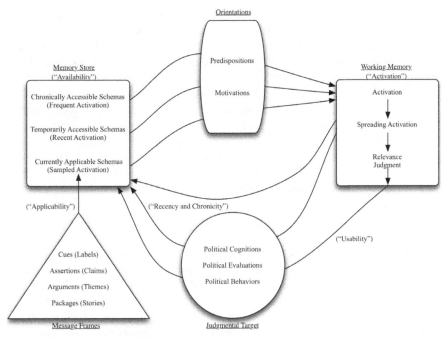

FIGURE 1.3. Message Processing Model (MPM).

Tewksbury, 1997). Once activated, these schemas may become more "accessible" for subsequent judgments and other cognitive tasks (Price and Tewksbury, 1997). Schemas that have been repeatedly activated in the past are more likely to be used in subsequent judgments, a phenomenon that has been called "chronic accessibility" (Roskos-Ewoldsen, 1997; Shah et al., 1996; Shen, 2004a). Likewise, cognitions that have been activated recently also remain available in memory and have a higher probability of accessibility in subsequent judgmental tasks. We refer to this as "temporary accessibility."

Whether these available and accessible schemas are actually activated and applied is a product of a number of other factors. First among these, as suggested by the MFM, are the orientations that individuals bring with them to any message processing experience. These predispositions and motivations influence whether cognitions available and accessible in long-term memory are activated for use in working memory. Individuals who are highly motivated may process information more deeply and make more of an effort to sample more fully from applicable cognitions. Individuals may be predisposed due to attributional biases or ideological preferences to rely on recently or chronically accessible constructs. Thus, these orientations, writ large, serve to condition which available cognitions are activated.

This model shares some commonality with the theory of affective intelligence, which asserts that people have active use of two systems: the dispositional (habitual) and surveillance (responsive) systems. These systems have an impact on how people think and act. For recurring events, individuals rely on the habitual processes to accomplish their goals, such as when people rely on partisan cues in voting decisions. However, under "novel and disruptive circumstances" people break free of habit and set out to examine information more fully. These conditions trigger a surveillance system (Armony and LeDoux, 1997; Gray, 1990; LeDoux, 2000). In particular, novel or dangerous circumstances encourage people to reconsider their thoughts and actions. Under familiar conditions of low anxiety, people rely on existing "heuristics" or "predispositions," since there is a "presumption of predictable continuity." Under less familiar conditions, people stop relying on existing predispositions and instead start processing contemporary information, regulating levels of political attention. Politicians can prompt processing of contemporary information, leading to the activation of existing thoughts and the integration of new ones (Marcus, 2000; Marcus et al., 2000).

Once thoughts are activated for use in working memory, a number of cognitive responses may occur. Activation may spread to constructs associated with the focal schema as the message was encoded in memory, with the linkages between constructs being strengthened each time they are activated in tandem. As the interconnections to any construct increase, so does the likelihood that it will be activated through this spreading or cascading process (Judd and Krosnick, 1989). This spread of activation process can influence cognitions even if the activated cognitions are not applied to a judgmental target. They can directly influence the recency and chronicity of schema accessibility by building connections between constructs. The stronger or more numerous the mental pathways between constructs, the greater the chance that thoughts activated to process information about one construct will cascade through memory to other constructs in the future, influencing evaluations and the formation of impressions (Lodge and Stroh, 1993).

Of course, the spreading activation process might also influence cognitions, evaluations, and behavior more directly. Before cognitive tasks are performed, the audience member may engage in an implicit judgment ("usability") about the appropriateness or relevance of applying the activated schemas to the cognitive task (Higgins, 1989; Higgins, 1996); in other words, not all activated thoughts are actually used for making subsequent judgments, nor are all activated thoughts equally relevant or important to a specific cognitive task (Hwang et al., 2007). When political messages inspire negative, aversive reactions of the disposition system, people typically show little further interest in the material, and, to the extent to which they do pay attention, seek messages that reinforce their own beliefs. On the other hand, when political messages induce anxious, uneasy reactions and activate the surveillance system, people become motivated to learn more about the issues involved, willing to seek out viewpoints other than their own, and more open to consider compromise remedies (Marcus, 2000; Marcus et al., 2005).

Other factors may further moderate the effects of a given message. For instance, the influence of an activated schema is dependent on its relationship to other available schemas. If no other schemas are applied to the cognitive task, the activated schema, if deemed usable, is likely to be influential. If the activated schema resonates with other consistent schemas, effects are accentuated; if competing or contradictory schemas accompany it, effects are reduced. The influence of other activated schemas is moderated by identifiable factors linked to prior schema development. For instance, partisanship influences the content of existing schema and the degree of consistency among available considerations. Likewise, political knowledge and issue involvement may be associated with greater cognitive complexity and schema availability. These factors may also be linked to message processing styles such as a greater tendency to reflect on messages, which would enhance spreading activation across schemas.

The MPM and Priming

In addition to the cognitive processes involved in regulating message effects, there are a host of other factors that shape the nature of effects. These factors include the nature of the message (as previously identified by the MFM), the nature of the medium carrying the message, the circumstances under which the message is delivered, and the temporal interval between the delivery of the message and the opportunity for response. Ultimately, the nature of message effects depends on what types of outcomes are being examined. Message effects include a variety of potential outcomes including knowledge gain, perceptual judgments, attitude change, and behavioral outcomes. In general, we can expect that message effects would be greatest on knowledge, diminishing as we move to effects on perceptions, attitudes, and behaviors. Regardless of the type of effect, our MPM articulates the various cognitive processes that mediate the nature of effects. It implies that the nature of message effects depends on the preexisting characteristics that audience members bring to the message reception, the nature of the message itself, and the receiver's orientations toward the message. In this sense, our model is consistent with Markus and Zajonc's (1985) O-S-O-R Model of message effects.

Many of the component processes of the MPM have been adapted from research on priming effects. Priming has been defined as a cognitive process in which a stimulus increases the accessibility of constructs stored in memory, which then has an impact on subsequent judgments (Higgins, 1996; Higgins and King, 1981; Krosnick and Kinder, 1990). The priming literature's emphasis on accessibility is based on the assumption that individuals are "cognitive misers" or limited-capacity information processors (Fiske and Taylor, 1991). That is, individuals make judgments and evaluations based on a small subset of all potentially relevant considerations, which are easily available and retrievable from stored memory without conscious and careful thought (Krosnick and Kinder, 1990). This accessibility emphasis has been reinforced by the fact that most past priming research examined constructs with clear applicability to subsequent cognitive tasks. As such, past priming research often overlooked the filtering processes such as the applicability of available and usability of accessible beliefs that regulate the influence of priming messages, even though many researchers have argued on behalf of their importance (Miller and Krosnick, 1996; Price and Tewksbury, 1997). In sum, priming research has emphasized the automatic activation of recently activated or temporarily accessible constructs, but downplayed the more active processes of availability, applicability, and usability.

Our MPM locates priming within a larger set of cognitive processes, which characterizes the interaction between audience predispositions, the message, audience orientations toward the message, and subsequent outcomes. For message effects to occur, the content of the message must resonate with an individual's preexisting schemas (availability and applicability). Further, activated schemas must be deemed usable, or relevant to subsequent judgments. In the context of political communication, priming studies have investigated how news media, as a primary source of political information, influence evaluations of candidates, politicians, and issues (Domke et al., 1998; Iyengar and Kinder, 1987).

To illustrate how the MPM applies to priming effects in the context of political communication, we will use the example of the effects of exposure to a news story about the faltering economy on presidential approval judgments. First, for such a priming effect to occur, the necessary belief structures must be available; in this case, it might be necessary to believe that a presidential administration's policy is among the factors that affect the health of the economy (availability). Second, the information contained in the news story must link to the relevant belief structure (applicability). Assuming this linkage occurs, the belief structure becomes more likely to be activated in working memory (activation), and thus accessible to subsequent evaluations of the president (accessibility). Finally, the relative strength of this primed belief structure in shaping evaluations (usability) may depend on the strength of competing belief structures. In the absence of strong competing structures, the activated structure may simply influence the judgment due to a recency effect (i.e., "top-of-mindedness"). Alternatively, other belief structures may be stronger or deemed more relevant to the evaluation. For example, an individual may see other factors affecting the economy as being more important (e.g., world economic disorder, business cycles, or acts of terrorism), or other factors as being more important to presidential evaluation (e.g., foreign policy issues or personal scandal).

Apart from the influence of the component processes of the MPM, it is important to recognize that the nature of priming effects is in large part a function of the content of the priming message. In the example described earlier, the influence of the priming message on presidential approval judgments, it is clear that effects might be different depending on whether the message portrayed the economy as faltering, recovering, or thriving. The MPM recognizes that the characteristics of a priming message can potentially differ, and that these differences matter when it comes to the outcomes of exposure to these messages. If we accept that priming messages can be framed in alternative ways, it becomes apparent that these processes overlap.

Applying the Models

By viewing framing effects through the lens of the MPM, we can see that framing and priming share the same basic effects process, reinforcing the contention of the MFM that the essential difference between frames and cues is the textual unit to which they apply. That is, while cues refer to the labels that are used to describe concepts (concept frames), frames are applied to larger textual units ranging from arguments/themes within the text to the entire text itself. The MPM also clarifies that both frames and cues can serve as primes that activate mental constructs. Moreover, when frames and cues are framed in different ways, they can produce different effects by activating different cognitions. However, the nature of these effects will differ depending on the structure of an individual's preexisting schemas. The MPM thus recognizes that audience members play an active role in understanding, interpreting, and applying message-relevant information to subsequent judgments, something that priming studies often overlook.

By putting the MFM and the MPM together, we provide the theoretical framework for the effects examined in our research. Essentially, we examine the effects of different textual units, framed in alternative ways as illustrated by the MFM, on subsequent judgments by the reader, which are outcomes of schema activation structured by the processes identified by the MPM. Across our studies, we examine whether the news story frames the target of government surveillance activities under the USA PATRIOT Act in terms of a specific individual or the collective of which they are a part, a framing distinction that is made at the news story or text level. We also manipulate cues (or concept frames) in different ways across our various studies. For instance, our research focusing on government surveillance of Arabs uses concept labels that frame them as either citizens or immigrants, and as either extremists or moderates.

In the case of our studies that use activists as the subjects of surveillance, we manipulate audience predispositions toward the group by having respondents randomly receive stories about groups whose cause they were inclined to either support or oppose. By systematically invoking predispositions, we experimentally engage different schemas. By using factorial experimental designs that counterbalance the applications of story frames and cues, we can examine not only the main effects of the application of these story elements, but also the effects of their convergence. Effects are likely to be most pronounced when frames and cues work together to activate similar schemas (Cho et al., 2006).

Framing Outcomes

The MFM and MPM leave some important questions unanswered: First, what are the potential outcomes of the effects of frames and cues? Second, what audience predispositions and motivations might affect the power of media frames and cues to influence these outcomes?

There are a variety of potential outcomes to media framing. As noted in our discussion of the MPM, frames and cues begin the effects process by activating certain cognitive schemas. Although the fact that different frames and cues activate particular schemas might be considered a basic cognitive effect, there are several potential consequences of that activation. For example, schema activation may influence the way in which messages are processed and new information is acquired. As such, one potential framing outcome is the acquisition of new information. In turn, this new knowledge may reinforce existing schemas or even add new cognitions to an individual's cognitive network. This may lead to the creation of new beliefs, the reinforcement of existing beliefs, or, in rare instances, the alteration of existing beliefs.

In actuality, effects on knowledge and beliefs are very similar. From a research standpoint, knowledge itself is inherently problematic as it implies that there is an objective standard for what is true. Beliefs, on the other hand, are what someone believes to be true. As such, it is difficult to establish clearly demarcated differences between framing effects on knowledge and on beliefs. Indeed, cognitively, the process is very much the same. That is, exposure to message frames and cues activates schemas, which influence message processing and the acquisition of new information, which may or may not be integrated into the existing cognitive structure. Thus, the effect is the integration of new information in the form of knowledge/beliefs, regardless of whether or not that knowledge is in fact true, or only believed to be true. This may manifest itself in more complex, integrated, or elaborated cognitions.

Other potential cognitive effects of message frames and cues include evaluations, perceptions, and attributions, which are somewhat easier to measure than knowledge and are thus frequently used as outcome variables for framing effects research. For example, McLeod and Detenber (1999) examined the effects of news stories about social protest on evaluations of the effectiveness of the protest and perceptions of the conduct of the protesters and police. Iyengar (1991) looked at framing effects on attributions of responsibility for the creation (causal responsibility) and resolution (treatment responsibility) of social problems.

While framing effects are generally thought of as being cognitive in nature, schema activation may lead to other outcomes such as the formation and change of attitudes, and the promotion and reinforcement of related behaviors. By activating certain schemas that promote a particular way of understanding situations, issues, and problems, media frames may influence such affective orientations as attitudes toward welfare, affirmative action, and homosexuals (Nelson and Kinder, 1996; Shen, 2004b) or such behaviors as political decision making (Druckman, 2001; Shah et al., 1996). All of these outcomes speak to the multilevel nature of framing effects, from the cognitive to the behavioral.

Framing Moderators

Whether one is examining cognitive, affective, or behavioral framing outcomes, the nature of effects is likely to be subject to the influence of moderating variables. Moderators are factors that either increase or decrease the strength of framing effects, or define the conditions under which framing effects will or will not occur. In Figure 1.3, these moderators are represented by the orientations (including motivations and predispositions) that shape the nature of message effects outcomes. In other words, moderating variables can suppress or enhance the influence of framing, priming, and cueing effects.

There are several potential moderators that can be linked to Petty and Cacioppo's (1986) Elaboration Likelihood Model (ELM). At the center of the ELM is issue involvement, as it increases both motivation and ability to process media content (Petty et al., 1991). As with knowledge, the nature of involvement's moderating role is complicated. On one hand, motivation may lead to more thorough message processing, thereby increasing message effects. On the other hand, involvement may be associated with stronger predispositions that are likely to be more resistant to message effects. In addition, both the ELM and Eagly and Chaiken's (1993) Heuristic-Systematic Model (HSM) suggest that involvement is related to the strategies that people use to process messages. High-involvement individuals are more likely to engage in "central route" processing, the conscious and systematic evaluation of a message's manifest content. Alternatively, low-involvement individuals engage in less effortful "peripheral route" processing by focusing on heuristic cues (e.g., the attractiveness of a message source) that are external to the message's manifest content. As such, the influence of the framing of a content element will affect high and low involvement individuals differently.

Shen's (2004a) study of the effects of political ads stressing either candidate issues or character showed that a message's potential to activate mental constructs was related to the degree of correspondence between characteristics of a message and the availability of preexisting schemas. Using a thought-listing technique to assess activation, this study found that issue ads elicited more thoughts from issue-oriented individuals and character ads activated more thoughts from people with more developed character schemas. In other words, messages that resonated with preexisting schemas were more powerful in eliciting reasons underlying respondents' voting decisions, indicating that mental structure plays an important moderating role in framing effects.

Shen's (2004a) research also provides an example of how predispositions may moderate framing effects. In fact, there are innumerable potentially moderating predispositions. These potential moderators include, but are not limited to, political predispositions (i.e., liberal vs. conservative ideology), issue predispositions (i.e., preexisting positions on issues featured in the message), actor predispositions (i.e., orientations toward individuals and collectives featured in the message), and media predispositions (i.e., media credibility, trust, and biased perceptions). All of these predispositions might come into play to regulate the impact of message frames.

In addition to the internal cognitive moderators described here, there are social variables that also regulate the nature of message framing effects. For example, Druckman and Nelson (2003) illustrate the influence of social interaction by providing evidence that the tendency to engage in conversations that include a diversity of perspectives reduces framing effects by creating greater potential for the activation of countervailing schemas. Given this finding, we might also expect that framing effects would be greater for individuals who operate within homogeneous social networks than for individuals who are part of heterogeneous social networks in which they are more likely to encounter diverse conversations.

A Framing Analogy Revisited

Near the start of this chapter, we introduced two analogies that past scholars have offered to illustrate the role of news frames: the picture frame (Bateson, 1972) and the building structure (Bock and Loebell, 1990). While we appreciate the usefulness of these analogies, we believe that they are limited in terms of their ability to capture the essence of news frames. In this section, we use the previous discussion of Figures 1.2 and 1.3 to extend previous analogies to a more comprehensive analogy to represent frames and their effects.

Our Message Framing Model (Figure 1.2) expands the notion of framing beyond the news story to other subunits of content contained within it. We note that the words chosen to represent concepts (cues) are framed in ways that connote meaning, as are the assertions into which they may be compiled. In turn, these assertions can be brought together to create themes, which ultimately may be used to construct news stories. Each of these hierarchical units can be framed in different ways to create different types of meaning. Though each hierarchical unit is to some degree independent of the others, certain framings of concepts lend themselves particularly well to certain assertions, which themselves are likely to be part of the development of particular themes, and so forth.

In this sense, the construction of frames is analogous to the construction of a house. The house has a certain structure or meaning that is the product of the meaning choices made at smaller levels of content. In constructing the news story, the journalist may be following an abstract mental blueprint that is the product of professional, organizational, and cultural socialization. This blueprint calls for the use of certain concepts (the building blocks or bricks). The bricks are assembled into walls (assertions) and rooms (themes), which ultimately give structure to the house (news story). Like building houses, there are infinite ways to construct news stories, but there are common patterns of story construction (such as using an individual as an exemplar to personalize and illustrate a more complex underlying topic or issue), just as there are common and fashionable building styles for houses.

While the house analogy is not entirely new, its utility can be advanced by applying it to framing effects. In this case, the audience member encountering a news story is like a visitor arriving at a house. The visitor has seen many houses before and is able to recognize the features that characterize the new house. The perspective from which the visitor approaches the house, the visitor's sightlines into the various rooms, and the path taken through the house provide different perspectives on the interior. The visitor's estimations of who lives in the house and what they are like is at least partly a function of the interplay between the structure of the house and the ways of seeing into it. The visitor brings predispositions to the experience (e.g., preconceptions, tastes, lifestyles, etc.). Thus, the past experiences and predispositions that are embedded in the visitor's cognitive framework shape the resultant experience and attributions. As a result, different visitors will experience the house differently (e.g., they will attend to different features and notice different things within it depending on their vantage points). In essence, reactions to the new house reflect in part the nature of the house, and in part the nature of the visitor. This is much like reactions to news stories, which are in part a reflection of the nature of the news story (its frame and the frames of its components), and in part the result of characteristics of the audience member (e.g., mental schemas) as they interact with content characteristics.

The research reported in this book adopts this perspective on the nature of framing effects. That is, we see news frames as the culmination of the meaning embedded in the story and its component parts, all of which can be framed in alternative ways. We hypothesize that news story effects will be a function of these content frames, as they interact with the predispositions of the audience. Moreover, framing effects are the result of cognitive processes in which message features activate available schemas, rendering them more accessible for subsequent judgments. We study these framing effects in the context of what has been a central political debate of the new millennium, the tension between national security and civil liberties.

2

Framing Surveillance and the War on Terror

"While our job is not finished, we have used the tools provided in the Patriot Act to fulfill our first responsibility to protect the American people. We have used these tools to prevent terrorists from unleashing more death and destruction on our soil. We have used these tools to save innocent American lives. We have used these tools to provide the security that ensures liberty."

– John Ashcroft
Former U.S. Attorney General
August 19, 2003

"The tour that the attorney general has started suggests that they've had enough criticism of what they've been doing that they've found it necessary to actually go out and defend the PATRIOT Act, with all of its intrusive measures. All the violations of people's privacy, doing things without the supervision of a court, doing things in a warrantless fashion, many of the things that are banned by our Bill of Rights, they're doing it."

– Larry Pratt
Executive Director of Gun Owners of America
August 21, 2003

Following the events of September 11, 2001, a core issue that lay dormant beneath the surface of everyday politics roared to life, confronting policymakers, journalists, activists, and citizens with what has arguably been the central civic dilemma of the new millennium. How do we strike an appropriate balance between concerns about guarding citizens against future acts of terrorism, while minimizing infringements on civil liberties? The Bush administration and certain members of Congress argued that fundamental changes in intelligence gathering and law enforcement were necessary to protect national security, an assertion that resulted in both the founding of the U.S. Department of Homeland Security and the passage of the USA PATRIOT Act in October of 2001.

The latter initiative has prompted serious criticism from both policymakers and activists, who assert that certain provisions compromised established civil liberties of American citizens. Indeed, evidence has accumulated that government agencies substantially overstepped the expanded powers of the PATRIOT Act, engaging in illegal surveillance activities. This dilemma, and the conflict that has unfolded around it, form the central issue of this book.

This chapter begins by tracing some of the most salient historical events where national security and civil liberties have come into conflict. This brief review shows that this debate has been a part of American politics and society since the Colonial era. It also illustrates a common pattern in which an external conflict provides an impetus for weakening civil liberties in the interest of national security, followed by a resurgence of civil liberties as the conflict subsides. The observation that, in the case of the USA PATRIOT Act and its associated domestic surveillance, the initial response was so strong and resurgence has taken so long and been relatively weak, is a major impetus for the research reported in this book.

The next section describes the emergence of the national security/civil liberties debate initiated by the passage of the USA PATRIOT Act following the September 11, 2001, terrorist attacks. We follow the story through more than a decade as information about government's surveillance practices began to trickle out through various leaks and investigative news stories (see Lichtblau, 2008). As the massive scope of the national security state was gradually revealed, including extensive domestic surveillance, debate within the power structure also emerged to the point where even Congressman James Sensenbrenner, Jr. (R-WI), the "architect" of the PATRIOT Act, sent a letter to U.S. Attorney General Eric Holder to complain that the surveillance activities had gone too far. We tie this discussion of the public policy arena to subsequent trends in public opinion, noting that public support for the policies of the War on Terror remained relatively strong throughout the decade that followed the 9/11 attacks, with the citizenry largely willing to surrender some personal freedom in order to reduce the threat of terrorism. It was only in 2013 that the public opinion pendulum exhibited a meaningful shift back in the direction of support for civil liberties, although support had been waning. This book seeks to shed light on why public support for these surveillance activities took so long to fade.

Because exposure to the events and issues related to the national security/civil liberties debate occurs largely through the news media for a vast majority of Americans, it becomes important to understand not only how the media covered this debate, but also how the public reacted to media coverage, which we explore in a series of experiments reported in subsequent chapters. Setting the stage for these studies, this section begins by addressing the role of the media as an intermediary between policymakers and the public, as mainstream news institutions respond in ways that support established authorities during periods of war and crisis. We then present results from two content analyses and descriptive evidence of how this post-9/11 debate was covered in the mainstream media, identifying some of the features of this news coverage, including news frames and cues thought to shape public beliefs, attitudes, and behaviors. Next, since the experimental stimuli that we used in our experiments were fictional news stories about Arab and activist groups subjected to surveillance under the PATRIOT Act, we review actual news stories that focused on the surveillance of such groups under the PATRIOT Act.

We conclude this chapter with a section that discusses the distinction between individual and collective framing in the context of news stories about domestic surveillance, identifying some the expected outcomes examined in our experiments. We argue that journalistic norms of personifying such stories by highlighting individual cases may accentuate the perceived threat of terrorism in a way that shapes audience reactions. We conclude this chapter by identifying key political outcomes related to the tension between national security and civil liberties – sophistication of thought, tolerance toward others, and expressive participation – and specify how they are likely to be influenced by the individual versus collective framing.

Thus, this chapter lays the contextual groundwork for the effects that we examine in our experimental research presented in subsequent chapters. We conducted this research with the theoretical expectation that certain persistent frames and cues contained in media representations of applications of the PATRIOT Act would shape the sophistication, tolerance, and participation of news consumers. Specifically, we hypothesized that the use of individual exemplars to frame stories about the government's surveillance of domestic groups might reduce citizens' complexity of thought, their openness to different social and political groups, and their willingness to engage in debate over civil liberties protections. These outcomes are consequential because they are essential elements of the democratic ideal of a thoughtful, open-minded, and responsive citizenry. Moreover, we recognize that media may simultaneously encourage one of these ideals, while discouraging others, fostering both intolerance and participation, for example. We explore these issues in the chapters that follow, but before we do so, some historical context is necessary.

National Security versus Civil Liberties

It would be a mistake to think that the tension between national security and civil liberties was born during the aftermath of September 11. In fact, there have been numerous specific instances in American history in which federal legislation and policies, initiated in the name of protecting national security, accentuated the fundamental tension between security and liberty.

In the late eighteenth century, under threat of war with France, Congress passed The Alien and Sedition Acts of 1798, which increased the residency requirement for citizenship from five to fourteen years, authorized the deportation of potentially dangerous nonresidents, sanctioned the wartime arrest and imprisonment of nonresidents under the influence of the enemy, imposed fines and prison terms against the printing of "false, scandalous and malicious" material, and criminalized false criticisms of the government, Congress, and the President (see Smith, 1999; Stone, 2004).

Similarly, during the Civil War, civil liberties were rescinded in the name of national security. In 1861, President Abraham Lincoln suspended the Writ of Habeas Corpus, leading to mass arrests of people suspected of being Confederate sympathizers. Under this suspension, the government could detain individuals without official justification. After reinstating Habeas Corpus in 1862, Lincoln suspended it again seven months later in order to deal with disloyalty among the Union troops and purportedly seditious newspaper editors. Lincoln did, however, intercede to reinstate the *Chicago Times*' right to publish after it had been closed by a Union general for criticizing Lincoln's leadership (see Neely, 1991; Smith, 1999; Stone, 2004).

Between the Civil War and World War I, there was a series of disputes between business and labor in which the government was complicit in repressive activities to suppress labor organizing and strikes in the name of protecting national security against domestic threats (see Goldstein, 2001). For example, during the Red Scare of 1873–1878, various initiatives empowered local police and the military to take action against communists, anarchists, unions, and immigrants. Four anarchists were executed in Chicago for merely advocating violence against police in 1888. Later, during the Communist-Anarchist-Labor Scare of 1892–1896, then President of the American Railway Union Eugene V. Debs was indicted for conspiracy, as newspapers painted him as seeking to lead a revolution that would install him as dictator. In other incidents, strike leaders and union members were indicted for treason and "aiding the enemies of the State of Pennsylvania" (Goldstein, 2001, p. 46).

During the twentieth century, there were numerous episodes that involved the clash of concerns about national security and civil liberties surrounding the presence of fascists and communists in the United States. During World War I, a host of legislative initiatives were enacted to suppress free speech and the press in the name of national interests. For example, Congress passed the Sedition Act of 1918, which punished individuals for criticizing the government and interfering with military activities such as recruitment, and sanctioned newspapers for publishing "false, scandalous, and malicious" information against the U.S. government. Though this act was repealed in 1921, the U.S. Postmaster General Albert Burleson extended the Espionage Act of 1917 to stop delivery of antiwar newspapers. President Wilson proposed an additional provision to the Espionage Act that would have permitted the direct censorship of newspapers; however, Congress rejected this proposal. This legislation was also used to prosecute and convict members of the Industrial Workers of the World (IWW) and other socialists in various trials around the country. During this period, the IWW defense teams were prohibited from using the mail and had their offices raided, meetings disrupted, team members arrested or deported, and advertisements suppressed (see Goldstein, 2001; Stone, 2004). In addition, the Trading with the Enemy Act of 1917 (TWEA) required foreign language publishers carrying news about the war to submit a translation to the Post Office before mailing.

In the immediate aftermath of World War I, fears about the spread of communism emboldened U.S. Attorney General A. Mitchell Palmer to lead a series of raids (known as The Palmer Raids of 1918–1921) against leftist radicals. In one such raid, 249 resident aliens, including feminist writer Emma Goldman, were deported on a ship to the Soviet Union (see Feuerlicht, 1971; Hoyt, 1969; Stone, 2004). In 1940, the Smith Alien Registration Act sanctioned fines and imprisonment for any individual who advocates or engages in actions to overthrow the U.S. government, a law that arguably conflicted with First Amendment free speech protections. The Smith Act (i.e., the Alien Registration Act of 1940) and the Espionage Act were used as the basis for prosecuting and curtailing the activities of Nazi sympathizers such as William Dudley Pelley and Father Charles Coughlin during the Roosevelt administration, and communists during the Truman administration (see Belknap, 1977; Pember, 1969; Stone, 2004).

During the middle third of the twentieth century, the House Committee on Un-American Activities (HUAC) investigated subversive elements, beginning with Nazi propaganda and Ku Klux Klan activities, and later shifting its attention to the presence of communists in American society, including the entertainment industry (see O'Reilly, 1983; Redish, 2005; Stone, 2004). A similar spirit guided the 1954 Army-McCarthy Congressional hearings into the alleged presence of communists in the military (see Bayley, 1982; Fried, 1990; Redish, 2005; Stone, 2004; Straight, 1954). Fears about foreigners espousing subversive ideas led to provisions of the McCarran-Walter Immigration and Nationality Act of 1952 that allowed the government to ban "ideologically dangerous individuals" (including such notable individuals as Pierre Trudeau, who later become Prime Minister of Canada; actor/singer Yves Montand; authors Graham Greene, Farley Mowat, and Jan Myrdal; Nobel Prize winning writers Gabriel García Márquez and Pablo Neruda; and economist Ernest Mandel) from entering the United States (see Mowat, 1985; Shanks, 2001), a policy that has been reinvigorated under the PATRIOT Act.

Because of concerns about national security during World War II, President Franklin Roosevelt issued Executive Order 9066, which forcibly relocated about 120,000 people of Japanese descent living on the West Coast, 62% of whom were American citizens, to detention camps. Relocated individuals lost property and other assets in the process (see Daniels, 1975; Harvey, 2003; Hayashi, 2004; Stone, 2004; Yancey, 1998). A smaller number of people of German and Italian descent were also interned. Similar concerns about safety and security were used to justify the relocation, and, in some instances, the extermination of Native Americans dating from the 1500s into the twentieth century. The Indian Removal Act of 1830 passed under President Andrew Jackson provides a salient example (see Garrison, 2002; Green, 1982).

During times of war, the U.S. government has a long history of engaging in surveillance and other efforts to repress the activities of antiwar groups. In addition to the aforementioned examples of wartime repression by President Lincoln during the Civil War and President Wilson during World War I, such activities also occurred during World War II under President Roosevelt. But perhaps the most vigorous surveillance and infiltration of antiwar movements occurred during the war in Vietnam when the FBI was engaged in a variety of counterintelligence programs (COINTELPRO) against such groups as the Southern Christian Leadership Council (SCLC), the Student Nonviolent Coordinating Committee (SNCC), the National Association for the Advancement of Colored People (NAACP), the Black Panthers, the Nation of Islam (Black Muslims), and the Students for a Democratic Society (SDS), as well as against various movement leaders and spokespersons such as Stokely Carmichael, H. Rap Brown, Elijah Muhammed, Malcolm X, Martin Luther King, Jr., Jesse Jackson, Benjamin Spock, Joan Baez, and William Sloane Coffin. These are but a few of a multitude of groups and individuals that were subjected to surveillance activities of the FBI, the CIA, the NSA, the IRS, the military, and other government organizations under the Johnson and Nixon administrations. This era also included numerous conspiracy trials of antiwar demonstrators, most notably the trial of the Chicago Eight, which included such notable defendants as Bobby Seale, Tom Hayden, Jerry Rubin, and Abbie Hoffman (see Goldstein, 2001; Stone, 2004).

There have been numerous cases in which the U.S. government has tried to use the national security argument to suppress press freedom to publish information. In 1917, under the authority of the Espionage Act, U.S. Postmaster General Albert Burleson refused to carry the August issue of the *Masses*, a countercultural monthly magazine that had been critical of the military draft and the U.S. involvement in World War I. The *Masses* successfully fought this policy when then U.S. District Court Judge Learned Hand ruled on First Amendment grounds that the Espionage Act could not be applied to the magazine's content (see Stone, 2004). This, however, was overturned on appeal. The Circuit Court of Appeals ruled that the postmaster's decision must stand unless clearly wrong, and further that speech is punishable if it encourages resistance to the law. The *Masses* case was the precedent that allowed Burleson to act almost without challenge (Chaffee, 1941).

In 1971, a Department of Defense employee Daniel Ellsberg leaked secret government documents to the *New York Times* and the *Washington Post*. When the newspapers began publishing the documents (known as the Pentagon Papers), which revealed unpublicized details about how the government had expanded the war in Vietnam, the Nixon administration filed for injunctions to stop both newspapers on national security grounds. Ultimately, the Supreme Court threw out the injunctions after failing to find sufficient grounds to merit prior restraint (see Ellsberg, 2002; Rudenstine, 1996; Stone, 2004; Ungar, 1989).

The government again attempted to use the national security rationale to suppress a story that included publicly available descriptions of how hydrogen bombs work, published in *The Progressive* magazine in 1979. The initial publication of the article was stopped by a federal district court injunction. However, when *The Progressive* appealed the injunction, the government abandoned the case as the bomb information was ultimately published in the *Madison Press Connection*, a short-lived daily formed by striking workers from the two Madison, WI daily newspapers (see De Volpi et al., 1981; Morland, 1981).

Each of these policies and proceedings represents an attempt by the government to infringe on the freedoms and civil rights of individuals and groups, investigating and surveilling them in the name of protecting national security. These are but a few of the more prominent examples among many instances in which these fundamental values have been pitted against each other.

Security and Liberty after 9/11

The dilemma raised by the PATRIOT Act is certainly not new. Nonetheless, it is clear that in this most recent instance, the government response to a domestic threat was widespread and encompassing – and may have even crossed the lines of legality – yet is in many ways less visible to the public. This may reflect the stark reality that Americans woke to on the morning of September 11, 2001, when two hijacked passenger planes were flown into the twin towers of the World Trade Center in lower Manhattan, causing them to collapse. A third plane slammed into the side of the Pentagon in Arlington, VA. A fourth plane never reached its intended target, instead crashing in a field near Shanksville, PA, after passengers attacked the hijackers. Over 3,000 people died as a result of these events, surpassing the death toll at Pearl Harbor on December 7, 1941. These events set a host of U.S. government initiatives in motion, including the "War on Terror," the invasions and occupations of both Afghanistan and Iraq, the consolidation of a variety of national security agencies under the auspices of the new Department of Homeland Security, and, of course, the enacting and implementation of the USA PATRIOT Act.

The longstanding tension between liberty and security was brought into sharp focus by the passage of House Resolution 3162, more commonly known as the USA PATRIOT Act, on October 24, 2001, by a vote of 357 to 66. The bill was approved by the Senate by a vote of 98–1 (Senator Russ Feingold [D-WI] was the lone dissenter) and signed by President Bush two days later (Lawrence, 2001). This act expanded the power of the Department of Justice, and its agencies such as the FBI, to investigate suspicious individuals and groups. It also set the stage for the National Security Agency to engage in the most extensive set of domestic surveillance programs ever witnessed on U.S. soil (Greenwald, 2013b). While administration officials under both Presidents Bush and Obama have repeatedly asserted that the new powers granted by the PATRIOT Act are essential to protecting national security in the post-9/11 era, critics have decried the broad authority ceded to the executive branch of government and its law enforcement officials and legal challenges have been initiated.

The PATRIOT Act granted greater latitude to government agencies to engage in domestic surveillance, while reducing requirements for judicial oversight. Many PATRIOT Act provisions were not newly developed in response to the September 11 terrorist attacks, but had previously been turned down by Congress on the grounds that they eroded civil liberties. The terrorist attacks merely provided the impetus to push through these changes, which were passed through Congress with little inquiry, deliberation, or debate. Opposition to the bill was suppressed with charges that the legislation's critics were impeding national security, during a time in which the public was feeling particularly vulnerable and dissent was being stifled.

The PATRIOT Act expanded the domestic surveillance capabilities of government in four domains: records searches (Section 215), secret searches (Section 213), intelligence searches (Section 218), and "trap and trace" searches (Section 214). The records search provision made it possible for the FBI to secure client records from doctors, libraries, bookstores, travel agencies, credit card companies, universities, phone companies, and Internet service providers, without having to demonstrate "probable cause," without judicial oversight, and without notification of the person under surveillance. The secret search provision permits federal authorities with a search warrant to engage in an unsupervised search and seizure on private property without notifying the owner, regardless of whether or not this activity has anything to do with combating terrorism. The PATRIOT Act also expanded the foreign intelligence exception in the 1978 Foreign Intelligence Surveillance Act (FISA), which permits intelligence agencies to conduct searches and wiretaps without first demonstrating probable cause, to include law enforcement regarding domestic criminal activities. Finally, the PATRIOT Act loosened restrictions on the "pen register/trap and trace" searches on tracking telephone and Internet communications. Previously, the FBI could get a warrant to monitor the origin and destination (but not content) of electronic communications without demonstrating reasonable suspicion. The PATRIOT Act expanded the power of such warrants by eliminating the locality restriction, making the warrant executable anywhere, and by allowing law enforcement agents to specify the monitoring locations unsupervised after getting the warrant. According to the ACLU, each of these provisions conflicts with previously established Fourth Amendment rights, and removes important layers of oversight and accountability for government law enforcement activities.

The Expanding Surveillance State

In addition to the expanded powers granted under the PATRIOT Act, as revealed through what began as a trickle of reports in the press and ultimately become a deluge in 2013, various government agencies have engaged in a range of surveillance activities in the name of protecting national security. In 2006, the *Washington Post* reported that the government has been using computers to monitor international faxes, e-mail messages, and telephone calls. The growth of digital technologies not only provides citizens with greater access to information and communication opportunities, but also offers the government far greater capability to engage in surveillance activities. Computers identify potentially suspicious messages for further scrutiny by human analysts. In most cases, these messages are cleared as being free of any illegal activity. Intelligence experts consider it a "triumph for artificial intelligence if a fraction of 1 percent of the computer-flagged conversations guide human analysts to meaningful leads." For example, of the estimated 5,000 individuals who have had their phone conversations and e-mail messages monitored by human analysts, "fewer than 10 U.S. citizens or residents a year . . . have aroused enough suspicion during warrantless eavesdropping to justify interception of their domestic calls" (Gellman et al., 2006).

Later that year, *USA Today* reported that the National Security Agency (NSA) has been compiling a phone call database designed to track all phone calls made within the United States. Three companies, AT&T, Verizon, and BellSouth, gave the NSA the records of millions of calls, though Qwest refused to comply. The NSA claimed at the time that the content of phone calls was not monitored as a part of this program, which was alleged to simply track the source and destination of phone calls, with a focus on personal calls made to and from international locations (Diamond and Cauley, 2006).

In 2007, the *Washington Post* ran a story about an internal government audit that revealed that the FBI broke the law and/or agency procedures over 1,000 times during the course of engaging in unauthorized surveillance of domestic phone calls, e-mail messages, and financial transactions. This number was considered staggeringly large at the time, considering that the audit only dealt with 10% of national security investigations (Solomon, 2007). Despite these allegations, reporting on the government's surveillance activities across the decade following passage of the PATRIOT Act typically focused on its application to specific Muslim citizens and immigrants, as well as particular political activists, a point we return to in the following section.

Among the notable journalists who were at the forefront of reporting on the expansion of the surveillance state and the massive monitoring of Americans (including Eric Lichtblau, Michael Isikoff, Barton Gellman, and Glenn Greenwald) were Dana Priest and William Arkin. These two reporters published a series of articles under the banner of "Top Secret America," first in a *Washington Post* series during 2010 and then in their book the following year, which detailed the exponential growth of the American intelligence apparatus (see Priest and Arkin, 2010a; Priest and Arkin, 2011). Based on a massive influx of funding and the organization of the Department of Homeland Security, they reported that the U.S. intelligence community had grown to 854,000 individuals with top-secret security clearances (roughly 1 of every 300 persons in the 2011 U.S. population), employed by 1,271 government organizations and 1,931 private companies in 10,000 different U.S. locations.

The surveillance apparatus created by this growth was divulged to be massive in scope. As early as 2010, Priest and Arkin were reporting that, "every day, collection systems at the National Security Agency intercept and store 1.7 billion e-mails, phone calls and other types of communications. The NSA sorts a fraction of those into 70 separate databases" (Priest and Arkin, 2010a). Since the 9/11 terrorist attacks, this monitoring included "the FBI, local police, state homeland security offices and military criminal investigators [participating in a system that was] the largest and most technologically sophisticated in the nation's history." Their sources revealed that the government "collects, stores and analyzes information about thousands of U.S. citizens and residents, many of whom have not been accused of any wrongdoing." Surveillance measures have included such technologies as infrared license plate scanning and surveillance cameras in public places. In many cases, these technologies, funded in the name of protecting against terrorism, have been used for purposes that go well beyond guarding against terrorism (Priest and Arkin, 2010b).

Adding to these claims of abuse of government power – that is, "Big Brother" – was Glenn Greenwald, first with *Salon* and then with the *Guardian*, whose disclosures about the scope of domestic surveillance presaged the Snowden leak. As early as April 2012, he was highlighting how much surveillance had increased under President Obama, reporting that the NSA held over 20 trillion transactions about U.S. citizens with other U.S. citizens (Greenwald, 2012). Whistleblower William Binney, who resigned from the NSA after almost 40 years of service in protest over the NSA's domestic spying, stated the following:

The data that's being assembled is about everybody. And from that data, then they can target anyone they want.... That... estimate only was involving phone calls and emails. It didn't involve any queries on the net or ... any financial transactions or credit card stuff.

Greenwald went on to contend that, "Obama's unprecedented war on whistleblowing has been, in large part, designed to shield from the American public any knowledge of just how invasive this Surveillance State has become." Senators Ron Wyden (D-OR) and Mark Udall (D-CO) have repeatedly warned that domestic spying under the PATRIOT Act has been broadened in a manner that would shock the American public. In light of the subsequent Snowden leaks, we now know that the scope of this unauthorized surveillance was actually larger and more intrusive than previously understood.

Yet despite these reports, claims, and concerns, the PATRIOT Act was not only renewed under the Obama administration in 2010, "even though the terrorist threat seemed less urgent" (Wallace-Wells, 2011), it was extended well beyond jihadist threats. For example, between 2006 and 2009, delayed-notice search warrants issued under the PATRIOT Act were mainly applied in drug crimes (1,618 cases) and fraud investigations (122 cases), as opposed to terrorist activities (15 cases) (Wallace-Wells, 2011).

Nonetheless, the need for these expanded powers was justified by Attorney General Eric Holder in late 2010, after the "Top Secret America" series, when he asserted the scope and nature of continuing threat of "homegrown" terror and making the case for continued domestic surveillance powers. Holder stated that "the terrorists only have to be successful once. . . . You didn't worry about this even two years ago – about individuals, about Americans, to the extent that we now do" (Cloherty and Thomas, 2010). This provides a clear example of an elite framing the threat of terrorism in individual terms, personifying the danger posed by individual "homegrown" radicals. Taking this framing a step further, he went on to link this risk to radical cleric and U.S. citizen Anwar al Awlaki, who, Holder said, "ranks right up there with Osama bin Laden" (Cloherty and Thomas, 2010).

Yet according to the New American Foundation, the number of "homegrown" jihadists either indicted or convicted decreased dramatically over a period of five years, from forty-one cases in 2009 to just six in 2013. The number actually plotting attacks within the U.S. also diminished from twelve in 2011 to just three in 2013 (Bergman and Sterman, 2013). Yet the visibility of individual threats remained prominent, partly due to a number of lethal attacks characterized as acts of domestic terrorism:

- In November 2009, Major Nidal Malik Hasan killed thirteen people and injured thirty-two at Fort Hood in Killeen, Texas. This attack was described by the U.S. Senate as "the worst terrorist attack on U.S. soil since September 11, 2001" (Lieberman and Collins, 2011).
- In August 2012, Wade Michael Page, a white supremacist, attacked a Sikh temple in Oak Creek, Wisconsin, killing six and injuring three. His ties to the Hammerskins, a neo-Nazi skinhead group, led this to be defined as an act of domestic terrorism.
- In April 2013, the Tsarnaev brothers allegedly planted bombs near the finish line of the Boston Marathon, killing four and wounding over 260 others, prompting an unprecedented manhunt that led to the killing of one brother and capture of the other.

The Snowden Revelations
In May of 2013, just after the Boston bombings, President Obama called for greater government powers to monitor the Internet, claiming that evolving communication technologies have allowed dangerous groups to elude government scrutiny. A General Counsel for the FBI, Andrew Weissmann, stated that "the proposal was aimed only at preserving law enforcement officials' longstanding ability to investigate suspected criminals, spies and terrorists subject to a court's permission" (Savage, 2013). The government's assertion about their dwindling

surveillance capacity and the reach of their activities was disconfirmed by a string of news reports, which included evidence of targeting whistleblowers.

On May 13, the *Associated Press* broke a story revealing that the Department of Justice had acquired two months of phone records from AP reporters and editors. According to Gary Pruitt, AP President and CEO of AP, this acquisition was a "massive and unprecedented intrusion" into how organizations gather the news, giving the government potential access to all confidential sources used during that period. This surveillance of journalists was linked to a government probe investigating who was leaking information to the press about antiterrorism activities in Yemen (Sherman, 2013). Little more than a week later, the *New York Times* reported that the Department of Justice was searching *Fox News* reporter James Rosen's e-mail messages as part of a separate inquiry investigating leaks about espionage activities in North Korea and threatening to prosecute him (Stelter and Shear, 2013).

With members of the news media subjected to electronic surveillance by the government, press concern about civil liberties infringements began to mount. On June 5, the *Guardian* broke the news that the U.S. government obtained a court order to collect the phone records of millions of Verizon customers, both domestic and international calls, even though the vast majority of those customers were not suspected of committing crimes (Greenwald, 2013a). The Obama administration subsequently defended the practice as "a critical tool in protecting the nation from terrorist threats" (Hosenball and Heavey, 2013).

As the news of this latest revelation spread, criticism from within the power structure surfaced from both the left and from the right. For example, in his letter to U.S. Attorney General Eric Holder, Republican congressman and author of the PATRIOT Act James Sensenbrenner expressed his opinion that government surveillance activities under the auspices of the act had gone too far: "These reports are deeply concerning and raise questions about whether our constitutional rights are secure." Former Vice President Al Gore called the indiscriminate surveillance "obscenely outrageous" (Roberts and Ackerman, 2013).

This report was immediately followed by new revelations published by other news organizations. The *Los Angeles Times* reported that "The federal government has amassed a database for at least seven years containing details on virtually every telephone call made within the United States or between this country and telephones abroad." While the report stressed that the surveillance did not include monitoring individual conversations, it noted that the government has been storing and analyzing the patterns of conversation networks in an attempt to identify suspicious activity (Dilanian and Lauter, 2013). At the same time, the *Washington Post* published a report revealing the NSA and FBI's secret PRISM program, which was "tapping directly into the central servers of nine leading U.S. Internet companies, extracting audio and video chats, photographs, e-mails, documents, and connection logs that enable analysts to track foreign targets" (Gellman and Poitras, 2013). Another report indicated that the NSA was collecting and analyzing customer data from fifty American companies, including phone companies, Internet service providers, credit card companies, and credit rating agencies (Ambinder, 2013). From this flurry of reports, it seemed evident that up until this point in time, the American public had only seen the tip of the surveillance iceberg.

Shortly after this flurry of reports surfaced, Edward Snowden, a former CIA employee and NSA contractor, revealed himself as the source of the documents that had been leaked to the news media. His disclosures vaulted the erosion of civil liberties in the name of security into one of the top stories of the year. *Time Magazine* listed Snowden as the runner-up for Person of the Year and his leaks as the fourth largest international story of 2013, noting that "The cache of documents released by NSA whistleblower Edward Snowden shed light on the extent of U.S. espionage operations in various parts of the world and threatened to damage U.S. relations with some key international players, who claimed in public to be furious with the U.S.'s snooping in their own countries" (Rayman, 2013). Concerned that the extent of civil liberties infringements of these surveillance programs had worsened under President Obama, Snowden released the details of the data mining activities to prominent news organizations (Gellman and Blake, 2013), asserting that Obama "closed the door on investigating systemic violations of law, deepened and expanded several abusive programs, and refused to spend the political capital to end the kind of human rights violations like we see in Guantanamo" (Cohen, 2013).

Among the tactics revealed by the documents that Snowden provided to the news media was an NSA domestic surveillance program called XKeyscore, which "allows analysts to search with no prior authorization through vast databases containing emails, online chats and the browsing histories of millions of individuals." XKeyscore training materials indicate that NSA analysts have the ability to track the content of Internet activity of U.S. citizens by providing a simple justification and without oversight from the courts or even other NSA personnel (Greenwald, 2013b). According to the *Wall Street Journal*, NSA surveillance has the potential to track about 75% of U.S. Internet traffic. "In some cases, it retains the written content of emails sent between citizens within the U.S. and also filters domestic phone calls made with Internet technology" (Gorman and Valentino-DeVries, 2013). The NSA defended the XKeyscore program, stating that the "NSA's activities are focused and specifically deployed against – and only against – legitimate foreign intelligence targets . . . to protect our nation and its interests" (Greenwald, 2013b).

Subsequent media reports revealed another surveillance program described in the Snowden documents in which the NSA was collecting almost 5 billion records each day recording the locations of cell phones, "enabling the agency to track the movements of individuals – and map their relationships – in ways that would have been previously unimaginable. The records feed a vast database that stores information about the locations of at least hundreds of millions of devices" (Gellman and Soltani, 2013). The *Washington Post* detailed the

NSA's MYSTIC telephone surveillance program, which was able to capture all foreign telephone calls for one month to permit analysts to review entire conversations. The Snowden documents revealed that in a 2011 test of the program, it collected all calls to and from an unnamed country, which analysts sampled for review (Gellman and Soltani, 2014).

Recent revelations have documented a host of additional surveillance techniques by the NSA and their British counterpart, the GCHQ. Both have used cookies (small files sent from a website and stored in a user's computer to track sites visited by the user) in order to identify suspicious individuals to target for more invasive spyware programs (Soltani et al., 2013). The *New York Times* reported that the NSA "has implanted software in nearly 100,000 computers around the world that allows the United States to conduct surveillance on those machines and can also create a digital highway for launching cyberattacks." (Sanger and Shanker, 2014). Intelligence agencies have even used smartphone apps such as Angry Birds to hack unsuspecting users in order to harvest personal data, message content, contact information, and geographic location to profile users, including their sexual preferences, social networks, and movement patterns (Ball, 2014).

These intelligence agencies also deployed a program called "Optic Nerve," which collected the webcam images of millions of Internet users, most of whom were not even suspected of any criminal activity. "In one six-month period in 2008 alone, the agency collected webcam imagery – including substantial quantities of sexually explicit communications – from more than 1.8 million Yahoo user accounts globally." Running from 2008 through at least 2012, Snowden documents reveal that facial recognition technology was used to identify individuals (Ackerman and Ball, 2014). Once identified, these images could be connected to databases containing personal information, communications, and personal data (Risen and Poitras, 2014).

A *Washington Post* investigation based on the Snowden documents provides an example of how Internet surveillance spread from suspicious targets to innocent individuals. For example, "If a target entered an online chat room, the NSA collected the words and identities of every person who posted there, regardless of subject, as well as every person who simply 'lurked'" (Gellman et al., 2014). By some estimates, NSA tactics examine the communications of nine innocent people for every "suspicious" person monitored, collecting and retaining a large cache, even though it consists of personal correspondence, intimate photographs, medical records, and other private data belonging to blameless people (Doctorow, 2014).

While some may justify these domestic surveillance activities on the logic that intelligence agencies focus on the activities of dangerous terrorists who are engaged in illegal activities, as journalist Glenn Greenwald points out, the government has a long track record of using surveillance methods against dissenters who are not suspected of any criminal or terrorist activity. Greenwald cites the examples of the surveillance of Martin Luther King Jr. and various social movements and activist groups by the FBI under the direction of J. Edgar Hoover. Indeed, the documents released by Edward Snowden confirm suspicions that such surveillance would be used against dissenting individuals and groups (Greenwald, 2014).

Personifying the Threat

As the Snowden revelations began to surface, government officials immediately counterattacked on two fronts: justification and vilification. First, they began to *justify* the PRISM surveillance program. General Keith Alexander, Director of the NSA, "told Congress that more than 50 potential terrorist attacks have been thwarted by two controversial programs tracking more than a billion phone calls and vast swaths of Internet data each day." Though he provided members of the House Intelligence Committee with a full list of the foiled attacks, he only released cursory details of two plots publicly, including the case of Najibullah Zazi, an Afghan-American, who planned a suicide bombing in the New York subway system (Parkinson, 2013). U.S. Attorney General Eric Holder called Zazi's planned attack "one of the most serious terrorist threats to our nation since September 11, 2001 and were it not for the combined efforts of the law enforcement and intelligence communities, it would have been devastating" (FBI, February 22, 2010). As such, Zazi became the personified representation of the success of the NSA surveillance programs in thwarting evil, one of a long list of individual cases that were used to illustrate the success of global antiterrorism efforts.

Parallel to this were efforts to *vilify* Snowden, who was labeled a "traitor" by House Speaker John Boehner. Republican strategist Karl Rove accused Snowden of making the world a "less safe" place (Frumin, 2013). In the weeks that followed the revelations, former NSA Director Michael Hayden compared Snowden to terrorists and called the leak, "the most serious hemorrhaging of American secrets in the history of American espionage... [revealing] our sources and methods, our tactics, techniques and procedures to people around the world who wish the American nation and the American people harm" (Kaplan, 2013).

The journalists who reported on Snowden's revelations countered this view, asserting that Snowden did not release his trove of documents directly to the public. Instead, he filtered them through reporters, asking them to hold back information that might disclose compromising details. As a consequence, many have labeled Snowden a hero, a whistleblower, and a patriot who has defended the Constitution, with calls for his clemency gaining strength due to "the enormous value of the information he has revealed, and the abuses he has exposed" (*The New York Times*, 2014). As journalist Ezra Klein (2013) noted, "There's simply no doubt that his leaks led to more open debate and more democratic process."

Only after these major revelations about the size and scope of the surveillance state did public opinion begin to exhibit a meaningful shift toward civil liberties, even though groups of policy makers and civil libertarians worked to oppose the PATRIOT Act during its enactment and renewals. At various stages, there was considerable outcry from advocacy groups, civil libertarians, and current and former members of Congress, with many of these concerns now substantiated by the Snowden revelations. When these concerns were voiced, often in the form of opposition from legislative or judicial branches, they gained little traction in the face of claims about national security interests.

Policy Debate and Public Opinion about the PATRIOT Act
Even during the initial passage of the USA PATRIOT Act, just forty-five days after the 9/11 terrorist attacks, there was vigorous debate over the extent to which practices sanctioned by this legislation would infringe upon the civil liberties of individuals and groups. Critics charged that the PATRIOT Act eliminated important safeguards that protect citizens from unjust persecution and invasions of privacy. Civil liberties advocates argued that the PATRIOT Act and other practices of the "War on Terror" fundamentally changed the balance between national security and civil liberties to a dangerous extreme, removing restraints on wire tapping, Internet monitoring, and other monitoring techniques, and that these changes posed a serious threat to personal freedoms and privacy rights. According to the ACLU, the door had been opened for government agencies to engage in "the same abuses that took place in the 1970s and before, when the CIA engaged in widespread spying on protest groups and other Americans" (American Civil Liberties Union, 2001; see also Garrow, 1983). Many complained the PATRIOT Act redefined acts of civil disobedience used by protest groups as acts of "domestic terrorism," allowing the government to curtail the First Amendment rights of political activists.

These concerns were lodged despite the fact that there was tremendous public support for granting the government increased power in the aftermath of the 9/11 attacks. Just over a month after the attacks, a FOX News/Opinion Dynamics Poll found that 71% of participants agreed that Americans would have to give up some personal freedoms to make the country safe from terrorist attacks. Indeed, when polled, they appeared to favor many of the policies enacted in the PATRIOT Act. The NPR/Kaiser Family Foundation/Kennedy School of Government Poll conducted in November 2001 found that considerable portions of the population supported surveillance activities: 69% for telephone wiretaps, 72% for e-mail interception, 57% for regular mail interception, and 82% for Internet-use monitoring. This same poll revealed that a majority of Americans agreed that it was acceptable to permit the government to access citizen records as part of the war on terror: 76% supported government access to educational records, 82% for telephone records, 79% for bank records, 75% for credit card purchase records, and 75% for tax records.

Polls conducted during the same period found that three-quarters of Americans backed wiretaps for conversations between terror suspects and their attorneys and random searches at large public events, whereas a majority favored enhanced search and seizure powers and looser trial rules (ABC News/Washington Post Poll, November 2001; Field Poll, September 2001). Although potential violations of due process rights, few Americans felt these policies represented a risk to their personal freedoms. Along these same lines, the NPR Poll mentioned earlier found that 58% of respondents supported government detention of suspects without formal charges for up to one week, a number that only dropped to 48% when respondents were asked about indefinite detention. When polled about applying these police powers against people of Arab descent, public support for national security measures was even stronger. A Gallup Poll from September of 2001 showed that 58% of Americans agreed that Arabs should be taken aside at airports and subject to more intensive security, while 49% supported requiring Arabs, including citizens, to carry special ID cards. It was within this policy and opinion climate that the PATRIOT Act was passed.

Since being enacted, the PATRIOT Act has faced legal challenges, required multiple amendments and reauthorizations, and continually spurred outcry about the erosion of civil liberties. In later years, concerns have stemmed from reports of abuses and comments from members of Congress, who have expressed doubts about the scope of the surveillance activities.[1] These concerns were amplified by the Act's vague definition of terrorism, which invited law enforcement agencies to apply these powers beyond the War on Terror to monitor the activities of a wide range of individuals and groups, potentially for political reasons. Indeed, FBI surveillance, interviewing, and infiltration of antiwar protest groups and other "political troublemakers" – both Arab and non-Arab – raised the concern that the PATRIOT Act could have a chilling effect on legitimate political activities, from organizing protests to signing petitions. According to one Department of Justice Inspector General's Report, there were 1,076 complaints regarding civil liberties infringements related to the PATRIOT Act (Bohn, 2003).

Driven by concerns for civil liberties, a bill repealing the PATRIOT Act provision that permitted the execution of "sneak and peak" secret search warrants was passed by the House of Representatives by a vote of 309 to 118. Notably, Representative Clement L. Otter, a conservative Idaho Republican, sponsored the bill (Lichtblau, 2003a). Though the bill never made it through the Senate, Senators Larry Craig (R-ID) and Richard Durbin (D-IL)

---

[1] Despite these concerns, the War on Terror was also used to justify new levels of government secrecy and the denial of judicial rights. In *Center for National Security Studies v. U.S. Department of Justice*, an appeals court found that a public interest group was not entitled to the names of more than 800 people detained after the September 11 attacks. In a 2–1 decision, the majority of the court agreed with the Justice Department argument that naming terrorism suspects would give the enemy insight into the government's knowledge and investigation of its activities (Lane, 2004).

cosponsored their own reform bill in 2003,[2] the Safety and Freedom Ensured Act or SAFE Act (S-1709), to limit such searches (O'Rourke, 2005). The House later passed another bill by a vote of 238–187 (with the support of 38 Republicans) that limits the ability of government to access library and bookstore records without a warrant from a criminal court judge (Allen, 2005), even in the face of a veto threat from President Bush. These initiatives all failed to curtail the government's surveillance activities.

Instead, the PATRIOT Act was reauthorized under the Bush administration, first in 2005 and again in 2006, amidst growing questions from the public about the potential infringement of civil liberties. The House of Representatives voted to reauthorize a revised version of the PATRIOT Act by a vote of 280–138 (just two votes more than the two-thirds majority needed for reauthorization). During the Senate's reauthorization debate, Russ Feingold, the Senate's lone dissenting vote on the original passage of the PATRIOT Act, summarized opposition as follows:

Over 400 state and local government bodies passed resolutions pleading with Congress to change the law. Citizens have signed petitions, library associations and campus groups have organized to petition the Congress to act, numerous editorials have been written urging Congress not to reauthorize the law without adequate protections for civil liberties. These things occurred because Americans across the country recognize that the Patriot Act includes provisions that pose a threat to their privacy and liberty – values that are at the very core of what this country represents, of who we are as a people. (Nichols, 2006)

Others senators, such as Barack Obama, John Kerry, and Chuck Hagel, expressed concern about specific provisions that "would allow the government to obtain library, medical and gun records and other sensitive personal information." They called for changes to "protect innocent Americans from unnecessary surveillance and ensure that government scrutiny is based on individualized suspicion, a fundamental principle of our legal system." When the Senate approved reauthorization by a vote of 89–10, none of these modifications were included. When President Bush signed it, 14 of 16 provisions became permanent and two others were extended for 10 years (Stolberg, 2006a,b).

These renewals only stoked opposition to the PATRIOT Act in policy circles and fostered questions in news media coverage.[3] Polls show that the public maintained support for the Bush administration's approach of "restricting civil

---

[2] At around this same time, Attorney General John Ashcroft, in response to mounting criticism and slipping support for administration policies, embarked on a multicity tour to generate support for the PATRIOT Act. While the tour garnered media coverage about the War on Terror, it also produced a wave of protests, critical editorials, and vigorous debate over the merits and liabilities of PATRIOT Act provisions (Lichtblau, 2003a).

[3] Senator Ron Wyden (D-OR), responding to the first effort to extend and expand the PATRIOT Act, stated that "we are deputizing the military to spy on law-abiding Americans in America" (Pincus, 2005a, p. A6).

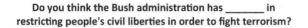

**Do you think the Bush administration has _____ in
restricting people's civil liberties in order to fight terrorism?**

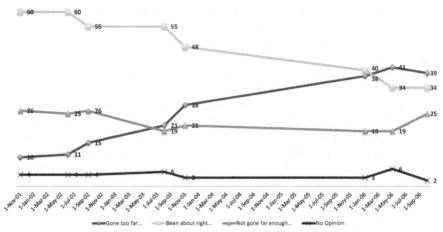

FIGURE 2.1. "Do You Think the Bush Administration Has Gone Too Far, Been About Right, Not Gone Far Enough in Restricting People's Civil Liberties in Order to Fight Terrorism?" (Gallup, Cable News Network, *USA Today* – Telephone Interviews of National Adults).

liberties in order to fight terrorism," albeit less and less so over the course of his second term (Figure 2.1). Notably, Americans expressed a growing sense that the sacrificing of civil liberties had "gone too far," though a majority still felt it had "been about right" or "not gone far enough." On the heels of these reauthorizations, the ACLU brought suit against the NSA's practice of monitoring international telephone calls of Americans without prior court warrants. On August 17 of 2006, U.S. District Court Judge Ann Diggs Taylor found that the NSA was indeed in violation of citizen protections provided under the Fourth Amendment, as well as the 1978 Foreign Intelligence Surveillance Act, which mandates that court warrants be obtained prior to conducting wiretapping inside the United States (Liptak and Lichtblau, 2006).[4] This decision was overturned by the U.S. Sixth Circuit Court of Appeals, which the Supreme Court later refused to consider on appeal.

The Democratic Congress elected in the 2006 midterm elections began to push back more forcefully against the Bush administration's surveillance efforts. As he was preparing to take the Chairmanship of the Senate Judiciary Committee, Senator Patrick Leahy (D-VT) voiced a commitment to provide closer oversight of the government's data-mining programs. His comments

---

[4] Prior to the passage of the PATRIOT Act, obtaining a court order for a wiretapping necessitated that the law enforcement agency show probable cause that the individual or group under surveillance are engaging in illegal activities.

were preceded by an AP story reporting that since 2002, the Department of Homeland Security's Automated Target System (ATS) has been generating and logging risk assessment reports on Americans and foreigners when they cross U.S. borders. American citizens are not allowed to review or challenge the information that will be stored on file for 40 years, even though state, local, and foreign governments and certain corporations may ultimately be granted access to this data. Though the Department of Homeland Security maintains that the ATS system and the information that it compiles is crucial to protecting national security, Leahy asserted that

It is simply incredible that the Bush administration is willing to share this sensitive information with foreign governments and even private employers, while refusing to allow U.S. citizens to see or challenge their own terror scores.... [This program] highlights the danger of government use of technology to conduct widespread surveillance of our daily lives without proper safeguards for privacy. (Sniffen, 2006, p. 1)

The legal showdown between Congress and the Bush administration came to a head in June 2007, when the Senate Judiciary Committee issued subpoenas demanding that the White House turn over documents related to the National Security Agency's warrantless eavesdropping efforts. By 2007, legislators for both parties "called for limits on antiterrorism laws in response to a Justice Department report that the FBI improperly obtained telephone logs, banking records, and other personal information on thousands of Americans" (Eggen and Solomon, 2007, p. A1). An audit of FBI activities revealed that the bureau made 143,000 information requests using national security letters on 52,000 people between 2003 and 2005 (almost half were American citizens or legal residents), though the numbers were reported as being much lower to Congress. The Justice Department audit revealed that 16% of the FBI's requests were without merit (Eggen and Solomon, 2007). Concerned about the erosion of civil liberties, former Republican Congressman Bob Barr, who had affiliated with the American Civil Liberties Union (ACLU), submitted testimony that the FBI had abused its authority in collecting personal information without court authorization. Bending to this pressure, the Bush administration agreed to allow judicial oversight of electronic surveillance activities, which it had been resisting prior to the 2006 election (Stout, 2007).

In response to the efforts of civil liberties organizations to publicize infringements on personal freedoms, the emerging attempts to make civil liberties a wedge issue, and legislation in Congress to revise the PATRIOT Act, the Bush administration worked hard to defend the act on the grounds of national security. Democrats made the defense of civil liberties part of their party platform in 2008, adopting the following language at the convention nominating Barack Obama:

We support constitutional protections and judicial oversight on any surveillance program involving Americans. We will review the current administration's warrantless wiretapping program. We reject illegal wiretapping of American citizens, wherever they

live. We reject the use of national security letters to spy on citizens who are not suspected of a crime. We reject the tracking of citizens who do nothing more than protest
a misguided war.... We will revisit the PATRIOT Act and overturn unconstitutional
executive decisions issued during the past eight years.

It surprised many, then, that President Obama reversed course and supported
the reauthorization of the PATRIOT Act, namely the provisions allowing rov-
ing wiretaps, records searches, and "lone wolf" surveillance that would have
expired (Conery, 2009; Mascaro, 2011; Savage, 2009). Indeed, a number of
critics have argued that President Obama not only continued but expanded
the very programs he critiqued, leading former Vice President Dick Cheney to
assert in early 2011 that "[Obama] learned that what we did was far more
appropriate than he ever gave us credit for while he was a candidate."

In 2013, the debate over the acceptability limits of government surveillance resurfaced in the aftermath of the Boston Marathon bombings and
again after the Snowden revelations. The Boston Marathon bombing seemed
to validate concerns about terrorism and the value of private surveillance cameras, though it also raised concerns about whether the government's massive
domestic surveillance apparatus developed to combat domestic terrorism was
effective.

Tracking of public opinion indicates that public shared this skepticism, with
Americans' willingness to give up some personal freedom in order to reduce
the threat of terrorism at the lowest level since the 9/11 attacks. The attack
did not rally more support for the surveillance state; rather, it appears to have
reduced support for these intrusive practices if they could not prevent attacks
by dangerous individuals. In fact, the 43% support for giving up some personal
freedoms gauged on April 16, 2013, was a drop of nearly 30 points from the
high of 71% in the weeks following 9/11 (Figure 2.2). And this was before the
Snowden leaks broke.

The revelations concerning the government's dragnet of phone hacking,
data mining, and movement tracking not only "provoked both fear and outrage – from liberal advocates and conservative libertarians alike – over the
government's seemingly aggressive snooping" (Frumin, 2013), they also gal-
vanized civil rights activists, religious groups and gun and drug advocates to
join together and file a lawsuit, seeking an injunction against the NSA, Justice Department, and FBI for what they called an "illegal and unconstitutional
program of dragnet electronic surveillance" (*Associated Press*, 2013). These
groups were bolstered by the release of a top-secret court ruling by FISA Court
Judge John D. Bates in which he criticized the NSA for "for gathering and storing tens of thousands of Americans' e-mails each year." He warned that the
NSA had repeatedly misrepresented their activities to the court by downplaying
the scope and volume of surveillance activities (Savage and Shane, 2013).

Many legal experts argued that the government programs violated basic
privacy protections provided by the Fourth Amendment and its safeguards
against unreasonable and warrantless searches and seizures (Barnett, 2013),

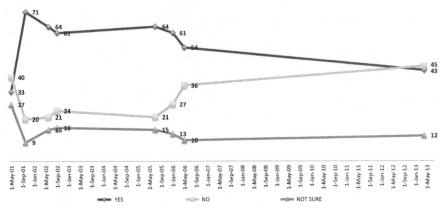

Would you be willing to give up some of your personal freedom in order to reduce the threat of terrorism?

FIGURE 2.2. "Would You be Willing to Give Up Some of Your Personal Freedom in Order to Reduce the Threat of Terrorism?" (Fox News/Opinion Dynamics – Telephone Interviews of Registered Voters).

although others disagreed, arguing the NSA's metadata collection was constitutional (Posner, 2013). Two judges, upon hearing these legal arguments, rendered opposing decisions on all major questions before them, "including the intelligence value of the program, the privacy interests at stake and how the Constitution figures in the analysis" (Liptak and Schmidt, 2013). The fact that the two courts offered such different legal interpretations on the NSA domestic surveillance programs would seem to indicate that the U.S. Supreme Court will ultimately be called upon to pass judgment (Horwitz, 2013).

As the NSA surveillance programs came under scrutiny on legal grounds, other critics began to question the effectiveness of these programs. Yochai Benkler, Berkman Professor at Harvard Law School, questioned the NSA's program on both grounds:

It implements a perpetual "state of emergency" mentality that inverts the basic model outlined by the Fourth Amendment: that there are vast domains of private action about which the state should remain ignorant unless it provides clear prior justification. And all public evidence suggests that, from its inception in 2001 to this day, bulk collection has never made more than a marginal contribution to securing Americans from terrorism, despite its costs. (Benkler, 2013)

Indeed, when pressed by Chairman of the Senate Judiciary Committee, Patrick Leahy, NSA Director Keith Alexander acknowledged that the actual number of terrorist plots foiled by the NSA's massive data dragnet could be counted on one hand, definitively only a single instance, and certainly not the fifty-four claimed repeatedly by the administration (Waterman, 2013).

This confluence of factors likely contributed to further erosion of public support for intrusive monitoring and surveillance practices, though it is important

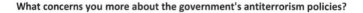

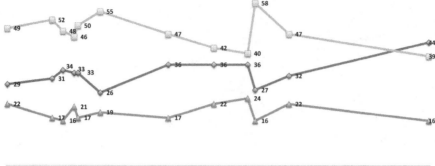

FIGURE 2.3. "What Concerns You More About the Government's Antiterrorism Policies: They Have Gone Too Far in Restricting the Average Person's Civil Liberties, or They Have Not Gone Far Enough to Adequately Protect the Country?" (Pew Research Center for the People and the Press- Telephone Interviews of National Adults).

to note that even with these explosive revelations, Constitutional questions, and marginal effectiveness, only a plurality of Americans (44%) expressed concerns that government antiterrorism policies had gone too far in restricting the average person's civil liberties, with 39% still maintaining they had not gone far enough to adequately protect the country (Figure 2.3). This was a considerable drop from the high of 58% who indicated that the government had not gone far enough to protect the country in the aftermath of the Fort Hood shootings.

In response to these changing circumstances, President Obama commissioned a presidential advisory committee to review NSA surveillance programs and balance concerns for protecting national security and civil liberties. The committee's subsequent report concluded that the NSA's surveillance programs have overextended their authority and made forty-six recommendations for constraining the agency's activities and increasing oversight (Sanger and Savage, 2013). Responding to the content of the report, a *New York Times* editorial asserted that the committee's report underscores a "lack of regard for the Constitution that has led those efforts, and the virtual absence of supervision and restraint by Mr. Obama and his predecessor, President George W. Bush" (*The New York Times*, 2013).

The Dynamics of Public Opinion
As the figures referenced earlier illustrate, public support for the PATRIOT Act exhibited a pattern of slow decline over the first dozen years following

the 9/11 attacks, from extraordinarily high levels initially to a divided opinion climate after the Snowden revelations. During the Bush administration (see Figure 2.1), concerns about civil liberties certainly increased, though most Americans continued to support domestic security initiatives. By the time of the Boston bombings, a plurality of Americans were no longer willing to give up their own personal freedoms in order to reduce the threat of terrorism, though nearly as many Americans remained willing to do so (see Figure 2.2). After the Snowden revelations, concerns about antiterrorism policies going too far finally eclipsed the view among Americans that they had not gone far enough to adequately protect the country (see Figure 2.3). This gradual erosion of public support for the surveillance state took over a decade, with large subsets of Americans continuing to express support for aggressive surveillance policies.

This might be expected from the literature on the rally-round-the-flag effect (Mueller, 1973). As the immediacy of the threat dissipated, the pendulum of public opinion started to swing back in the direction of civil liberties. For public opinion researchers, the PATRIOT Act and its implementation offer an interesting case study in which to study opinion dynamics. The public opinion literature provides ample reason to suspect that, at least initially, public opinion would support the PATRIOT Act.

First, the suddenness and magnitude of the September 11 attacks, combined with the continual visual reminders through the media, made for a highly charged environment, conducive to pushing the pendulum of public opinion toward national security (Cho et al., 2003). Such external conflicts, even with an elusive enemy such as Al Qaeda, tend to produce a rally-round-the-flag effect of public support for the President (Mueller, 1973). Though originally proposed to explain presidential support, rally effects have been shown by other research to apply to administration policies as well (McLeod et al., 1994).

Second, research on the "elite cueing" effects (Berinsky, 2007; Berinsky, 2009) finds that public opinion follows the lines of elite discourse as members of the public take cues from partisan elites. For conflict issues in which elites are largely in consensus (such as the PATRIOT Act as evidenced by the aforementioned lone dissenting vote by Senator Feingold), public opinion will reflect little dissent. Entman (2003) elaborates the process by which elite cueing influences opinion as administration message frames "cascade" through elite hierarchies to the mass media and on to the public. Their influence on public opinion is largely mediated by the extent to which these frames are contested as they move through elite and media channels. Given the "dominance" (see Entman, 2003) of the national security frame in elite circles following the September 11 attacks, it is not surprising that subsequent opinion polls showed that the public was largely willing to sacrifice rights and liberties for increased safety.

Third, research on threat and trust perceptions has sought to understand processes related to judgments about the national security versus civil liberties tradeoff. For example, Huddy et al. (2005) show that the degree of threat perception specifically (but not more general terrorism-related anxiety) increases public support for various antiterrorism policies such as government surveillance. Similarly, the results of research by Davis and Silver (2004) raise concerns about American's willingness to cede civil liberties, particularly under threat of terrorism. The extent to which individuals perceived terrorism as a threat was associated with lower concern about the loss of civil liberties. Political ideology was also predictive of support for civil liberties, as liberals were more concerned about the loss of civil liberties, though this effect was diminished by perceived terrorism threat, a finding that has important implications for the framing of the threat that we discuss in the following section. This research also showed that the relationship between threat and decline in support for civil liberties was moderated by trust in government. Research by Gross et al. (2004) indicates that exposure to television news increased levels of systemic trust (consistent with the rallying effects of an external threat). This suggests that, by priming trust in government, television coverage enhanced the pendulum swing in the direction of national security, an effect that diminishes with temporal distance from the threat incidence. For further discussion of the trade-off between civil liberties, national security, and other political orientations, see McClosky and Brill (1983), Peffley et al. (2001), and Sniderman et al. (1996).

Media and the National Security/Civil Liberties Debate

In the concluding section of this chapter, we turn to the role of the news media as the key intermediary between the government and the populace – as in the case of the public policy domain and public opinion described earlier. The vast majority of the public experienced the national security/civil liberties debate through media presentations of the events of 9/11, the passage of the PATRIOT Act, and reports on the government's domestic surveillance activities. The factors that tie the mainstream news media to powerful institutions such as the government, particularly in the context of a terrorist threat, induce a degree of homogeneity in coverage in ways that tend to support the status quo. Common patterns and conventions of news stories about such events and policies, such as framing coverage at the individual level, are likely to be influential in shaping audience reactions. As such, they may be partially responsible for why the swing of the public opinion pendulum back toward civil liberties was so gradual after 9/11. Research that we report on in subsequent chapters largely supports this contention.

Our discussion of the media begins with a look at their role in times of crisis, where ties to powerful institutions under the conditions of an external threat generate news stories that "cover Big Brother" by sustaining support for domestic surveillance. We then report on the results of our computer-assisted and manual content analyses, which document patterns in news coverage of the tension between national security and civil liberties, as well as how media framed the targets of government surveillance. This is followed by a series of examples of news reports documenting the government's selective targeting of Arabs/Muslims and activists for surveillance. We then identify several examples of individual framing that personify the target of government surveillance.

The Role of Mainstream Media in Times of Crisis

In the aftermath of September 11, journalists were not only charged with the responsibility of explaining these events and their ramifications, but were also faced with the task of constructing meaning around the official responses of government institutions. Of course, responses by the federal government to the War on Terror soon included a shift in the balance between national security and civil liberties. It is important to consider how mainstream media conduct moved from the immediate repercussions of the attacks to the unfolding reduction of civil liberties in the name of security raised by the PATRIOT Act. That is, media had to decide how to frame the controversies surrounding the PATRIOT Act.

Before we can address how the media responded to the implementation of the PATRIOT Act, we first must consider what kinds of normative expectations we might have for the media. That is, how might we expect the media to respond in order to serve their democratic responsibility to society? As a starting point, Gurevitch and Blumler (1990) identified eight normative ideals for news media in a democratic society: (1) surveillance of relevant events; (2) identification of key issues; (3) provision of platforms for advocacy; (4) transmission of diverse political discourse; (5) scrutiny of institutions and officials; (6) activation of informed participation; (7) maintenance of media autonomy; and (8) consideration of audience potential. In the specific context of the aftermath of September 11, we might reorganize these normative expectations for the media into three broad categories: (a) spread information and encourage sophisticated understanding among the citizenry; (b) support democratic virtues while respecting national security; and (c) encourage democratic expression and action.

These normative expectations encouraged monitoring the relevant events of September 11 and the actions of policymakers and law enforcement agencies as well as identifying the key underlying issues that structure public discourse surrounding these events and the subsequent policies that transpired. Of course, these ideals also support the defense of civil liberties even in the face of threats to security; the media must question the agenda and dogma of official institutions and avoid being swept up in the nationalistic fervor that follows such attacks. In addition, the goal of encouraging expression and action involves mobilizing the citizenry to get involved in the efforts of the nation to recover from the attacks and to be engaged participants in subsequent debates over the policies of the War on Terror. By providing platforms for dialogue, the media help audience members realize their potential as active and informed participants in democratic processes. Satisfying these ideals is a great deal to expect from the media, especially given what we know about media dependence on official sources (Bennett, 2001; Fishman, 1980; Gans, 1980; Sigal, 1973; Soley, 1992).

Post-9/11 coverage exemplifies several important principles about governance and the role of media in times of conflict. First, the government propagates concerns about a vilified enemy and spreads fear about potential threats to national security in a manner that constitutes a powerful force of social control, generating support for presidential administrations and government policy initiatives. This phenomenon is certainly not new; the Cold War, for example, provided a long-standing source of vilified enemies and security threats that fostered the growth of the military-industrial complex. Second, the media play an important role in this process by serving as a conduit for social control messages. Media scholars have argued that by taking cues from official government sources, the media transmit information that steers public attention toward an agenda that fits the interests of the power elite (Altschull, 1984; Donohue et al., 1985; Paletz and Entman, 1981). Noting the factors that tie media to the interests of the government, Herman and Chomsky (1988) go so far as to propose that the mainstream media serve as a propaganda agent of the U.S. government. Along these lines, Glassner (1999) argues that the media promote a "culture of fear" that exaggerates certain threats and ignores others.

While there have been quite a few scholars who have written about the mutually supportive relationship between government and media in fostering social control, McQuail (1987) distinguishes these perspectives into three different camps:

One is the view that the media act generally, but non-purposively, to support the values dominant in a community or nation, through a mixture of personal and institutional choice, external pressure and anticipation of what a large and heterogeneous audience expects and wants. Another view is that the media are essentially conservative because of a combination of market forces, operational requirements and established work practices. A third view holds that the media are actively engaged on behalf of a ruling (and often media-owning) class or bourgeois state in suppressing or diverting opposition and constraining political and social deviance. (p. 285)

So it is clear that American mainstream media, particularly in times of international conflicts, support the interests of the U.S. government. What is less clear is how the media counter these pressures when they come into conflict with the First Amendment, for which they have considerable self-interest. Ultimately, the media may be more reluctant to follow the lead of government when national security concerns are pitted against civil liberties in policy debates such as the controversy surrounding the USA PATRIOT Act.

What is needed, given the range of theories of press responses during periods of crisis, is a synthetic framework of news production that reflects the complexities of press performance when national security and civil liberties are at odds. Unlike typical press responses during periods of war or external conflict, which are marked by "rallying 'round the flag" and the reduction of counterinstitutional reporting, when civil liberties are at stake, we would expect that news media would be motivated by their role as guardians of expressive rights to question the government. However, the news media remain constrained by professional norms and news values, which likely influence the reporting on such controversies in several predictable ways.

First, given that journalists tend to follow the lines of power in their use of information sources and construction of information, we expect that coverage of the enforcement of the PATRIOT Act is likely to highlight the issue of national security over civil liberties. The focus on national security is likely to be enhanced during a conflict or crisis such as was the case in the aftermath of the 9/11 attacks. That is, media coverage is likely to exhibit the same type of rally around the President that characterizes public opinion (see Mueller, 1973). As a result, we expect coverage of this value conflict will tilt toward the side of national security. Second, we expect that the slant toward national security will fade as the external threat dissipates with temporal distance from the 9/11 attacks, as dissent within the power structure emerges (see Hallin, 1986), and as the media's self-interest in civil liberties issues starts to reassert itself. Finally, we expect that journalists are likely to structure their press accounts around certain professional conventions in order to simplify news production and ease audience understanding of complex issues, which become more digestible when presented in these terms (Shah et al., 1996). Specifically, we expect media coverage to adopt personifying individual frames over collective frames, which is one of the central theoretical distinctions of the framing effects research presented in this book, and important to understanding sustained support for security measures.

News Coverage of the National Security/Civil Liberties Debate

In order to test these expectations, we analyzed news coverage of domestic applications of the PATRIOT Act by using two different forms of content analysis: computer-assisted and manual content analysis. The computer analysis examined the balance of attention between national security and civil liberties, and whether that balance changed over time. The human content analysis explored how stories framed the target of government surveillance.

The sample for these analyses was drawn from the LexisNexis Academic news database. We pulled every article appearing in the *New York Times*, the *Washington Post*, *USA Today*, and the *Associated Press Newswire* in which the phrase "Patriot Act" appeared within the same paragraph as either the phrase "national security" or "civil liberties" during the entire tenure of the Bush administration (January 20, 2001, to January 20, 2009), the period that saw the strongest support for national security powers and served as the context in which our experimental testing took place. This process yielded a total of

TABLE 2.1. *Concept Frames Indicating Attention to National Security and Civil Liberties Used in the Computer-Assisted Content Analysis*

National Security Concept Frames	N	Civil Liberties Concept Frames	N
Fear	96	Abuses	153
Hijacker	3	Amendment Rights	19
Homeland	142	American Liberties	6
Safe	80	Civil Libertarians	39
Terror	431	Civil Liberties	1137
Terrorist	630	Civil Rights	181
Threat	247	Constitutional Rights	54
Weapons of Mass Destruction	32	Constitutionality	28
		Constitutionally	19
		Human Rights	46
		Privacy Protections	19
		Privacy Rights	48
TOTAL	1661		1749

858 articles (237 from the *New York Times*, 252 from the *Washington Post*, 71 from *USA Today*, and 298 from *The Associated Press*).[5]

The Computer-Assisted Content Analysis

All 858 articles were subjected to computer-assisted content analysis using the VBPro text analysis program to examine whether paragraphs in the story focused on the national security or civil liberties angle of the story. We also examined whether the balance of attention to national security and civil liberties changed over the course of the Bush administration (2001 to 2009).

Specifically, the computer analysis identified the use of terms that we identified through a manual examination of the stories as being indicative of attention to national security and civil liberties issues. These indicators, which have been referred to as "cues" in the literature, are examples of what we call "concept frames" in our Message Framing Model. These concept frames representing national security and civil liberties are listed in Table 2.1.

The use of these terms in the coverage was tabulated by year from 2001 through 2009. In terms of the raw use of these concept frames (Figure 2.4), the pattern is fairly clear across time. They increase annually from 2001 to 2005

---

[5] We chose the *New York Times* and *Washington Post* because they are two of the most influential news organizations in setting the news agenda in the United States. These news organizations were also at the forefront in breaking many of the stories about how the PATRIOT Act was being applied in the surveillance of individuals and groups. *USA Today* was included because of its national circulation and the fact that it also contributed original coverage of PATRIOT Act applications. Finally, we analyzed *Associated Press* coverage because it is the dominant wire service in the U.S. and it provided much of the coverage of this debate that found its way into newspapers across the country.

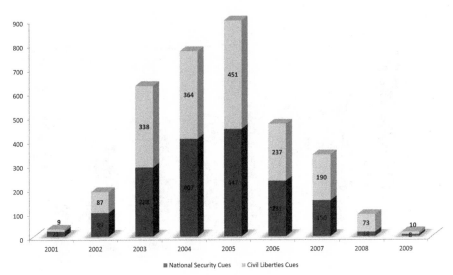

FIGURE 2.4. Number of national security and civil liberties cues in PATRIOT Act stories appearing in the *New York Times, Washington Post, USA Today*, and the *AP Newswire* by year.

(peaking at 898 total cues), and then exhibit a fairly steady decline through inauguration day in 2009. This reflects an overall rise and fall in the number of stories across this period. The number of stories increased from 2001 to 2005, first in response to the stories that were breaking regarding how the Bush administration was enforcing the PATRIOT Act, and then in 2005 in response to the Congressional deliberations over the act's reauthorization. After 2005, stories and the use of concept frames declined.

As illustrated in Figure 2.5, the proportion of national security cues to civil liberties cues shifts across the time period (2009 content was omitted because the sample size was very small). The proportion of national security cues ranged from a high of 70.0% in 2001 to a low of 19.8% in 2008 with a relatively stable plateau that hovers around 50% in between. Across time, there was a growth in the proportion of civil liberties cues that would be consistent with the dissipation of the rally effect of the 9/11 attacks. The trend is also consistent with a pendulum swing back toward civil liberties as critics of the PATRIOT Act began to emerge and stories surfaced about how the PATRIOT Act was being used for domestic surveillance.

This pattern fits the rally-round-the-flag effect identified by Mueller (1973), as there was an overall decline in the emphasis on national security as the attacks of 9/11 moved further into the past. Initially the media, like members of the general public, swung to the side of national security, providing little criticism of the War on Terror on either the global or domestic fronts. As the immediate shock of the attacks subsided and the war in Iraq

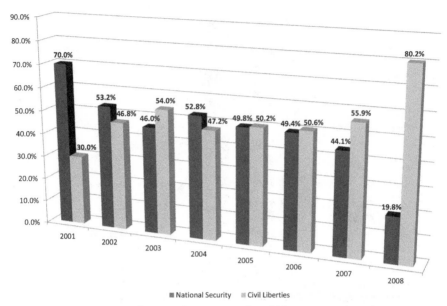

FIGURE 2.5. Proportion of national security and civil liberties cues found in PATRIOT Act stories appearing in the *New York Times, Washington Post, USA Today,* and the *AP Newswire* by year.

bogged down, concerns about infringements on civil liberties began to appear, especially in the elite media, as reporters such as the *New York Times'* Eric Lichtblau and *Newsweek's* Michael Isikoff began reporting on the government's domestic War on Terror. These news reports began to lift the veil on government surveillance of individuals and groups inside United States. As such, it is natural that the rally effect that swept public opinion and the media up in a frenzy of support for national security measures would dissipate over time.

The Manual Content Analysis

In order to examine the practice of individual and collective framing, we conducted a manual content analysis of news articles. To reduce the burden of human coding, a subsample of the articles from each of the four news organizations was taken by drawing every third article. This produced 280 articles for analysis (78 for the *New York Times,* 81 for the *Washington Post,* 24 for *USA Today,* and 97 for the *Associated Press*). A trained graduate student researcher coded the selected articles. A subset of these articles were double-coded by a faculty researcher in order to assess intercoder agreement. All variables exceeded the .75 standard for Krippendorff's Alpha, a common intercoder agreement coefficient.

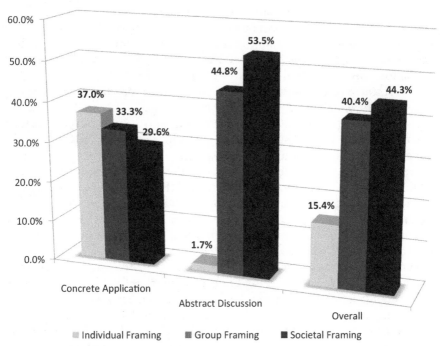

FIGURE 2.6. Individual, group, and societal frames found in PATRIOT Act stories appearing in the *New York Times, Washington Post, USA Today,* and the *AP Newswire* by concrete versus abstract discussion of PATRIOT applications.

Of particular interest for the manual content analysis was whether the article framed the target of government surveillance under the auspices of the PATRIOT Act in terms of individuals, groups, or society as a whole. That is, did new stories identify a particular person targeted by surveillance activities (i.e., individual framing), or did they merely identify a particular targeted group or type of person (i.e., collective framing)? Alternatively, stories could address the national security or civil liberties implications of the PATRIOT Act without referring to targets (i.e., societal framing, a distinction not addressed in our experimental research).[6]

Results from our content analysis showed that there was quite a bit of variance in terms of the way that journalists framed news stories about government surveillance (Figure 2.6). Across all sampled coverage, we found that 15.4% of news articles used an individual exemplar as the target of government surveillance. Another 40.4% of articles identified only a particular group

---

[6] This target-framing variable is related to one of the key theoretical concepts used in the experimental research presented in the later chapters of this book – individual versus collective framing. That is, in the context of news stories about the PATRIOT Act, the framing of the target of the government surveillance is a primary indicator of individual versus collective framing.

without identifying an individual as the target. No specific target was identified
in 44.3% of stories. These proportions were relatively stable across the four
news organizations. For example, the proportion of stories using individual
framing was 15.4% for the *New York Times*, 11.1% for the *Washington Post*,
16.7% for *USA Today*, and 18.6% for the *Associated Press*.

At first, these results would seem to indicate that individual framing in this
context is not widely practiced. However, there are a few important factors
to consider. First, of the 280 articles analyzed, only 38.6% of them focused
on concrete discussions of surveillance applications of the PATRIOT Act. The
remaining articles dealt with national security or civil liberties implications
of the policy in a purely abstract manner. When the stories about concrete
applications of the PATRIOT Act were isolated (Figure 2.6), 37.0% engaged in
individual framing, 33.3% in group (collective framing), and 29.6% in societal
framing. When these were further broken down into the story types that were
used in our experimental analysis, we find that 52.6% of stories engaged in
individual framing, while 47.4% exhibited collective framing.

Results also showed that the proportions of target framing were relatively
stable over time, and thus the selection of individual, collective, or societal
frames do not seem to be influenced by the rally effect. They were stable across
news organizations and stable over time, indicating that such patterns are a
function of factors such as news routines and professional practices rather than
a function of news organization practices or situational conditions.

Selective Targeting for Surveillance

The empirical findings presented here do not provide the full account of how
the War on Terror was presented to the U.S. public in the years after the
9/11 attacks, and how this contributed to the public's willingness to accept the
erosion of civil liberties for such a lengthy period. To do so, one must first
understand how the threat of "homegrown terrorism" was constructed by the
government and covered by the media. Although it is true that the framing
of the War on Terror often focused on individuals targeted for government
surveillance, with many of those featured in stories serving as a personification
of either dangerous actors or government abuses, episodic framing (see Iyengar,
1991) does not explain this phenomenon, as individual cases illustrating an
elusive condition may work against the notion of a longstanding and ongoing
threat. Instead, what is needed is the continuous personification of the threat as
a way to provide cover for Big Brother. This coverage focused on both domestic
and international targets, including Arab-Americans and political activists.

It is also important to realize that this coverage often followed the application of the PATRIOT Act to groups well beyond the external threat posed
by international networks of jihadists such as al-Qaeda. These included "street
theater companies, church groups, and antiwar organizations" (Dwyer, 2007,
p. 1), along with gay rights, environmental protection, animal rights, and
antiabortion activists (Johnson, 2007). Among the more shocking examples

was the definition of three anti-nuclear pacifists, including an 82-year-old nun, as terrorists, for their protest activities (Schneier, 2013). In recent years, this included the monitoring of the Occupy movement and thirty-five world leaders, allegedly including German Chancellor Angela Merkel (Ball, 2013). Snowden himself wrote, in an open letter to Brazil seeking asylum, that the NSA's "programs were never about terrorism: they're about economic spying, social control and diplomatic manipulation. They're about power."

Surveillance of Arabs and Muslims

Many of the examples of possible civil rights infringements have involved Arab-American citizens, immigrants from the Middle East, and Muslims. Still other examples have focused on political activist groups, such as antiwar protestors. It is these two types of groups, Arabs and activists, that were featured in the stimulus stories used in the framing experiments reported in this book. Since passage of the PATRIOT Act, mainstream media have exposed some of the details of these questionable government activities targeting Arab and activist groups.

To begin with, the FBI engaged in the practice of targeting selected individuals for surveillance and interviews, which some critics have labeled ethnic profiling. The Department of Homeland Security compiled lists of Arab-Americans broken down by zip code and country of origin, echoing similar records that were employed for the internment of Japanese-Americans during World War II (Clemetson, 2004). The FBI interviewed roughly 5,000 people of Middle Eastern descent in a search for information to identify terrorism suspects (Cohen, 2002). Leaders of Muslim groups were specifically targeted for interviews. Many of those interviewed complained that the interviews were conducted in their workplace and contributed to community fears. Immigrants were particularly fearful because thousands of immigrants were deported during the early days of the War on Terror (Sheridan, 2004). Many other Arabs and Muslims were detained by authorities as part of efforts to combat terrorism. By one estimate, about 1,200 Arabs and Muslims were arrested following the September 11 terrorist attacks and held in custody without the standard legal protections (Hamud, 2003).

Reporting included the fact that the military sought to expand its power to conduct domestic intelligence gathering. Since the 1970s, when Army surveillance of antiwar protesters was made public, the Privacy Act of 1974 has blocked military personnel from gathering information on domestic civilians without first identifying themselves and their purpose. In 2004, following a Defense Department request, the Senate Intelligence Committee approved Senate Bill S.2386, which exempts military personnel from complying with the Privacy Act in the interest of preventing terrorist attacks against U.S. installations (Isikoff, 2004; Regan, 2004). That same year, *Newsweek* reported that Army intelligence officers approached officials from the University of Texas Law School seeking a list of participants at an Islamic law conference. The

Army defended its actions saying that it was seeking to identify students who had been asking "suspicious questions." The Army later admitted that its agents had overstepped their authority (Isikoff, 2004).

Surveillance of Activists

It is clear that the government's surveillance efforts have not been limited to the profiling of Arabs and Muslims. In fact, there have been many cases of surveillance against activist groups, especially those who have been critical of the government's antiterrorism policies and the wars in Afghanistan and Iraq. On numerous occasions, the news media reported on the widespread monitoring of nonviolent civil liberties and antiwar organizations. The FBI maintained files on a variety of groups that engaged in no unlawful conduct, but were critical of the Bush administration, including 1,173 pages on the ACLU and 2,383 pages on Greenpeace. Files also were kept on other groups such as United for Peace and Justice (a coalition of over 1,300 antiwar organizations), and the American Indian Movement of Colorado in connection with a 2002 Columbus Day protest in Denver (Lichtblau, 2005; Sherman, 2005). The FBI also compiled exhaustive information on "the tactics, training and organization of anti-war demonstrators" and issued a memorandum to local police agencies to notify the FBI's counterterrorism squads (Lichtblau, 2003b).

U.S. intelligence agencies created a massive information database called Terrorist Identities Datamart Environment (TIDE) to track individuals who the government considers a potential security threat. For instance, the TIDE database was used to create the travel watch lists that prevent over 30,000 people from flying in the United States. From 2004 to 2007, the number of files in this database expanded from less than 100,000 to 435,000, so large that security experts worry that its effectiveness has been diluted. Not only does the size of the database lead to problems of finding needles in a haystack, but it also leads to errors such as cases of mistaken identity and incorrect information. Nearly half of the airline travelers who have been tagged by a watch-list hit were misidentified, according to the Government Accountability Office. For instance, on multiple occasions, Catherine Stevens, the wife of former Senator Ted Stevens (R-AK), was pulled aside at airports, misidentified as Cat Stevens, a pop singer who converted to Islam, renaming himself Yusuf Islam, and who was banned from the U.S. (DeYoung, 2007).

On December 14, 2005, the Pentagon announced that it was conducting an internal review of its Talon database, which tracks information about U.S. citizens considered to be a threat to defense facilities. NBC News reported "that a sample of about 1,500 'suspicious incidents' listed in the database included four dozen anti-war meetings or protests, some aimed at military recruiting" (Pincus, 2005b, p. A1). One such group tracked by the Talon program as a potential threat to national security consisted of ten protesters who passed out peanut butter and jelly sandwiches to employees outside Haliburton Headquarters to draw attention to the corporation's "war profiteering." The Talon database also kept records on People for the Ethical Treatment of Animals (PETA) and Greenpeace. *Newsweek* reported on a Pentagon memo from Deputy Defense Secretary Paul Wolfowitz admitting that the database inappropriately included files on U.S. citizens and organizations (Isikoff, 2006).

Other media reports detail government infiltration, interrogations, and investigations of social protest groups. The Colorado Coalition Against the War in Iraq, a group that planned nonviolent demonstrations, was twice infiltrated by undercover police officers conducting surveillance of the group. Law enforcement agents interrogated antiwar protesters in New York and kept databases on their political associations (Goldberg, 2004). During the period leading up to the 2004 Republican National Convention, the FBI interviewed political activists about their knowledge of plans to disrupt the event in New York. One FBI employee filed an internal complaint regarding the policy's broad definition of suspicious activity that included legitimate political speech (Lichtblau, 2004). At the same time, undercover New York City police officers traveled the United States, Canada, and Europe to infiltrate and spy on potential convention protesters (Dwyer, 2007, p. 1). In another example, Drake University was served with a subpoena issued by a federal prosecutor seeking the records of the Drake University Chapter of the National Lawyers Guild and the names of participants in an antiwar conference (Goldberg, 2004).

Following the lead of federal agencies, state agencies got into the national security frenzy. For example, Alabama became the first state to establish its own state-level Department of Homeland Security. In its fervor to identify potential terrorists, it posted a list of groups that harbor "single-issue" terrorists. Among the groups included on this list were gay rights, environmental, animal rights, antiabortion, and antiwar organizations (Johnson, 2007).

Finally, in 2012, documents released by the FBI in response to a Freedom of Information Act (FOIA) request revealed that the agency was coordinating a nationwide program to "investigate and monitor the Occupy Wall Street movement." The documents indicated that the FBI was repeatedly characterizing Occupy and its participants' protest activities as "criminal activity" and "domestic terrorism" (Hines, 2012). The FBI was working with antiterrorism units around the country to engage both traditional and digital surveillance, which included accessing private records from financial institutions. According to Mara Verheyden-Hilliard, executive director of the Partnership for Civil Justice (who filed the FOIA request), "This production [of documents], which we believe is just the tip of the iceberg, is a window into the nationwide scope of the FBI's surveillance, monitoring, and reporting on peaceful protestors organizing with the Occupy movement" (Wolf, 2012).

News Frames and Their Effects on the Public

While reporters exhibited some variance in terms of how they portrayed government activities that were related to the PATRIOT Act, we did find evidence that journalists were influenced by the news norms of personalization and exemplification. That is, consistent with past research, journalists frequently use individual exemplars in part because of the belief that the "human interest" angle make stories more engaging to audiences than stories that focus on groups or more general issues (Iyengar, 1991; Shah et al., 2004). So within the value conflict, journalists had a choice about how to "profile" the targets of government surveillance activities even as they were critiquing this policy. They could choose to present them as individuals, who were singled out for government attention, or as a collective that represented many like-minded individuals. In a significant number of cases, coverage emphasized the value conflict between national security and civil liberties by personifying the targets of government surveillance.[7]

Past research has shown that framing issues in individual terms has substantial consequences for information processing, social attributions of responsibility, and broader attitude formation processes (Iyengar, 1991; Shah et al., 2004). In this book, we extend and expand on this work by examining how

---

[7] For instance, when the media reported on possible civil rights infringements against Arab and Muslim citizens and immigrants, they often used individual exemplars to demonstrate how the FBI's practices affected individuals. Here are three examples: (1) "When they came for Adham Hassoun, America's counterterrorism forces took no chances. Federal agents and sheriffs' deputies circled his car in a quiet residential area not far from his home in Sunrise, Fla., and whisked him into custody.... Now, 15 months later, Hassoun has yet to be charged with a violation of any US law. Nonetheless, he remains behind bars – and fears he is about to lose everything he has ever loved and worked for during 13 years in America. Hassoun's experience is not unlike that of other immigrants of Middle Eastern or Islamic heritage swept up in a post-Sept. 11 dragnet aimed at disabling terrorists before they strike again. It is a nationwide anti-terror campaign with tactics including preventive detention, coercive interrogation, and secret deportation hearings, targeting a community of noncitizens in America now living in silent dread of a knock at the door" (Richey and Feldmann, 2003, p. 1). (2) "The FBI now issues more than 30,000 national security letters a year, according to government sources, a hundredfold increase over historic norms. The letters – one of which can be used to sweep up the records of many people – are extending the bureau's reach as never before into the telephone calls, correspondence and financial lives of ordinary Americans." The article goes on to discuss the case of Magdy Nashar, a North Carolina State University student, whose confidential student records were obtained by the FBI using a national security letter (Gellman, 2005, p. A1). (3) In covering a story about how President Bush authorized the National Security Agency (NSA) to monitor phone calls and e-mail inside the United States without getting warrants, reporters illustrated the policy with the case of one Iranian-American doctor who had his phone calls monitored. Like most targeted individuals, he was never connected to acts of terrorism (Risen and Lichtblau, 2005).

Many of these media reports were framed around the targeting of individual protesters, such as this *Newsweek* report on Michael Connole, who in this case was falsely accused by law enforcement officials: "The FBI arrested an anti-war protester and raided a vegan commune in Pomona, CA on September 12, 2003, after they mistakenly suspected that the group was involved of arson at four Hummer dealerships. Michael Connole was questioned in custody for days before being released. The FBI latter admitted the mistake and paid $100,000 to settle a wrongful arrest lawsuit" (Isikoff, 2005).

the framing of news about the conflict between national security and civil liberties at the individual or collective level can influence political sophistication, social tolerance, and democratic participation. Although others have touched on aspects of this distinction, especially in the formulation of episodic framing (see Iyengar, 1991), our work focuses specifically on the characterization of the protest group that is the subject of the news story and distinguishes between whether that entity is presented (i.e., personified) through the exemplar of an individual or portrayed as a collective (Shah et al., 2004).

Iyengar (1991) asserts that the journalistic norm of constructing social issues around instances and individuals (episodic framing) encourages "attributions of responsibility both for the creation of problems or situations (causal responsibility) and for the resolution of these problems or situations (treatment responsibility)" to the subjects of press reports (Iyengar, 1991, p. 3). He contrasts this with news that frames the issue in broader trends and social conditions (thematic framing). Interpreting issues in terms of an occasional unfortunate occurrence to an isolated individual is thought to diminish a sense of shared responsibility and suppress collective action. As persuasive as this theory seems, experimental studies concerning crime, poverty, and unemployment provide only some support for these claims, with many tests of the central hypothesis, while directionally consistent, failing to achieve statistical significance.

Shah et al. (2004) suggest that the lackluster results of Iyergar's testing may be the result of:

the confounding of two distinct frame dimensions in the contrast between episodic and thematic coverage. That is, episodic coverage not only favors specific instances over enduring problems (i.e., time span), it also emphasizes individual situations over societal conditions (i.e., social level). From an attribution perspective, a sense of shared responsibility for solving social problems should be minimized when audiences encounter stories featuring an individual struggling with a persistent problem. Thus, the crosscutting frame dimensions may have countervailing effects, reducing observed differences. (p. 104)

They go on to explain that shifts of perspective from the individual to the societal level likely operate in tandem with other media frames and cues, which may be in competition for audience attention (see also Chong and Druckman, 2007a,c; Shah et al., 2010). The interplay of frames, cues, and other textual features may "create contexts in which audiences are particularly likely (or unlikely) to generate inferences about the causes, components, and consequences of social problems" (Shah et al., 2004, p. 104).

We believe this shift from individual to collective presentations of protest groups implicates principles of entitativity, which considers the degree to which a social aggregate is perceived as having "the nature of an entity, of having real existence" (Campbell, 1958, p. 17) and explores the influence of these perceptions on social attributions. This perception has implications for tolerance. Perceived entitativity, the degree to which an observer perceives social units as being cohesive and consistent, ranges from very high for individuals, to lower for small groups, to even lower for larger populations. Perceived entitativity is related to two corresponding principles regarding the perceptual judgment process.

First, judgments about an entity are likely to be rendered more readily when the target is presented as an individual rather than as a collective. People feel more comfortable in making trait inferences and related judgments about entities presented as individuals. When making judgments about a collective, however, the lower perceived entitativity makes rendering judgments more difficult, as these trait inferences are not as available to apply to evaluation, resulting in greater reliance on basic considerations. As a result, individuals are quicker to make trait inferences and related judgments about an entity presented as an individual as opposed to one presented as a collective (Hamilton and Sherman, 1996).

Second, when evaluating an individual entity, observers expect a greater degree of consistency between the perceived opinions of the entity and subsequent behaviors. Individuals are seen as more likely to act on underlying attitudes, and as such behavioral outcomes are less likely to be moderated by other group members. In the case of political activists, observers are more likely to perceive individuals as being more extreme in comparison with the collective and more strongly associate these evaluations with other attitudes linked to the group.

These principles are supported by research by Susskind et al. (1999), who concluded that "in comparison with those forming impressions of a group or an aggregate, participants in individual target conditions made stronger (more extreme) trait judgments, they made those judgments faster, and they made them with greater confidence" (p. 190). This is because they view an individual as a coherent and unified psychological unit that is more likely to act on impulses. In this case, when making judgments about individuals under government scrutiny, perceivers assume great consistency between beliefs and actions and therefore assume the best or the worst about these individuals. By contrast, social judgments are less likely to depend on such extreme inferences when the target is a group because evaluations of collectives are tempered. Relying on this argument, we expect that the individual-frame conditions will amplify the effects of cue convergence. Specifically, we predict that individual story frames will amplify the correlations between group evaluations and associated judgments.

In summary, past research on entitativity indicates that judgments are amplified, or more extreme, when aggregates are perceived as unified entities, which is more likely to happen when stories that involve groups are framed in individual terms. As such, groups presented in individual terms are more likely to be judged harshly than those presented as a collective, especially when they are seen as representing outgroups or advocating causes the observer is predisposed to oppose. This is related to stereotyping, particularly the degree to which behavioral information about one group member is applied and transferred to other group members. For this reason, it is especially relevant for research on tolerance and civil liberties. Coverage framing the value conflict over the application of the PATRIOT Act in individual rather than collective terms is likely to exacerbate predisposed differences and polarize an already divided citizenry. Notably, these effects may be attenuated or amplified by other factors, such as cause predisposition, group liking, and ideology, and may interact with other cues found in media content.

Political Judgments Related to Security and Liberty

Readers exposed to messages, such as news stories with national security and civil liberties implications, respond in numerous ways as they process and integrate new information. Following the Message Processing Model (see Chapter 1), we propose that the new information triggers applicable and accessible schema, which are then activated subject to the moderating influences of the receiver's predispositions, to shape relevant responses to the message. That is, judgments concerning the national security versus civil liberties tradeoff may be influenced by the nature of news messages that an individual was exposed to prior to making the judgment. In turn, the degree of influence that these news messages have depends on predispositions of the individual. For example, authoritarianism is one likely moderator of judgments related to the conflicting concerns of national security and civil liberties (Feldman, 2003), a factor that may be accentuated in the face of external threats (Feldman and Stenner, 1997; Lavine et al., 2005). In this case, highly authoritarian individuals would be expected to gravitate toward the conformity position of supporting national security and more likely to exhibit lower tolerance for activist and immigrant groups, which are perceived as challenging the social consensus.

Response judgments relative to the national security versus civil liberties tradeoff may include the development of political cognitions, the formation of political judgments, and the propensity to engage in political behaviors. Cognitions, judgments, and behaviors are likely to be influenced by features of the message, especially the events, issues, and targets featured in the story. Among the large number of responses relevant to the issues examined in this book, we focus on the sophistication of activated thoughts, message influences on security concerns and tolerance judgments, and expressive forms of political participation. Sophistication, tolerance, and participation are all important components of the democratic ideal of a thoughtful, open-minded, and responsive citizenry. However, these three ideals may be at odds with one another, with increases in one reducing others. In fact, message features that enhance sophistication or tolerance may diminish participation, or those that reduce acceptance of others tied to action.

The most fundamental of these is political sophistication, the complexity and organization of an individual citizen's thoughts on a topic. Although sophistication is related to knowledge, they are by no means synonymous. Rather political sophistication is understood as the integration of activated thought, the complexity of individuals' mental models, and the association between attitude structures. Deliberative reasoning in a participatory democracy is often a product of how related relevant cognitions are to one another and the complexity of those interconnections. Past research has shown that framing can influence the cognitive complexity and the degree of integration among mental elements (Shah et al., 2004; Shah et al., 2010). Certain framing devices increase complexity because they lead to a spread of activation from highly centralized nodes. Values are very central and highly accessible. Of course stereotypes are also quite central and easily activated (Devine, 1989). As a consequence, more complex and interconnected cognitions do not guarantee more tolerant judgments.

Tolerance and the support of civil liberties are also desirable in a diverse democratic society, given the necessity of interaction between different ethnic and social groups and among those espousing different political perspectives. Tolerance reduces social conflict and is necessary for deliberative processes and social integration, especially in heterogeneous contexts. Some scholars have defined political tolerance in terms of one's willingness to permit speech from outgroup members or from political perspectives that one personally opposes (Marcus et al., 1995). We largely adopt this perspective here, but also consider how individuals manage the tensions between liberty and security when they encounter government encroachment on the civil rights of groups whose causes they endorse. This leads us to conceive of tolerance as a set of judgments about the extent of speech and social freedoms that should be afforded to a range of threatened groups. The manner in which news media frame protest groups may reduce tolerance toward them, as suggested by past research (McLeod, 1995; McLeod and Detenber, 1999). This intolerance may also be tied to increased participation by tapping on people's strong feelings about the topic and their sense of threat from outgroups.

Accordingly, even though intolerance may spur participation, active engagement in pressing social issues by citizens is critical to democratic functioning. Western societies rely on civic actions – letter writing, platform oratory, volunteerism, and participating in campaigns – as a way to provide direction to governmental institutions and address collective problems. Media, especially television, have been implicated in declining rates of participation (Putnam, 2000), though news consumption via print, broadcast, and online sources has been found to spur political expression, deliberative reasoning, and public-spirited engagement (Shah et al., 2005). In terms of framing effects, some studies have considered such political outcomes as perceptions of shared responsibility for solving social problems and cynicism about government and politics (Cappella and Jamieson, 1997; Iyengar, 1991). Understanding media effects on political participation and related attitudes is key to countering the rising rates of democratic inaction and disengagement. In this study, we are particularly concerned with the willingness to speak and act in favor of or against protest groups targeted by the PATRIOT Act. This form of participation directly engages the conflict between civil liberties and national security, with some seeking to support limits on the liberties of groups perceived as a threat, and others acting to protest a different type of threat – encroachments on civil liberties.

These ideals of a healthy democracy and of a vigorous citizenry – sophistication, tolerance, and participation – may be particularly at odds within the national security and civil liberties debate. For example, individuals who are able to activate a wide range of thoughts about a protest group may not always be the most tolerant of that group, especially if the activation yields thoughts about the group that are at odds with their own political preferences. In cases where one actively opposes a protest group, intolerance may motivate the search for counter information, which contributes to cognitive complexity surrounding relevant issues. Similarly, such intolerance may also encourage participation. Political participation such as writing letters to politicians, circulating petitions, protesting, and the like often results from dissatisfaction with the status quo. For example, activists may engage in participatory behaviors as a result of uncompromising disagreement with those who oppose them.

Framing and Political Judgments
As the public's main source of information about applications of the PATRIOT Act and other forms of domestic surveillance activities, media representations that encourage audiences to perceive ethnic or activist groups as radicals have the potential to sway thoughts, judgments, and actions. Understanding this role of media framing may help to explain the nature of the American public's slow response to incursions on civil liberties. This book contends that media, by their preference for certain framing devices over others, tip the balance between security and liberty in the minds of certain citizens. The tension between providing security and preserving liberty has long animated political debates and fostered contentious politics. What is new here is the understanding we provide regarding the role of the media in amplifying this tension and animating this dynamic.

Specifically, we present four research chapters that are based on the data collected in two separate studies of news story effects in the context of the national security and civil liberties debate. A primary manipulation of both of these studies was individual versus collective story framing. We examined whether framing a story about FBI surveillance – focused on either people of Arab descent or members of activist groups – in a manner that emphasized an individual exemplar or the larger collective influenced subsequently measured sophistication, tolerance, and expressed willingness to participate. Moreover, we examined the extent to which these frames interact with other manipulated factors, such as (1) the concept labels that were used to present Arab targets as citizens or immigrants, and as extremists or not, or (2) whether the target of the surveillance was liked or disliked by the audience members. In addition, we measured other predispositions that were likely to play a role in moderating the influence of the manipulated factors.

Ultimately, the data analyses that are reported in the research chapters of this book yield evidence that contributes to the literature on many levels. First, the findings tell us about the influence of story and concept framing on thoughts, attitudes, and actions, and they examine several factors that may moderate these relationships. Second, the results provide examples of applications of our Message Framing Model and Message Processing Model (see Chapter 1) as they help us to understand what past research has labeled framing and cueing effects, as well as the influence of their interactions. Thus, the results contribute specific knowledge about the nature of these particular observed effects, but also demonstrate more abstractly how this type of approach might provide an alternative to the debate between the idealistic and pragmatic approaches to studying framing effects. Finally, these results inform us about the nature of audience opinions related to the debate between national security and civil liberties.

While many pundits and scholars have speculated on the impact of media coverage of the War on Terror on public opinion, few studies have examined how the nature of coverage actually influences audience reactions. This book provides such evidence by showing that alternative media frames of news stories do shape the cognitions, evaluations, and behaviors of the audience. The evidence presented reveals that such media effects are not simple, intuitive, direct effects. To the contrary, the impact of new frames is complex, depending on the predispositions and characteristics of the message receiver. The evidence provides not only a deeper understanding of how coverage of the tension between security and liberty affects the audience, but also advances the way that scholars think about the nature of framing effects.

PART II

FRAMING EFFECTS RESEARCH

3

Designing the Studies

"Police arrested an American-born Muslim in St. Louis early Sunday and took him to a police station where FBI agents questioned him about his anti-war activities and whether he was planning any attacks against the U.S. government. Bret Darren Lee, whose Muslim name is Umar ben-Livan, said... he is active in Muslim and anti-war groups and acknowledged that he holds views that may be considered outside the political mainstream. But Lee said he is far from a terrorist.... While Lee was still in custody, FBI agents returned to Lee's apartment about noon Sunday and spent a half-hour questioning his wife about whether he was a terrorist, his thoughts about the Taliban, and whether he was planning to take part in any more anti-war protests."

– Phillip O'Connor
St. Louis Post-Dispatch
February 11, 2003

"An FBI counterterrorism unit monitored and apparently infiltrated a peace group [the Thomas Merton Center] in Pittsburgh that opposed the invasion of Iraq, according to internal agency documents released Tuesday.... The documents make no mention of illegal activities, noting only that the group advocated 'pacifism,' opposed an invasion of Iraq, doubted the U.S. rationale for war, and had ties to an Islamic group with no known links to terrorism. The disclosure raised new questions about the extent to which federal authorities have been conducting surveillance operations against Americans since the Sept. 11 attacks."

– Jonathan S. Landsay
Knight Ridder Newspapers
March 15, 2006

The quotes above are from news stories that reflect the central theme of this book: the tension between the contending values of protecting national security and defending civil liberties. Both stories involve actions by the FBI as part of the War on Terror that are seen by some as expanding the scope of surveillance to include groups that are not threats to national security. Both deal with activists who have connections to Muslim groups, but apparently have no linkages to terrorism. Yet they also differ in important ways – ways that highlight the effects of message frames that we explore in the studies reported in this book. The first article is framed around the story of Bret Darren Lee, also known as Umar ben-Livan. It illustrates how the surveillance of Muslims and Arabs are typically presented in the media, providing an example of coverage framed around the case of an individual who is the target of FBI surveillance. The second article is about the Thomas Merton Center, a peace and justice collective from Pittsburgh. This article exemplifies news coverage of the surveillance of domestic activists framed around the case of a collective that was the focus of government scrutiny.

There are a number of important differences between these stories. First, there is the obvious difference in focus, one on a Muslim and the other on a domestic activist group. Second, there is a shift from a focus on an individual to a focus on a collective, which is the core framing distinction we explore in these studies. We examine the first of these distinctions between studies; with the first study we report focusing on coverage of Arab groups (Chapter 4) and the rest focusing on coverage of domestic activist groups (Chapters 5, 6, and 7). We explore the second of these distinctions within each of these studies by manipulating the frame of the news account between a focus on individuals to a focus on collectives. Before we present the specific design of these studies and the corresponding measurement of key concepts, we first discuss the value of our approach to studying framing effects using experimental methods.

Examining Framing Effects

So how do we examine news framing effects on audiences? Mass media scholars have a variety of techniques and methods at their disposal to study framing effects of the news media. Some choose to conduct content analysis of the news in order to identify the kinds of frames media favor when they cover an issue, assuming effects if certain frames are particularly prevalent. Of course, such trends in content are no guarantee of effects on audiences. Thus, other scholars have employed survey research to connect information about the content of news media with people's media consumption patterns and their perceptions, attitudes, and behaviors about issues. Efforts to connect exposure patterns to certain news frames in this way, and then to connect exposure to outcomes, can be problematic. One cannot conclude that frames influence audience members' understanding of political reality simply by associating media consumption with measures of potential audience outcomes, as the causal direction of such observed relationships would be indeterminate. That is, the observed audience outcomes could simply be unaffected audience predispositions that shape the nature of media exposure decisions.

Content analysis and survey-based approaches have several additional limitations. Perhaps most important, these methods do not allow the researcher to isolate those factors in news content that are causing the effects. Since numerous different features, including message frames, characterize news media, it is impossible to rule out the possibility that some feature of the news message other than the news frame may actually be influencing audiences' opinions. It is possible that a specific news frame may be systematically associated with other message factors, which may influence audiences independently or jointly with the news frame. In addition, if a certain frame is disproportionately employed in TV news, for example, differences in audiences' attitudes and behaviors with regard to an issue may result from the preexisting attributes of audiences since TV news users differ in significant ways from those who get their information through other channels. Coupled with the difficulty in assessing the causal flow of the linkage between behaviors (media consumption) and potential outcomes (audience perceptions), these methods pose some serious limitations for scholars interested in examining framing effects.

In contrast, an experimental approach has several advantages over other research methods for examining framing effects. In spite of common limitations such as artificiality and the use of nonrepresentative participant pools, experimental methods allow researchers to examine issues of causality among variables, all the while maintaining great control over other, potentially confounding, content features. Experimental methods can be used to isolate the effects of specified content differences while holding other message features constant. By exposing different groups of respondents to alternative versions of the message, one can assess effects by comparing the means of exposure group responses for relevant outcome variables. When a researcher is examining the effects of news media, and message frames in particular, an experiment allows the researcher to establish the three criteria required to make judgments about causal order: (1) the purported cause must precede the effect, (2) the cause and effect must be associated with one another, and (3) third variables that may create a spurious relationship must be controlled. We consider each of these criteria in turn and relate them to the features of experimental design.

First, experiments give researchers the ability to move beyond simple, observed relationships by accounting for the temporal order of variables. That is, within an experimental design, the researcher manipulates the assumed cause before observing the expected outcomes. By controlling the order in which the two factors appear, the researcher can isolate the potential causal variable to examine whether it actually produces the hypothesized effects on the outcome variable, not the other way around.

Second, for statements about cause and effect to be true, the two variables in question must be associated, which is possible to demonstrate within an experimental design by comparing individuals across discrete experimental conditions to demonstrate that there are differences in the outcome of interest.

By demonstrating such differences across experimental conditions, the cause and effect can be associated with one another.

Third, experiments allow the researcher to control for the effects of other potential causes, which increases the internal validity of the study by ruling out alternative explanations. By randomly assigning research participants to different experimental conditions, the researcher can distribute other potential sources of influence related to individuals' preexisting attributes equally among the treatment groups. With this random assignment procedure, the researcher can minimize the possibility that any observed differences in the designated outcome variables are the result of something other than differences in experimental treatments.

Within the experimental manipulation, the researcher can directly control for a range of potential causes by focusing on a specific factor of interest while holding other features of the message constant. By careful manipulation of these news messages, the researcher can isolate one causal effect at a time and also examine complicated interactions between the causal factors.

Research Design

Procedures
For both of the data collections used in this book, the experimental stimulus (a news story that contained the experimental manipulations) was delivered to respondents by embedding it in an online survey. The Web-based nature of the experiment afforded two significant methodological benefits and allowed for a more complex, dynamic, and realistic experimental manipulation.

First, Web technology allowed us to create an algorithm that used respondents' answers to questions from the pre-test stage to tailor elements of the manipulation to specific individual predispositions. In the second study, participants were asked a series of pre-test questions that tapped their feelings toward certain activist groups operating in the United States. Respondents were given a list of real groups, such as the National Rifle Association and Greenpeace, and were asked to identify their least-liked and most-liked groups. Based on these responses and the experimental condition to which they were assigned (see the following section for more detail about the experimental factors), respondents were presented with experimentally manipulated news articles in which the subject of the news story was a member of a fictional group that sounded ideologically similar to, but was more extreme than, the groups the respondents identified in the pre-test stage. For example, individuals who identified the NRA as their least-liked group were presented with a fictional news story about the "Arm America Front."

By being able to target these stimulus elements to more closely match the respondent's own predispositions, we were able to tap our outcome variables, such as tolerance and group evaluations, more finely. The tolerance literature has demonstrated that the nature of the target group in question has great importance when gauging an individual's stated level of tolerance. For example, Marcus et al.'s (1995) landmark tolerance studies and those that followed indicated Americans had become more tolerant of communists and communist groups since the Cold War era. Hidden in the conclusion that Americans were becoming increasingly open-minded was the fact that communism and communists no longer represented the threat they once did. It was not that Americans were more tolerant, but rather that communism was less of a concern. When presented with other groups that had not declined in their level of perceived menace, Americans were just as intolerant as they had been in the 1950s. The dynamic, tailored nature of our experimental design allowed us to tap into respondents' potential feelings of intolerance more effectively by making sure that they were presented with a group for whom they held little to no sympathetic feelings.

Second, because our experiment was embedded in an online survey, we were not bound to the traditional lab or classroom setting. Instead, because respondents could participate at their convenience and on their own computers, it allowed for a more realistic, more relaxed, and more authentic delivery of the stimulus material. This method is more consistent with how individuals consume and process mass media messages in the real world. It is particularly true for online media content, which people can access on demand at a time and place of their choosing.

By using an online survey, we were able to take measurements of processing time and response latency unobtrusively. For example, we could measure how long a respondent spent reading the experimentally manipulated news story and how long it took the respondent to answer questions. This was particularly useful for the open-ended post-test questions that asked respondents to offer reasons for their thinking. By measuring the time it took respondents to elaborate on issues (i.e., their response latency), we were able to get an indication of not only how complex their reasoning was but how quickly they were able to present their reasoning.

Experimental Manipulations

The experiments used to collect the data for this book were carefully designed to meet the criteria for establishing causality. The findings presented in the following chapters are based on two phases of experiments, collected and analyzed between fall 2002 and spring 2004. Both experimental studies dealt with the ongoing clash between national security and civil liberties that was debated among politicians, the mass media, and members of the general public during the months, indeed years, following the attacks of September 11, 2001. Both experiments involved the manipulation of specific frames and cues in news stories about the USA PATRIOT Act, or its proposed (but never implemented) extension, the VICTORY Act. These studies focused on Arab groups subjected to FBI scrutiny or on domestic activist groups such as environmental or gun-rights proponents targeted under surveillance programs. A number of factors were manipulated in these experimental designs, though most prominent among these was the shift from the individual to the collective framing of the target of government attention. For a summary of the methods used in these two data collections, see Table 3.1.

In all cases, participants read and responded to an experimentally manipulated, fictional news story about potential civil liberties restrictions. This story began with a main section that framed the monitoring of an Arab or activist group around an individual member or the collective as a whole. Regardless of the target of the frame, the reason for the FBI surveillance was an unspecified possible threat. At the end of each brief story, respondents had four choices. They could continue with the survey, or they could read more information in one of three categories: tracking and monitoring, search and seizure, or secret arrest. Each section contained information about additional FBI efforts regarding the featured individual or collective. At the end of each section, respondents could read more about that topic, switch to a different topic, or continue with the survey. Each topic had separate story segments, each of which went into more detail on the issue meaning that respondents could read up to nine additional story segments (beyond the main section) if they chose to do so.

The Arab Study: FBI Scrutiny of Arab Groups

In the case of the Arab Study, three manipulations were embedded within these stories. The first experimental factor dealt with how the story was framed. In the individual condition, subjects read about a particular member of the selected group who was quoted in the story and featured as the object of FBI scrutiny. The story made frequent references to that "individual" rather than to the "group." In the collective condition, respondents read a story in which the targeted group was presented as a whole as the subject of FBI scrutiny. The group was discussed as a unit, and any quotes came from an anonymous spokesperson for the group. Where possible, the story made reference to the "group" rather than an "individual" group member.

The second factor concerned the citizenship status attached to the subject of FBI scrutiny; the subject was described as an Arab-American group in New York founded by U.S. citizens of Arab descent for one condition and an Arab group in New York founded by immigrants from Arab countries for the other condition. For those assigned to the individual frame described earlier, the name of the individual was altered slightly to invoke the individual's citizenship. In the citizen condition, the individual was named Joseph Hazim, and in the immigrant condition, the individual was named Youssef Hazim.

A third experimental factor concerned whether the target of government scrutiny was defined as representing either extremist or nonextremist views. Language cues such as "extremist" and "Front" were used in the story to describe the radical target (e.g., "Arab Solidarity Front, a New York-based

TABLE 3.1. *Summary of Methods for the Arab Study and the Activist Study*

	The Arab Study	The Activist Study
Sample Characteristics	College Students	College Students and RDD-recruited Adult Sample
Sample Size (N)	N = 578	N = 650 (College Students = 413 and Adults = 237)
Research Design and Manipulations	2 × 2 × 2 1. Story Frame (Individual Frame vs. Collective Frame) 2. Immigrant Group vs. Citizen Group 3. Extremist Group vs. Non-Extremist Group	2 × 2 × 2 1. Story Frame (Individual Frame vs. Collective Frame) 2. Cause Predisposition (Most-liked Group vs. Least-liked Group) 3. Cue Manipulation (Liberal Think Tank vs. Conservative Think Tank)
Pre-Manipulation Measures Used in Research Chapters (Chapters that used measure)		Control Variables: • Materialism Index (5, 6) • Post-materialism Index (5) • Interpersonal Trust Index (6) • Newspaper Hard News Use Index (6) • TV Hard News Use Index (6) • Interpersonal Discussion Index (6) • Media Use Index (7)
Post-Manipulation Measures Used in Research Chapters (Chapters that used measure)	Closed-ended Dependent Variables: • Group Evaluation Index (4) • Tolerance for Extremists Index (4) • Support for Immigration Index (4) • Minority Empowerment Index (4) • Response Latency Measures (4)	Dependent Variables Constructed from Open-ended Responses: • Number of Unique Concepts (5) • Level of Elaboration (5) • Overall Cognitive Complexity (5) • Statements about National Security (5) • Statements about Civil Liberties (5) Closed-ended Dependent Variables: • Tolerance for Extremists Index (5) • Tolerance for Targeted Group Index (6) • National Security Concerns Index (6) • Group Evaluation Index (7) • Willingness to take Expressive Action (7)

(*continued*)

TABLE 3.1 *(continued)*

The Arab Study	The Activist Study
	Control Variables:
	• Number of Story Segments Viewed (5)
	• Gender (6)
	• Income (6)
	• Education (6)
	• Age (6)
	• Evaluations of the FBI Index (7)
	• Support for National Security Index (7)
	• Political Ideology Index (7)

extremist group" versus "Arab Solidarity League, a New York-based group"). See Table 3.2 for the full rendering of the experimental news stories used in the Arab Study.

The Activist Study: FBI Scrutiny of Activist Groups

Three manipulations were also tested in the study involving domestic activist groups. As with the Arab Study, the first factor dealt with how the story was framed; specifically, whether the target of FBI monitoring was presented as either an individual or a group. In the individual condition, participants read about a particular member of the selected group, named Greg Anderson. The story included direct quotes from Anderson, and the story made frequent reference to the "individual" rather than to the "group." In the collective condition, respondents read a story in which the selected group, as a whole, was the subject of FBI scrutiny. The group was discussed as a unit, and any quotes came from an anonymous spokesperson for the group. Where possible, the story made reference to the "group" rather than an "individual" group member. The fact that the individual versus collective frame was operationalized across seven different issue contexts demonstrates that this framing distinction is "transcendent" (as described in Chapter 1). Moreover, the design of the Activist Study allowed us to create dummy codes for each fictional group, thereby permitting an implicit test of this transcendence. That is, results showed that effects were not isolated to a particular fictional group, thus providing evidence of the transcendent nature of these frames and their effects.

The second factor concerned whether the activist targeted by the government represented a cause that the respondent supported or opposed. This was determined by establishing respondents' policy preferences by gauging their attitudes toward several real activist groups. Early in the survey, respondents were presented with six mainstream activist groups and were asked toward

TABLE 3.2. *Stimulus Messages for the Arab Study*

Individual Story Frame	Collective Story Frame
BUSH ADMINISTRATION DRAFTS EXPANSION OF ANTI-TERRORISM ACT	**BUSH ADMINISTRATION DRAFTS EXPANSION OF ANTI-TERRORISM ACT**
The Bush administration has prepared a comprehensive sequel to the USA PATRIOT Act that would give the government broad new powers to increase domestic intelligence-gathering, surveillance, and law enforcement prerogatives in the fight against terrorism.	The Bush administration has prepared a comprehensive sequel to the USA PATRIOT Act that would give the government broad new powers to increase domestic intelligence-gathering, surveillance, and law enforcement prerogatives in the fight against terrorism.
Proposed by Attorney General John Ashcroft, the Vital Interdiction of Criminal Terrorist Organizations Act of 2003, also known as the Victory Act, is designed to expand the powers of the FBI to monitor certain individuals considered to be potential threats.	Proposed by Attorney General John Ashcroft, the Vital Interdiction of Criminal Terrorist Organizations Act of 2003, also known as the Victory Act, is designed to expand the powers of the FBI to monitor certain groups considered to be potential threats.
While the administration claims that such measures are crucial for the safety of the nation, the plan has drawn criticism from members of groups such as the [*Arab / Arab-American*] Solidarity [**Front / League**], who worry such sweeping powers infringe on civil liberties and privacy.	While the administration claims that such measures are crucial for the safety of the nation, the plan has drawn criticism from groups such as the [*Arab / Arab-American*] Solidarity [**Front / League**], which worry such sweeping powers infringe on civil liberties and privacy.
For instance, [*Youssef / Joseph*] Hazim of the [*Arab / Arab-American*] Solidarity [**Front / League**], a New York-based [**extremist / no modifier**] group founded by [*immigrants from Arab countries / U.S. citizens of Arab descent*], said he has been under FBI surveillance in recent months. Hazim said he is unable to express his opinions in public and must watch what he says for fear of being taken the wrong way.	The [*Arab / Arab-American*] Solidarity [**Front / League**], a New York-based [**extremist / no modifier**] group founded by [*immigrants from Arab countries / U.S. citizens of Arab descent*] has been under FBI surveillance in recent months. Members say they are unable to express their opinions in public and must watch what they say for fear of being taken the wrong way.
The Victory Act would grant the FBI greater latitude to engage in electronic surveillance, conduct searches without a warrant, and make secret arrests without seeking judicial review.	The Victory Act would grant the FBI greater latitude to engage in electronic surveillance, conduct searches without a warrant, and make secret arrests without seeking judicial review.

(continued)

TABLE 3.2 (*continued*)

Individual Story Frame	Collective Story Frame
BUSH ADMINISTRATION DRAFTS EXPANSION OF ANTI-TERRORISM ACT	**BUSH ADMINISTRATION DRAFTS EXPANSION OF ANTI-TERRORISM ACT**
The Justice Department proposed the expansion of FBI powers out of concern that certain individuals may be plotting acts of violence and terrorism. "We need to be more vigilant in stopping people who pose a threat to the security of our nation," Ashcroft said.	The Justice Department proposed the expansion of FBI powers out of concern that certain groups may be plotting acts of violence and terrorism. "We need to be more vigilant in stopping people who pose a threat to the security of our nation," Ashcroft said.
[**Front / League**] member [*Youssef / Joseph*] Hazim is concerned his situation may worsen if the new legislation is passed. "What's to keep government officials from claiming that [*immigrants / citizens*] like me pose a threat so they can use these new police powers against us?" Hazim asked.	[**Front / League**] members are concerned their situation may worsen if the new legislation is passed. "What's to keep government officials from claiming that [*immigrants/citizens*] pose a threat so they can use these new police powers against us?" a spokesperson for the [**radical / no modifer**] group asked.
Ashcroft said the expansion of the original PATRIOT Act is necessary to protect national security.	Ashcroft said the expansion of the original PATRIOT Act is necessary to protect national security.
According to the draft, the Victory Act would strengthen the power of federal agencies to expand domestic intelligence gathering techniques including discretionary wiretaps and Internet monitoring. The Act would also authorize greater search-and-seizure powers for the FBI and would allow it to detain individual [*immigrants / citizens*] without judicial review.	According to the draft, the Victory Act would strengthen the power of federal agencies to expand domestic intelligence gathering techniques including discretionary wiretaps and Internet monitoring. The Act would also authorize greater search-and-seizure powers for the FBI, and to detain [*immigrants / citizens*] without judicial review.

Note: Cue manipulations are in brackets (citizenship status cues are italicized; extremism cues are bolded). At the bottom of the story, hyperlinks provided options to read additional material in three areas: (1) surveillance, (2) search and seizure, and (3) secret arrests. Reading patterns did not produce significant effects and were not used in the analyses.

which one they felt most positive and toward which they felt most negative. The answers to these questions were used to generate the target of the experimental stimulus stories that were presented later in the survey, with half of the participants assigned to read about a targeted group they were predisposed to support (the most-liked group condition) and the other half assigned to

TABLE 3.3. *List of Activist Groups Used to Establish Cause Predispositions (Most-Liked and Least-Liked Groups) and Fictitious Activist Groups Used in Experimental Stimuli*

Cause	Real Activist Group	Fictitious Activist Group
Bringing a faith-based agenda to politics	The Christian Coalition	United Christian Front
Preventing environmental degradation	Greenpeace	Earth Defense Front
Protecting the rights of gun owners	National Rifle Association	Arm America Front
Ending the practice of abortion	National Right to Life	Unborn Defense Front
Advancing the rights of gays/lesbians	Outproud	United Queer Front
Promoting the humane treatment of animals	People for the Ethical Treatment of Animals	Animal Liberation Front

read about a target group that they were predisposed to oppose (the least-liked group condition). However, to minimize the influence of existing knowledge about real groups and to help mask this manipulation, the group mentioned in the story was an "extremist" offshoot group with similar beliefs to the existing activist group. For example, if respondents listed Greenpeace as their most-liked group and were assigned to the predisposition-to-support condition, they would read a story that mentioned the more radical "Earth Defense Front" (see Table 3.3 for a list of groups).

A third experimental factor concerned the ideological cue attached to a fictional think tank, the Liberty Institute. Throughout the story the institute was used to provide a counter to FBI claims, discussing the merits of civil liberties protections and the need for government restraint. As a cue to subjects, the institute was described at multiple points in the story as "liberal" for one condition and "conservative" for the other condition. This manipulation is not the focus of this study and was therefore controlled in all tests of hypothesized relationships. Also, to ensure that it did not condition the effects of either of the other two experimental factors, tests were run to confirm an absence of interactions. Notably, no interactions were observed between this factor and the other two manipulations, so it was simply included as a covariate. See Table 3.4 for a full text of the stimulus material.

For both data collections, experienced professional journalists wrote the fictional news stories that contained the experimental manipulations. As an additional step to maximize their perceived authenticity, the fictional stories were also modeled on real newspaper articles covering similar topics. These real stories provided additional guidance as to the appropriate language and content to include. In terms of presentation, the experimentally manipulated

TABLE 3.4. *Stimulus Messages for the Activist Study*

Individual Story Frame	Collective Story Frame
FBI PUTS EXTREMIST GROUP UNDER SURVEILLANCE	**FBI PUTS EXTREMIST GROUP UNDER SURVEILLANCE**

Individual Story Frame

When Greg Anderson makes a telephone call or sends an e-mail from home, he knows the FBI is eavesdropping. As a member of [name of group that shares issue with predetermined *most-liked / least-liked* group], an extremist [insert issue] group, Anderson has been placed under surveillance by government agents in recent months.

The FBI fears that Anderson may be plotting acts of violence. "Targeting individuals who are potentially dangerous is important for the security of our nation," said Christopher Stark, an FBI representative.

However, the Liberty Institute, a [**conservative / liberal**] civil rights watchdog group, cautioned that the government should balance security issues against personal rights.

"The goal of domestic security is important, but we're concerned that perhaps the government is infringing on individuals' civil rights," said Sean Ward, a spokesperson for the Liberty Institute. "Where do we draw the line?"

Anderson said he is unable to express his opinion in public and must watch what he says on the phone or in e-mail because he is afraid it might be taken the wrong way.

Ward, the spokesperson for the [**conservative / liberal**] Liberty Institute, also feels the government is wasting its resources monitoring the activities of individuals. "The FBI's time would be better spent following due process in investigations," Ward said.

Collective Story Frame

When members of the [name of group that shares issue with predetermined *most-liked / least-liked* group] make a telephone call or send e-mail from home, they know the FBI is eavesdropping. As members of [name of *most-liked / least-liked* group], an extremist [insert issue] group, they have been placed under surveillance by government agents in recent months.

The FBI fears that the [name of *most-liked / least-liked* group] may be plotting acts of violence. "Targeting groups that are potentially dangerous is important for the security of our nation," said Christopher Stark, an FBI representative.

However, the Liberty Institute, a [**conservative / liberal**] civil rights watchdog group, cautioned that the government should balance security issues against personal rights.

"The goal of domestic security is important, but we're concerned that perhaps the government is infringing on individuals' civil rights," said Sean Ward, a spokesperson for the Liberty Institute. "Where do we draw the line?"

The [name of *most-liked / least-liked* group] said they are unable to express their opinions in public and must watch what they say on the phone or in e-mail because they are afraid it might be taken the wrong way.

Ward, the spokesperson for the [**conservative / liberal**] Liberty Institute, also feels the government is wasting its resources monitoring the activities of individuals. "The FBI's time would be better spent following due process in investigations," Ward said.

Note: Cue manipulations are in brackets (cues for the most-liked versus least-liked manipulation as determined by responses to premanipulation survey questions are italicized; cues for the liberal versus conservative watchdog group are bolded). At the bottom of the story, hyperlinks provided options to read additional material in three areas: (1) surveillance, (2) search and seizure, and (3) secret arrests. Reading patterns did not produce significant effects and were not used in the analyses.

stories appeared as though they were written by the Associated Press, adhered to AP style, and followed conventional hard news structure, including a general inverted pyramid form that emphasized the most important elements of the story first.

Experiment Participants

The Arab Study
Participants for the Arab Study were recruited from enrolled in courses at the University of Wisconsin, who received extra credit for participating in a research experience. All potential participants were contacted by e-mail and given the Web address of the online survey. A total of 578 students completed the survey experiment.

The Activist Study
Participants in the Activist Study were recruited from two populations. The first population was students enrolled in courses at the University of Wisconsin. Participants received extra credit from their instructors for participating. A second group of participants was recruited using a probability sampling variation of random-digit dialing to contact residents of Dane County, WI. These participants were offered a chance to win one of five $50 cash prizes for participating. Students in an upper-division research methods course contacted sampled households and spoke to a randomly selected adult within each household. Of the eligible adults who were contacted, 37.2% provided an e-mail address.

All potential participants were contacted by e-mail and given the Web site of the online survey. Nonstudent participants who provided an invalid e-mail address were recontacted by telephone, and every effort was made to obtain a legitimate e-mail address to use for recruitment. In order to receive extra credit or be included in the prize drawing, participants were required to provide their e-mail addresses at the start of the survey. Individuals who failed to respond to our initial e-mail contact received an e-mail reminder. Approximately 65% of recruited students completed the survey, for an N of 413. In addition, 51% of nonstudent respondents who provided e-mail addresses took the survey, for an N of 237. In total, 650 individuals participated in the Activist Study.

Measurement of Variables

In terms of measurement, although the two studies shared some common variables, each study also included a large number of unique measures. In this section, we describe variables featured in the subsequent data analysis chapters. The reasons for including each of these measures will become clear in the context of each of the four results chapters. Complete question wordings and scale performance information for both studies are listed in Appendix A and B for the Arab Study and Appendix C and D for the Activist Study.

Measures Used in the Arab Study

After reading the manipulated stories, participants answered a series of questions focusing on evaluations of the group featured in the manipulated story, as well as a series of questions addressing tolerance judgments. In terms of group evaluations, participants assessed the group targeted by the FBI according to four semantic differential scales (foolish/wise, unfair/fair, threatening/ nonthreatening, and dangerous/harmless). Participants were also asked questions to assess their tolerance for extremists, support for immigration, and attitude toward minority empowerment.

For the Arab Study, results also included an analysis of response latency for each of the aforementioned items. Response times for these items were recorded in the Web experiment log file, which was used to create measures of response latency for each set of responses. When analyzing these time measures, we first identified abnormal outliers, which we defined as responses two standard deviations higher than the mean score. It is likely that these outliers are attributed to time away from the online experiment to engage in other activities – such as answering a phone call – a limitation from which most Web-based experiments suffer. These outliers represented only a small fraction of responses ($N = 6$) and were equally distributed across experimental conditions.

Measures Used in the Activist Study

As described earlier, after being presented with a list of real activist groups (Christian Coalition, Greenpeace, the National Rifle Association, the National Right to Life, OutProud, and People for the Ethical Treatment of Animals), participants were asked to choose their most-liked and least-liked group. These responses were later used to assign respondents to a stimulus news story about a fictitious group that shared a cause with either their most-liked or least-liked group. Other measures in the Activist Study included tolerance for extremists, tolerance for the targeted group, national security concerns, group evaluation, and willingness to take expressive action for or against the targeted group.

Several variables were used as additional factors in data analyses, including maternalism and interpersonal trust based on research demonstrating that such dispositional factors are influential to political cognition processes (Ball-Rokeach and Loges, 1994; Kinder and Sears, 1985; Krosnick et al., 1994; Sotirovic and McLeod, 2004). In addition, recent research has highlighted the connection between nurturing maternalism and social tolerance (Lakoff, 2004). Sullivan et al. (1981) demonstrated that people who trust others displayed higher levels of political tolerance.

A second set of variables looked at newspaper hard news use, television hard news use, and interpersonal discussion. These three communication variables might also be considered potential confounds for a study of political tolerance. Although there has not been much research directly addressing the relationship between communication and tolerance, news consumption and interpersonal discussion are thought to promote political tolerance (Sullivan et al., 1981).

Through various communication channels, citizens can be exposed to diverse people, and learn the democratic principle that the "free exchange of ideas is necessary and that to be different is not necessarily to be dangerous" (Sullivan et al., 1981, p. 94). In addition, a media use index was developed for use in selected analyses.

Respondents in this study had the option of reading additional information – up to nine more stories – about the fictional news events presented in the first story. Most respondents bypassed this opportunity. Nonetheless, a variable indicating total number of stories viewed was included in analyses for control purposes, since it potentially increased the dosage of the manipulations and added to the cognitive complexity of activated thoughts on the topic.

A last set of control variables included political ideology as well as the standard battery of demographic measures: gender, income, education, and age. Previous researchers have found that political tolerance tends to be associated with these basic demographic variables (Marcus et al., 1995; Stouffer, 1955; Sullivan et al., 1981). Specifically, those who were female, younger, and of high social status exhibited higher tolerance.

Analysis of data from the Activist Study also included measures created from open-ended responses that were coded into various categories. Open-ended responses were prompted by the following question: "If you were explaining this issue to a friend, what would you tell them?" Respondents were encouraged to imagine themselves writing to a friend who was unsure what to think about the news story and wanted to know the respondent's thoughts and feelings about the issue. Following extensive training, four coders analyzed these responses to code for response structure. Focusing on manifest content only, responses were coded for three characteristics: number of unique categories mentioned, level of elaboration, and degree of integration.

For the first characteristic, the number of unique conceptual categories mentioned, coders focused on nine conceptual categories that had been identified from a preliminary examination of the open-ended responses. The nine conceptual categories derived from the open-ended questions were: (1) group/individual liking, support, allegiance; (2) group/individual disliking, opposition, disassociation; (3) government liking, trust, patriotism; (4) government disliking, distrust, criticism; (5) national security, safety; (6) rights, constitution, freedoms; (7) participation, collective action; (8) U.S. role in world; and (9) information needed/uncertainty/judgment avoidance. Finally, an "other" category was established to account for concepts that might be present in a specific answer, yet unrepresented in our nine conceptual categories.

The second characteristic was based on coding for the level of elaboration (i.e., the degree of embellishment for each concept). Coding categories ranged from a mere mention to a single-sentence elaboration to a multisentence elaboration.

The third characteristic was integration (i.e., the cognitive complexity or interconnectedness of the various conceptual categories mentioned in the response), taking into account the total number of conceptual categories listed. When more than one category was mentioned, coders judged whether the linkages between the concepts were evident (high integration) or not (low integration).

Summary

Using the data collected in these two online experiments, we were able to test a number of hypotheses as reported in Chapters 4 through 7. The results reported in Chapter 4, which are based on an analysis from the Arab Study, examine the confluence of frames and cues on attitude consistency and response latency, as they reflect an underlying spread of activation. The following three chapters use data from the Activist Study. Chapter 5 focuses on framing's impact on cognitive complexity as indicated by open-ended responses about the national security/civil liberties conflict. In Chapter 6, we examine the interaction between framing and individual predispositions as they influence tolerance judgments regarding the activists featured in the stimulus news story. Finally, Chapter 7 analyzes the differential effects of individual versus collective framing on readers' willingness to take expressive action supporting or opposing the featured targets of government surveillance. Through these experiments, we not only contribute empirical evidence to the literature on framing effects, but also illustrate how we can begin to put the framing effects models that we introduced in Chapter 1 into research practice.

4

Converging Cues and the Spread of Activation

"The USA PATRIOT Act and Homeland Security, while aimed at immigrants especially from the Middle East, is a threat to the civil rights and liberties of all people. How do you end racial profiling and stop police racist harassment in this atmosphere? How do you end racist discrimination when someone can be picked up, their phones can be tapped or they can be kicked off airplanes because they look Middle Eastern?"

– Jarvis Tyner
Executive Vice Chair, American Communist Party
February 16, 2002

"The federal government can and must protect Americans from the threat of terrorism without eroding our constitutional liberties. Today, Arab Americans are especially vulnerable to abuses of government power. Yet ultimately all Americans are put at risk when our rights come under attack. We must work to preserve our constitutional rights and roll back the most egregious infringements of our individual freedoms."

– Congressman Dennis Kucinich (D-OH)
2004

The above quotations share a common concern that the war on terrorism has exacerbated perceptions that people of Arab descent constitute a threat to public safety. Moreover, such threat perceptions have provided an impetus to generate public support for the policies of the USA PATRIOT Act that in turn has threatened the civil liberties of Muslims and Arab-Americans. For most citizens, the mass media provide the primary source of information upon which to base judgments about potential threats. As such, the nature of news coverage and its effects become important concerns for researchers seeking to understand the dynamics of political judgments.

In the discussion of our integrated Message Framing Model (Figure 1.2) in Chapter 1, we noted that news frames and cues have much in common in that they both describe ways in which journalists give meaning to text. They differ in terms of the unit of text to which they are applied. Both frames (i.e., organizing devices used by journalists to structure press accounts) and cues (i.e., the labels used to characterize issues, groups, and figures in the news) have received considerable attention from mass communication researchers interested in understanding how subtle changes in news reports influence audience understanding (Shah et al., 2002). Research on the cognitive effects of mass media find that both frames and cues can shape how people think about issues, groups, and figures by influencing mental activation and social evaluations (Domke et al., 1998; Kuklinski and Hurley, 1994; Mondak, 1993; Price and Tewksbury, 1997).

Most framing studies consider simple, direct effects of news framing and cueing on a range of social judgments, without considering how these content elements might work together to influence the thinking of the audience. Some research has examined the nature of frame-cue interactions (e.g., Shah et al., 2004; Shah et al., 2010). In this chapter, we examine the interactive effects of the frame and cues from our Arab group study. Specifically, we examine whether certain cues in news texts may resonate with another cue and generate stronger reactions among audience members, and the extent to which news frames condition the effects of cue interactions, amplifying or attenuating the observed relationships.

As a context for this study, we explore the cues used to characterize Arabs in coverage concerning the war on terrorism in the aftermath of the September 11 attacks. Criticisms of media coverage of Arabs had been made long before the events of September 11, 2001. For example, literary critic and social commentator Edward Said examined journalistic, literary, and academic representations of Arabs three decades ago. In his book, *Orientalism*, Said contended that portrayals of Arabs emphasize their traditionalism, even orthodoxy, and reinforce notions of "otherness" and opposition to Western ways of being and thinking. Since 9/11, according to Said's (2003) more recent analysis, Arabs are increasingly represented as backward, fundamentalist, unpredictable, dangerous, and at odds with the West.

Reflecting the images of Arabs portrayed in news (e.g., danger and otherness), our Arab Study manipulated different cues to simultaneously depict Arab groups as more or less threatening by presenting them in ways that highlighted their status as out-group or in-group and as extremists or moderates. Defining the subject of a story as an outsider or a radical seems likely to foster threat perceptions and trigger related thoughts. Guided by our Message Processing Model (Figure 1.3), we examine whether the co-occurrence of these cues fosters perceptions of threat, thus encouraging the spread of activation (a central feature of the model) to other tolerance-related judgments (i.e., intolerance for the group's expressive rights, and negative attitudes toward immigration and minority empowerment). Further, we also consider whether news framed in *individual* or *collective* terms amplifies cue convergence effects.

Mental Networks and Associative Priming

Scholars concerned with interattitudinal structures argue for a conception of memory as a network of interconnected cognitions (Anderson, 1985; Anderson and Bower, 1973; Collins and Loftus, 1975). These scholars maintain that any one concept is associated with other constructs when encoded in memory, and the linkages between constructs are strengthened each time they are activated in tandem. Further, as the number of separate linkages between constructs increases, so does the likelihood that one will be activated indirectly by the invocation of the other due to an "implicational relation" (Judd and Krosnick, 1989).

As a result, Berkowitz and Rogers (1986) argue, "When a thought element is activated or brought into focal awareness, the activation radiates out from this particular node along the associative pathways to other nodes" (pp. 58–59), increasing the probability that related constructs will come to mind. Drawing from these perspectives, theories of "spreading activation" contend that the stronger or more numerous the mental pathways between constructs, the greater the chance that thoughts activated to process information about one construct will cascade through memory to other constructs, influencing subsequent evaluations and the formation of impressions (Lodge and Stroh, 1993).

Only a few scholars, however, have examined how cognitions activated by media coverage may spread to other constructs via mental pathways. Schleuder et al. (1991) examined how linkages among mental constructs influence the retrieval of information about candidates from memory; they concluded that media effects research should more thoroughly consider the outcomes of spreading activation. Building on these insights, Domke et al. (1998) found that individuals with well-developed cognitive connections among mental constructs produced more coherence among a range of evaluations when spurred by certain types of media content. That is, individuals exposed to certain message features displayed strengthened associations among directly primed and related elements, suggesting that for these individuals, activation spreads more readily among the nodes comprising their mental networks.

These findings share some similarity with Neuman's (1981) notion of integrative complexity. Typically assessed using content coding of open-ended responses, Neuman's measures have been confounded with loquacity (Luskin, 1987). Other researchers have tried to develop alternate methods for assessing the interconnection between cognitive elements, including closed-ended measures (Eveland et al., 2004). For this study, we adopt an approach similar to that of Sniderman et al. (2004), who examine the intercorrelation among various perceptions under different experimental conditions, and to Fazio et al.

(1986), who assess response latency as an indicator of the degree of integration between objects and their evaluations.

We consider these two approaches to gauging the spread of activation as complementary; each one provides unique insights into the nature of spreading activation resulting from interaction with news texts. Specifically, measures of associational strength provide some indication of the degree to which cues trigger the cascade of activation to related cognitions, thereby offering some insight about the structure of the mental network, as a greater correspondence is seen between constructs activated through an "implicational relation." On the other hand, measures of response latency reveal whether the spread of activation resulting from situational triggers alters the actual accessibility of these cognitions as can be observed in more rapidly accessible cognitions.

Cue Convergence and Threat

The presence of particular cues, then, may encourage the application of certain cognitions, which then trigger other aspects of long-term memory as activation spreads through the cognitive network. The convergence of cues and the resulting activation of applicable constructs may encourage particular avenues of thought (Wyer and Srull, 1986; Wyer and Srull, 1989). This perspective is consistent with Edelman (1993), who argues that the public's understanding of political issues and social groups is often swayed by transparent "categories" offered up by political elites. These categories constrain a range of potential realities, shaping political "enthusiasms, fears and antagonisms" when presented as natural, self-evident, or simple descriptions rather than carefully constructed linguistic and rhetorical choices (Edelman, 1993, p. 232). These cues have the potential to shape evaluations beyond the issue or group at hand, providing criteria for a range of other judgments. As this suggests, media may broadly influence the nature of responses and the coherence among a range of elements.

Of course, the effectiveness of the cue depends on its construction – the more complicated the cue, the less effective it will be. At their most powerful, cues are "contestable metaphors" found in word choices such as "freedom fighter" (as opposed to "insurgent rebel") or "pro-choice" (as opposed to "abortion advocate"). In the case of Arabs, cues concerning residence status (*immigrant* versus *citizen*) and radicalism (*extremist* versus *moderate*) may be particularly powerful descriptors. Indeed, these cues may work in combination to shape a range of thoughts that are connected to evaluations of Arabs in the minds of audience members, including thoughts about civil liberties and multi-culturalism. In Europe, for example, a surge in Arab immigration has heightened these representations and sparked disputes over notions of nationality, civil liberties, and minority empowerment. As Sniderman et al. (2004) note, these changes have "triggered intense debate about the nature of citizenship" (Favell, 1998), "the claims – and limits – of multiculturalism" (Barry, 2001; Parekh, 2000), and even "the scope of free speech" (p. 35). The connections among these discrete judgments further suggest that the presence of particular cues may align a range of judgments.

Drawing on the reviewed research, the analysis presented in this chapter explores the interplay of different news cues on the structural coherence of group evaluations, judgments on civil liberties, and attitudes toward immigration and minority empowerment, as well as the speed with which these judgments are made. Specifically, we contend that the convergence of cues that reinforce stereotypes of Arabs as the "radical other" creates a context in which activation resulting from evaluations of Arabs becomes particularly likely to spread to connected constructs such as intolerance for speech or opposition to immigration for those with existing linkages among these mental elements. This assumes that many individuals have cognitive connections between beliefs about Arabs, civil liberties judgments, attitudes toward immigration, and feelings about minority power in the United States. In this case, the co-occurrence of two cues, Arabs as immigrants (as opposed to citizens) and Arabs as extremists (as opposed to moderates), should trigger this associative priming effect and lead to greater coherence, indicated by stronger correlations, among unfavorable evaluations of the group, opposition to speech freedoms, reduced support for immigration policy, and negative feelings about minority power.

Likewise, if, as we expect, activation spreads through the cognitive network to related nodes, the convergence of stereotyping cues should not only lead to heightened correlations between the primary evaluation (i.e., group evaluations) and other judgments (i.e., opposition to freedom of speech, immigration, and minority empowerment), but also among these judgments, which we expect are all interconnected for many people. That is, under a situation in which an individual encounters the convergence of immigrant and extremist cues, associative priming will likely increase the degree of association among these previously mentally linked elements, such as the second-level correlation between immigration attitudes and minority empowerment that exists distinct from the linkage to group evaluations.

As noted earlier, we further theorize that the process underlying these predictions involves associative priming through the spread of activation. If in fact the effects of cue convergence on these evaluations are the result of an associative priming process, people should make related judgments more rapidly. As Fazio and colleagues (1986) observe, response latency should be facilitated when there is "a strong association between the attitude object and an evaluation of that object" (p. 229). That is, people should render speedier responses concerning civil liberties, immigration, and minority power if there is a strong cognitive connection between these constructs and the primary evaluative object, which should be most likely to occur when the two cues (immigrant and extremist) co-occur. In this study, we consider response latency for these related judgments to be unobtrusive evidence of the strength of their association with evaluations of the targeted group. Accordingly, we predict that people will require less time to render judgments when there is a convergence of stereotyping cues.

Effects of Framing and Cueing in Social Judgment

Individual versus collective framing is likely to moderate cue convergence effects. As noted in Chapter 2, individual and collective frames invoke different conceptions of entitativity, which then moderate cue convergence effects on subsequent judgments. First, such judgments are more easily rendered when an entity is represented as an individual rather than as a collective. Thus, response times will be quicker and judgments more consistent in the individual-frame condition than in the collective-frame condition. Second, relying on these arguments, we expect that the individual-frame conditions will amplify the effects of cue convergence. That is, individual story frames will strengthen the correlations between group evaluations and associated judgments.

Testing cueing and framing effects on the structure of thoughts requires comparing the strength of associations among concepts rather than paying attention to mean differences across experimental conditions. Thus, Pearson correlations were calculated among the indices of group evaluation, expressive tolerance, support for immigration policy, and support for minority empowerment. The correlation coefficients (r) were statistically compared across the manipulations using Fisher's r-to-z transformation statistic. As described in Chapter 3, which provides the methodological information for our research, subjects in our experiment were allowed to continue reading more news stories after reading the main news story. This potentially different amount of self-opted exposure to experimental treatment could potentially affect the results of our research. To address this concern, we created a variable for the number of stories read after being exposed to the main story and included it as a control variable for all correlation analyses reported below.

Before testing our ideas formally, we performed a series of ANOVA tests to detect whether the experimental manipulations created any significant mean differences in the four variables of concern. Results showed no significant differences, indicating that the changes in the story did not have a notable influence on respondents' mean scores concerning evaluations of the group under FBI suspicion, tolerance for expression, support for immigration policy, or minority empowerment more generally. Thus, the manipulations did not sway the extent of these evaluations, though they did produce a more subtle set of effects.

Cue Convergence and Heightened Correlations

As predicted, the relationship between evaluations of the group and the other three variables – expressive tolerance, support for immigration, and minority empowerment – differed depending on the cue combinations to which the

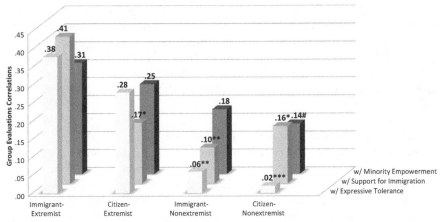

FIGURE 4.1. Correlations with group evaluation by condition, including difference tests. Correlations within outcome that are different from the immigrant-extremist condition at $p < .001$ are marked ***. Correlations within outcome that are different from the immigrant-extremist condition at $p < .01$ are marked **. Correlations within outcome that are different from the immigrant-extremist condition at $p < .05$ are marked *. Correlations within outcome that are different from the immigrant-extremist condition at $p < .10$ are marked #. All are one-tailed tests.

participants were exposed (see Figure 4.1). More specifically, the correlations in the Immigrant/Extremist (henceforth, IE) condition were higher than those in the other experimental conditions, suggesting that threat evaluations of this group were linked more strongly to speech intolerance, opposition to immigration, and minority disempowerment. We consider the correlations between group evaluations and each assessment in turn and test whether they are significantly different across experimental conditions. Note that case counts for each correlation ranged from $N = 131$ to $N = 148$.

Group Evaluation and Expressive Tolerance

Under the IE condition, the Pearson correlation between group evaluation and expressive tolerance was .38, while correlations for Citizen/Nonextremist (henceforth, CN) and Immigrant/Nonextremist (henceforth, IN) conditions were .02 and .06 respectively. Note that while this correlation is positive because of the affirmative coding of the variables, the implication of this stronger correlation in the cue convergence condition is that negative evaluations of the group were more strongly linked to speech intolerance. Once we compared the correlation score in the IE condition to those in the CN and the IN conditions, z-statistics indicated that the differences were statistically significant ($z = 3.18$, $p < .001$ for the IE and the CN comparison; $z = 2.87$, $p < .01$ for the IE and the IN comparison). When the story characterized the FBI target with cues of citizen and extremist (CE), the correlation between group evaluation and expressive tolerance was .28. Although the correlation in the CE condition is weaker than that in the IE condition, the formal test comparing the two correlation coefficients did not achieve statistical significance. Overall, when the extremist cues were emphasized, the group evaluation and expressive tolerance correlations were stronger. But when "extremist" cues were used along with "immigrant" cues (IE condition), the strength of the correlation increased dramatically.

Group Evaluation and Support for Immigration

Similarly, the correlation between group evaluations and support for immigration was strongest ($r = .41$) in the IE cue combination. Again, this positive correlation reflects the direction in which the variables were coded, with positive versus negative evaluations of the group positively related to support versus opposition to immigration. This relationship had much weaker correlations under the CN ($r = .16$), IN ($r = .10$), and CE ($r = .17$) conditions. When the IE correlation was statistically compared with the correlations obtained in the other experimental conditions, the z-statistics confirmed that differences were statistically significant ($z = 2.23, p < .05$ for IE vs. CN; $z = 2.81, p < .01$ for IE vs. IN; $z = 2.16, p < .05$ for IE vs. CE). Moreover, not even one of the z-statistic tests comparing the strength of the correlations among other three experimental conditions was significant, providing implicit support for our prediction.

Group Evaluation and Minority Empowerment

This general pattern continued in the correlations between group evaluation and minority empowerment. The correlation was strongest in the IE condition ($r = .31$). The other experimental conditions – CN, IN, and CE – revealed a somewhat stronger set of associations relative to the prior comparisons ($r = .14$, $r = .18$, and $r = .25$, respectively). As a result, z-statistics comparing the correlations did not achieve statistical significance. Thus, although the differences are directionally consistent with our expectations, formal tests do not provide support in this case.

To summarize, the pattern of results shows that the correlations between group evaluations and the other assessments were largely stronger in the condition where respondents were exposed to the combination of immigrant and extremist cues. Indeed, the formal tests indicate that the correlations in this condition are significantly higher than the other three conditions in five out of nine tests. As this suggests, under the condition where the stereotypic cues converged, liking or disliking for the groups became more tightly aligned with a range of other seemingly linked judgments about civic liberties, immigration, and minority power.

Further, we examined whether there was a difference between conditions in the strength of the correlations among expressive tolerance, support for immigration, and minority empowerment depending on whether the cue

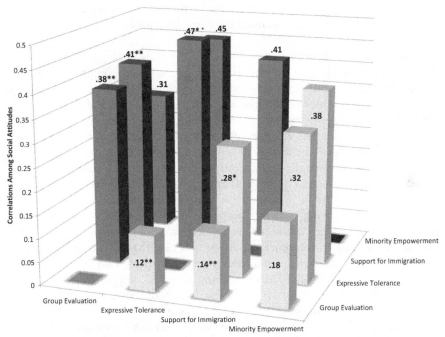

FIGURE 4.2. Correlations among social attitudes contrasting immigrant/extremists (cue convergence = above diagonal/darker) with others (cue divergence = below diagonal/lighter). Paired correlations that are different from one another at $p < .01$ are marked **. Paired correlations that are different from one another at $p < .05$ are marked *. All are one-tailed tests.

combination was convergent, as in the IE condition, or divergent, as in the other conditions. Figure 4.2 presents the patterns of intercorrelations, with the cue convergence condition above the diagonal (N = 131 to 132) represented by the darker columns, and the cue divergence conditions below the diagonal (N = 431 to 435) represented by the lighter columns.

First-Level Correlations

As observed earlier, the pattern of findings indicates that group evaluations were more strongly correlated with each of the other measures in the cue convergence condition than in the cue divergence conditions. Given the larger cell sizes, the differences in the size of correlations across experimental conditions achieved statistical significance for group evaluation and speech tolerance ($z = 2.22$, $p < .01$) and group evaluation and support for immigration ($z = 2.96$, $p < .01$). Likewise, the correlation between group evaluation and minority empowerment was stronger when cues converged ($r = .31$) than when they diverged ($r = .18$), but z-statistics for this comparison did not reach statistical significance. Again, all of these positive correlations reflect the association of favorable or unfavorable evaluations of the group with tolerance or intolerance for their speech, support or opposition for immigration, and minority empowerment or suppression, respectively, with the cue convergence condition exhibiting strengthened connections between these judgments.

Second-Level Correlations

The first-level correlations indicate that cue convergence strengthens the association between negative group evaluations with intolerance, opposition to immigration, and minority suppression. The results also reveal that the inter-correlations among the second-order variables (i.e., intolerance, immigration opposition, and minority suppression) were also stronger in the cue convergence condition than in the cue divergence conditions, but not always to an extent that was statistically significant. Specifically, the cue convergence condition produced stronger correlations among expressive tolerance and support for immigration in ($r = .47$) than the cue divergence conditions ($r = .28$), with the z-statistic being statistically significant ($z = 2.25, p < .05$). Similarly, the correlation between expressive tolerance and minority empowerment was stronger in the cue convergence condition ($r = .45$) than in the cue divergence conditions ($r = .32$), but the z-statistic comparing these two coefficients was not statistically significant. The correlation between support for immigration and minority power exhibits a similar pattern, with correlation between the two variables slightly higher in cue convergence conditions ($r = .41$) than in cue divergence conditions ($r = .38$), though this small difference did not achieve statistical significance and is likely not meaningful.

Nonetheless, the overall pattern is consistent; participants who read news stories with convergent cues – that is, featuring an immigrant presented as an extremist – exhibited a stronger relationship between the four variables than those who read news stories with divergent cues, strengthening ties between their evaluation of the group and their judgments about speech tolerance, immigration, and minority rights. In addition, statistical comparisons of the size of the correlations found that they were significantly different in three out of six tests.

Cue Convergence and Response Latency

Furthermore, time measures recorded in the web experiment log file were analyzed to test whether participants in the cue convergence condition (IE condition) would generate faster responses to the postmanipulation survey questions tapping the four variables of interest than those in the other experimental conditions. As reported in Figure 4.3, the results of a series of t-tests indicate a clear pattern in which participants spent less time answering questions under the cue convergence condition than under the cue divergence conditions.[1] Specifically,

---

[1] The only exception to this pattern was found for *group evaluation*; time spent answering the questions of group evaluation was virtually equal in the two experimental conditions, cue convergence and cue divergence. This finding was not reported in Figure 4.3 because the comparison

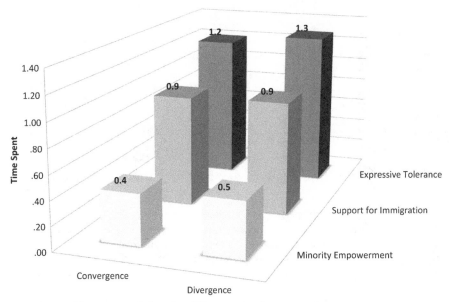

FIGURE 4.3. T-tests examining the difference in time spent between cue convergence and divergence conditions. Entries are normalized seconds calculated by dividing time spent responding to item battery by time spent answering preexperimental items. T-tests: The differences for "Minority Empowerment" and "Expressive Tolerance" were statistically significant.

responses to the items tapping *expressive tolerance* were reported faster under the cue convergence condition than under the cue divergence conditions ($t = 1.7$; $df = 575$; $p < .05$, one-tailed). Similarly, participants in the cue convergent condition spent less time responding to the *minority empowerment* items than those in the cue divergence conditions ($t = 2.58$; $df = 575$; $p < .001$, one-tailed). Although the t-test for *support for immigration* was not statistically significant, the result of mean differences in time spent was consistent with the expected pattern in that responses were faster under the cue convergence condition than the cue divergence conditions.

The Individual Frame, Cue Convergence, and Correlations

Figure 4.4 presents correlations between group evaluation and each of the other three variables across the different cue-frame combinations. If, as we expect, individual frames contribute to more extreme judgments, the correlations between group evaluation and each of the other three variables should be stronger when convergent cues coincided with individual frames.

of time spent for group evaluation, a judgment directly grounded in the manipulated news story, was not of interest to this study.

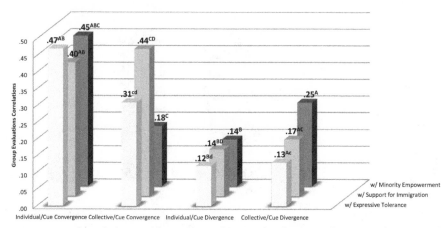

FIGURE 4.4. Correlations with group evaluation by frame and cue conditions with difference tests. Correlations within outcome that are different from one another at $p < .05$ share the same uppercase superscript; correlations within outcome that are different from one another at the $p < .10$ share the same lowercase superscript. All are one-tailed tests.

Group Evaluation and Expressive Tolerance

The correlation between group evaluation and expressive tolerance was strongest when the FBI target was described as an individual member of an extremist group founded by Arab immigrants ($r = .47$). When compared with correlations in the other cue-frame combinations, the correlation in the cue convergence and individual-frame condition was significantly higher than those in the cue divergence, individual-frame conditions ($r = .12$, $z = 2.75$, $p < .01$) as well as in the cue divergence, collective-frame conditions ($r = .13$, $z = 2.72$, $p < .01$). The correlation between group evaluation and expressive tolerance in the cue convergence, collective-frame condition was somewhat tempered ($r = .31$) and its difference from those in the cue divergence conditions, regardless of whether they received the individual or collective frame, was weaker ($z = 1.33$, $p < .10$ for the cue divergence, individual-frame condition; $z = 1.29$, $p < .10$ for the cue divergence, collective-frame condition).

Group Evaluation and Support for Immigration

The correlation between group evaluation and support for immigration in both of the cue convergence conditions ($r = .44$ for the cue convergence, collective-frame condition; $r = .41$ for the cue convergence, individual-frame condition) were found to be higher than those in the cue divergence conditions ($r = .17$ for the cue divergence, collective-frame condition; $r = .14$ for the cue divergence, individual-frame condition). Z-statistics indicate that the correlations in the two cue convergence conditions were significantly different from their counterparts in the cue divergence conditions, confirming the findings from Figures 4.2 and 4.3.

Group Evaluation and Minority Empowerment

For this last pair of variables, the pattern becomes more distinct. The most robust correlation between group evaluation and minority empowerment was found in the cue convergence, individual-frame condition ($r = .45$). The rest of the cue-frame combinations, the cue divergence, collective-frame condition; the cue divergence, individual-frame condition; and the cue convergence, collective-frame condition, revealed associations that were much more moderate ($r = .25$, $r = .14$ and $r = .18$, respectively). Z-statistics confirmed that the correlation in the cue convergence, individual-frame condition was significantly different from those in cue divergence, collective-frame condition ($z = 1.65$, $p < .05$); the cue divergence, individual-frame condition ($z = 2.46$, $p < .01$); and the cue convergence, collective-frame condition ($z = 1.67$, $p < .05$).

Overall, the results observed across these comparisons provide some support for the expectation that individual framing amplifies the effects of cue convergence. In seven out of nine tests, the individual-frame, cue convergence condition combination yielded statistically stronger correlations than the other frame-cue combinations. In contrast, the collective-frame, cue convergence condition produced correlations that were stronger than other conditions in only two of nine tests. As such, it seems that framing moderates cue convergence effects, with the individual frame amplifying convergence effects. In other words, subjects' evaluations of the group aligned more closely with their attitudes about speech tolerance, immigration, and minority rights when encountering individual framing and the presence of convergent "othering" cues.

Conclusions

People who encountered the Arab portrayal with the convergent cues of the immigrant extremist most closely connected their evaluations of the group featured in the news story to other judgments involving civil liberties, immigration, and minority empowerment. Specifically, when these two cues were present together in the stimulus story, favorable group evaluations became more closely aligned with tolerance for mediated expression of extreme perspectives, opposition to restrictive immigration policies, and minority empowerment, whereas unfavorable evaluations of the group became more closely linked to intolerance for such expression, support for immigration restrictions, and opposition to minority empowerment. The results further revealed that the correlations among these other variables grew when the cues converged to portray the Arab as the "radical other," such that intolerance, immigration opposition, and minority disempowerment were more tightly interrelated.

When coupled with the fact that we did not observe differences in mean scores on these variables across experimental conditions, these findings become more interesting. Traditional approaches to analyzing experimental data would not have revealed these effects. We examined these effects because of the expectation that spreading activation (see Figure 1.3) and associative priming would tighten the intercorrelations among these related evaluations. Many individuals appear to have mental networks that contain cognitive connections among these constructs, yet it was under the conditions of cue convergence that we observed more coherence among these evaluations. Thus, measures of associational strength provide some evidence of the degree to which cues and frames can trigger the cascade of activation to related cognitions, offering insights about the structure of the mental network, as a greater correspondence is seen between constructs activated through "implicational relations."

These conclusions are bolstered by the results of the response-time analysis, which revealed that participants who encountered the Immigrant/Extremist cue combination generated the fastest normalized responses to the postmanipulation survey questions concerning civil liberties, immigration, and minority power. This assessment of response latency suggests that the spread of activation resulting from situational triggers altered the actual accessibility of these cognitions as can be observed in more rapid accessibility. Specifically, participants spent significantly less time responding to items pertaining to expressive tolerance and minority empowerment under the IE condition as compared with the other experimental conditions. In sum, when coupled with the results of correlation analyses, these findings that people spend less time rendering judgments under certain cue combinations lend additional support to our claim of cue convergence effects on knowledge activation and associative priming.

Finally, this study finds that frames and cues can have interactive effects in a manner consistent with other recent framing research. That is, framing news about civil liberties restrictions in individual terms amplified the effects of cue convergence, with correlations between group evaluations and the other assessments strongest under these circumstances. This result suggests that media effects may be enhanced when journalists integrate consistent and mutually reinforcing frames and cues within news stories. It also implies that researchers who adopt the idealist approach (see Figure 1.1) to studying framing effects may underestimate the true power of news frames by stripping them of associated textual elements that convey particular meanings through the framing of smaller linguistic units (i.e., cues), elements that enhance the effect of the story frame and contribute to its power.

There are two possible reasons why certain frames and cues may have interacted to influence the connections individuals made between attitudes: (1) certain combinations may have caused research participants to consciously feel more motivated to think about and respond consistently with a range of activated constructs, and (2) certain combinations may have triggered increased associations with existing mental structures, thus activating a greater number of constructs when responding more or less automatically, absent the motivation to process. The most likely explanation of the data seems to be a combination of the two.

Regardless, these data indicate that the interaction between frames and cues has implications for cognitive responses. Research on media framing and cueing has only begun to discover how subtle elements of news content interact to produce effects (see Chong and Druckman, 2007a,c; Shah et al., 2004; Shah et al., 2010). A recognition that multiple frames and cues exist in all news stories – especially in contexts where democratic competition involves elites offering different labels for issues – and a dedicated effort to understand how they may interact with one another are clearly required.

On a related point, examinations of communication framing and cueing effects are aided by looking beyond mean scores to consider the associations among variables and the latency of responses under different experimental conditions. These approaches allow the researcher to observe the most basic consequences of framing and cueing on cognitive processing and attitude expression. They provide some insight into the structure of expressed thoughts and the cognitive processes underlying these expressions. A particularly important innovation of this research is the application of response latency techniques outside the laboratory, which provides a new direction for future survey and survey-experimental work in communication.

In addition, these findings suggest that content analyses of media should determine the relative frequencies and co-occurrence of various cues and frames. If the relationship among frames and cues within news stories is important, then analyses that identify frame-cue patterns and determine the relative frequencies and co-occurrence of such content are also necessary. Indeed, in environments featuring elite competition over issue framing and journalists working to cover different story angles, this sort of co-occurrence is to be expected.

These findings also obviously have implications for media portrayals of Arabs and research on minorities and the media. In the wake of September 11, 2001, media representations of Arabs have varied widely, presenting a range of Arab and Muslim groups as more or less threatening. Our finding that cues highlighting their status as an outgroup rather than as an ingroup and as extremists rather than as moderates interact with audience members' existing cognitions to produce the observed effects is notable on a number of fronts. First, it seems that a range of intolerant, xenophobic, and prejudiced attitudes are linked to the notion of the Arab as the radical outsider. While portrayals of Arabs were simply the context for this study, this certainly has implications for those interested in how media coverage of Arab groups may be reinforcing intolerant beliefs. Second, and perhaps more important, this research suggests that the cueing of race and ethnicity can have important, albeit subtle, effects on audience thinking.

As a whole, this analysis provides a promising avenue for future research. It remains to be discovered whether such interactions occur across other topics and for other groups, as well as whether the co-occurrence of these cues can be systematically cataloged in the media production process. Nevertheless, it is clear that frames and cues, acting together, have effects that go beyond what would be predicted by examining the individual outcomes of the components.

This lends a new layer of complexity to our understanding of how the choices and patterns present in media texts may contribute to the cognitions and ultimately the behaviors of individuals. It also underscores the utility of factorial designs that allow for the layering of frames and cues in experimental research for examing framing and cueing effects.

5

Cognitive Complexity and Attitude Structure

"Our enemies operate secretly and they seek to attack us from within. In this new kind of war, it is both necessary and appropriate for us to take all possible steps to locate our enemy and know what they are plotting before they strike."

– U.S. Attorney General Alberto Gonzalez
Testimony before the U.S. Senate Judiciary Committee
February 6, 2006

"I know for an absolute fact that we have not been involved in anything related to promoting terrorism, and yet the government has collected almost 1,200 pages on our activities. Why is the ACLU now the subject of scrutiny from the FBI?"

– Anthony. D. Romero
ACLU Executive Director
July 16, 2005

As the United States government took actions to engage in surveillance of activist groups, the discourse surrounding this action straddled both sides of the national security/civil liberties dichotomy. Some officials, such as Attorney General Alberto Gonzalez (quoted above), made the argument that such government activities are necessary to protect the safety and security of the American public. On the other hand, civil rights advocates such as Anthony Romero, the ACLU's Executive Director, questioned whether activist group surveillance wasn't motivated by political rather than security concerns. As discussed earlier, this national security/civil liberties debate was played out for public consumption through the mass media. Audience members seeking to understand the debate over government surveillance activities had to make judgments about what was happening on the basis of information reported in the media. This led us to ask questions about how the audience would make sense of this controversy in response to the news stories that they encounter.

In this chapter, we examine how different frames used to construct such new stories affect audience understanding and cognitions. As we noted in Chapter 1, frames are likely to affect people differently according to the predispositions that they bring to the processing of news stories. As such, this chapter examines the interplay of news frames and political predispositions on audience reactions to news stories. For this analysis, we used data from the Activist Study in which research participants read news stories about the surveillance of political advocacy groups under the USA PATRIOT Act. Specifically, we are interested in how the news frame, whether individual or collective, and the audience member's predisposition toward the targeted cause influenced what readers had to say about the issues covered in the news story in terms of the elaboration and complexity of their responses.

News Framing and Impression Formation

Most framing research begins with the assumption that by constructing social and political issues in specific ways, media convey a particular understanding of the situation and provide a basis on which subsequent judgments can be made (Iyengar, 1991; Shah et al., 1996). Scholars working in this domain assert that frames trigger the application of cognitive heuristics and biases that then encourage certain patterns of construct activation (Price and Tewksbury, 1997). For example, the journalistic tendency to frame news reports around particular instances and individual exemplars is thought to initiate certain attributional processes (Iyengar, 1991).

That is, the news media's preference for episodic frames (i.e., focused on discrete events and their manifestation at the individual level) over thematic frames (i.e., focused on social issues and their implications at the community level) is thought to influence how viewers attribute responsibility for solving social problems. Episodic framing fosters individual attributions of responsibility "for the creation of problems or situations (causal responsibility) and for the resolution of these problems or situations (treatment responsibility)" (Iyengar, 1991, p. 3). By contrast, framing the issue in more general terms encourages a sense of shared responsibility and motivates a collective response to the issue. Experimental studies concerning crime, poverty, and unemployment, however, provide only weak evidence to support these claims, suggesting an underlying conceptual issue.

Speculating on why the empirical support was not stronger, Shah et al. (2004) assert that the distinction between episodic and thematic framing confounds two frame dimensions. Episodic coverage not only favors specific instances over enduring problems (i.e., time span), it also emphasizes individual situations over societal conditions (i.e., social level). This second factor, the distinction between individuals and collectives, is particularly relevant for the social inference and impression formation processes.

Shifting the story frame from individual to collective terms implicates a particular type of attributional process involving the principle of entitativity, (Hamilton and Sherman, 1996). As Keum et al. (2003) emphasize, entitativity concerns the degree to which a social unit is perceived as being cohesive and consistent, ranging from very high in individuals to very low in population aggregates. People tend to attribute more volatile and extreme behavioral outcomes to more cohesive and consistent entities. In contrast, large groups are not only seen as hard to coordinate and mobilize into action, but also as more able to moderate the more extreme behavior of individual members. As a consequence of these perceptions, people tend to integrate and organize information more rapidly, process the incoming information more thoroughly, and recall more information when forming impressions (McConnell et al., 1994; Susskind et al., 1999).

Hamilton and Sherman (1996) found support for entitativity theory by providing evidence that people are quicker to make trait inferences about individuals than about groups, and that these inferences are more pronounced, which shares some similarity with the results presented in the previous chapter. Consistent with this work, Susskind et al. (1999) reported that individuals put more effort toward resolving inconsistencies in the information about an individual target than inconsistencies in the information about a group target. Further, they find that "in comparison with those forming impressions of a group or an aggregate, participants in individual target conditions made stronger (more extreme) trait judgments, they made those judgments faster, and they made them with greater confidence" (p. 190). This has major implications for journalists' preference for personifying issues.

Cause Predisposition and Affective Reactions

The political predispositions that individuals bring to processing news coverage about civil liberties controversies have the potential to sway the nature and extent of their information processing and subsequent judgments (Marcus et al., 1995). This research attempts to understand how individuals respond when confronted with disliked groups. It finds that when people encounter reviled groups – organizations whose goals they strongly oppose – the resultant sense of threat encourages deeper information processing and cognitive elaboration (Forgas, 1992; Sullivan and Marcus, 1988; Sullivan et al., 1979; Sullivan et al., 1981).

Marcus et al.'s (1995) technique of identifying experimental subjects' "least-liked group" revealed that disliked groups fostered a sense of threat, which became a critical factor in explaining patterns of information processing and social judgments. However, the focus on least-liked groups shifted attention away from public responses to liked groups and supported causes. If the presence of a disliked group fosters negative reactions, does the presence of a liked group encourage favorable perceptions, and thereby reduce the inclination to process information deeply? To answer this question, we must also consider how people respond to targets whose cause they support. Accordingly, we consider reactions to both liked and disliked groups to test the role of perceived threat.

For this chapter, we are interested in the conditions under which people are inclined to engage in effortful and elaborated cognitive processing. In particular, we focus on the direct and conditional effects of news frames spurred by political predispositions. We suspect that people become most inclined to process information deeply when two conditions are met: (1) they are motivated to form more coherent and consistent inferences because they encounter individually framed news accounts, and (2) they feel threatened because they encounter a target that opposes their political predispositions. We believe when both conditions are met, individuals become particularly likely to draw information from networked memory into active thought.

Associative Network Models of Memory

The conceptualization of the human mind as a network of interlinked or associated concepts is frequently used as a basis for social and cognitive science research (e.g., Acton et al., 1994; Carley, 1986; Carley and Palmquist, 1992; Lazo et al., 1999). These models assume that behind all information processing is a mental system made up of networks of associated nodes. Within this system, the activation of one node can spread through the network of interconnected units, leading to the activation of related nodes. Prompted by theories of spreading activation, social scientists have become interested in extracting activated mental models in order to illuminate the relationships among memory, social inference, and human behavior (Carley, 1986; Lazo et al., 1999; Novak and Gowin, 1984).

Many methods for deriving mental models rely on content analysis of verbatim responses to deduce the causal and categorical connections among relevant cognitions (e.g., Langston and Kramer, 1998; Rye and Rubba, 1998; Wallace and Mintzes, 1990). These data can be used to represent the structure of activated memory for analysis. As Carley and Palmquist (1992) note, this approach assumes that (1) mental models are representations of associations in memory, (2) language is the key to understanding these associations, and (3) these models can be represented as networks of activated concepts.

Common to most of these studies is an interest in the complexity of mental models, particularly the differentiation of unique elements and their integration with one another (Neuman, 1981). For example, Lazo et al. (1999) proposed that the overall level of detail (elaboration of specific categories), depth (causal connections among categories), and width (the discreet categories that serve as the foundation for these causal connections) could function as a measure of the complexity of mental models (see also Carley and Palmquist, 1992; Novak and

Gowin, 1984). As we discuss, the examination of the complexity of activated mental models may be useful for understanding news framing effects.

News Frames, Cause Predisposition, and Cognitive Complexity

Past research on framing, especially work focusing on the application of cognitive biases that encourage certain inferential processes, suggests that framing news in individual rather than collective terms will have important implications for mental processing (Iyengar, 1991). Coupling these insights with findings on entitativity (i.e., the perceived cohesiveness and consistency of entities), individual news framing should foster more extensive and more effortful inferential processing than collective frames. Accordingly, we expect more complex mental models to be generated when people encounter individual news frames, and expect less complex mental models for collective frames.

Likewise, perceptions of threat are thought to motivate deeper mental processing (Forgas, 1995). Bearing in mind that our experiment involves exposing people to targets of government surveillance that they are predisposed to support or oppose, the exposure to targets who stand in opposition to an individual's political preferences should generate greater perceptions of threat, which should then motivate deeper processing and the production of higher levels of cognitive complexity.

Furthermore, a combination of an individual frame and exposure to a story about a disliked group should interact to foster even deeper processing. The effects of individual framing on social judgments should be amplified by political predispositions against the group featured in the news story. When both conditions are met, each should amplify the effect of the other (i.e., the threat perception working with entitativity to produce an interactive effect).

Effects of the News Frame and Cause Predisposition

We begin our analysis by examining whether the combination of individual frames and cause opposition activates more thoughts and produces more elaboration on these thoughts. To test the influence of the news frame and cause predisposition, we used data from the Activist Study. After exposure to the manipulated news stories, respondents answered an open-ended question, in which they were first asked to imagine that "the news story you just read was sent to you by a friend" who wanted to know your thoughts about it. We coded open-ended responses to this question for three factors: the degree of differentiation (i.e., the number of discrete cognitive categories mentioned), the average elaboration (i.e., the extent of detail provided for each mentioned category), and integration (i.e., the interconnectedness of the various cognitive categories mentioned) in the answers provided by respondents. For details concerning the coding process, see Chapter 3.

We examined the interplay of news frames and political predispositions on the complexity of open-ended responses – that is, the number of unique concepts mentioned, the level of elaboration of these concepts, and the integration of these concepts into a naïve theory – using a two-way Analysis of Covariance (ANCOVA), in which we assessed not only the main effects of our experimental factors (news frame and cause predisposition manipulations), but also their interactive effects. Our analyses controlled for the remaining experimental manipulation (i.e., source cue) and the number of story segments the respondents viewed.

This analysis revealed a consistent and statistically significant main effect of the frame manipulation on all three outcome variables examined. Participants in the individual frame condition exhibited a higher level of cognitive complexity than those in the collective frame condition: for the total number of unique concepts expressed, $F(1, 211) = 7.68$, $p < .01$; for the level of elaboration, $F(1, 211) = 4.05$, $p < .05$; and for the level of integration of the responses, $F(1, 211) = 4.59$, $p < .05$. By contrast, we did not find any significant main effects of cause disposition. However, interaction effects between frame manipulation and cause predisposition were found to be significant for the number of unique categories ($F[1, 211] = 3.81$; $df = 1,211$, $p = .05$) and level of integration among these categories, ($F[1, 211] = 4.59$, $p < .05$), but not for the average elaboration of unique categories. Overall, these results suggest that the effects of news frames differ depending on cause predisposition.

To interpret the nature of interaction effects more easily, we plotted the adjusted means for the number of unique categories (see Figure 5.1) and for level of integration (see Figure 5.2), while holding all covariates constant. The vertical distances between the two corresponding points indicate the effects of the frame manipulation for the two different conditions of cause predisposition (most-liked group vs. least-liked group). Clearly, in both figures, the mean differences between the individual and collective frame conditions are relatively small in the most-liked group condition. Only in the least-liked group condition did frame manipulation generate substantially large mean differences. Further, these large differences were mainly due to particularly high mean scores marked at the combination of the individual frame and the least-liked group condition. These patterns of mean distribution suggest that the effects of news frames are highly conditional and dependent on predispositions toward the target group under surveillance; individuals who encounter individual frames tend to generate substantially higher levels of cognitive complexity than those who encounter the collective frame, but only when the featured target group stands in opposition to participants' political predisposition.

Taken together, our ANCOVA results suggest that the individual frame fosters deeper processing and generates more elaborate and complex mental models than did the collective frame. However, this kind of framing effect was shown to be conditional, depending on cause predisposition. In two out of three tests we conducted, individual frames produced the effects only when the

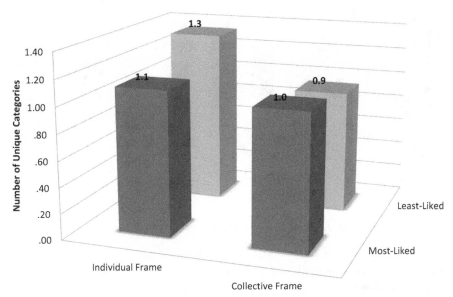

FIGURE 5.1. Number of unique categories by individual/collective frame and cause predisposition.

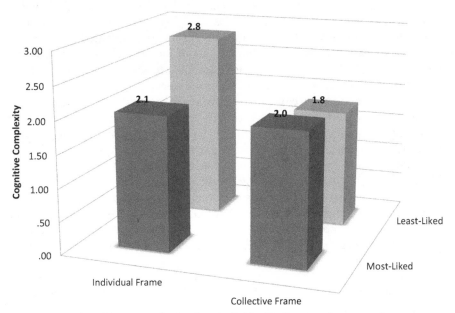

FIGURE 5.2. Cognitive complexity by individual/collective frame and cause predisposition.

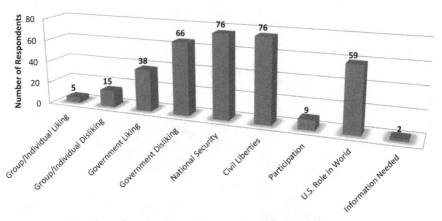

FIGURE 5.3. Number of respondents who mentioned each concept.

individual frame was combined with a featured target group whose goals those individuals opposed.

Framing and the Nature of Activated Thoughts

It is important to go beyond simply looking at the number of unique thoughts activated and the degree to which these thoughts were elaborated and integrated to look more specifically at the content of these activated thoughts. In other words, what were readers thinking about immediately after reading the news story (as reflected in open-ended responses to the question of what the participant would tell a friend about the news story)?

Figure 5.3 shows the frequency with which participants mentioned various content categories. The fact that national security and civil liberties were the two most frequently mentioned content categories shows that the news stories were clearly triggering activation of these schemas among respondents. Moreover, Figure 5.4 demonstrates that national security and civil liberties had the highest amount of elaboration among activated constructs.

These conflicting considerations were activated by exposure to the news stories. Our next question is, once activated, how were these thoughts about national security and civil liberties used in the process of making tolerance judgments? In the rest of this chapter, we draw a broader picture of framing effects on the attitude formation process.

As Rokeach (1968) argues, cognitions and attitudes are deeply rooted in beliefs and values. Among the diverse values individuals hold, materialism and postmaterialism are especially relevant for tolerance judgments toward extreme groups because materialist values emphasize economic and physical security, a strong national defense, and law and order, while postmaterialist values prioritize self-expression and democratic values (Inglehart, 1971;

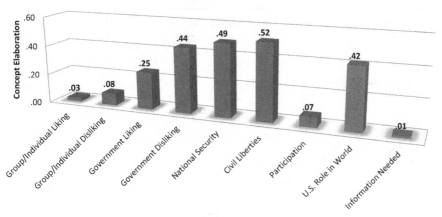

FIGURE 5.4. Average elaboration of each concept.

Inglehart, 1977). As such, these values were included in our models of tolerance judgments not only because they are important in the judgment process, but also because they illustrate the role of values in such a decision-making model.

In constructing these models, we build on existing theory and research that suggests that attitude judgments involve two different, though intersecting, modes of cognitive processing (Chaiken, 1980; Eagly and Chaiken, 1993; Petty and Cacioppo, 1986). The basic difference between the two modes – that is, central or peripheral, systematic or heuristic – centers on the extent to which individuals engage in effortful cognitive processing when they form attitudes. According to these theories, individuals may follow a low-effort route in which they rely on salient cognitive constructs, or heuristics, and subconsciously apply them to the formation of attitudes. Alternatively, individuals may consciously and effortfully process relevant cognitive elements that in turn affect their attitudes.

As discussed earlier in this chapter, message framing can be one of the factors determining cognitive processing modes. That is, collective framing may lead to automatic and simple memory retrieval modes of attitude formation without effortful cognitive elaboration, while individual framing may facilitate effortful attitude formation through extensive cognitive processing, which may be further enhanced by activated values (see Figure 5.5), as our results suggest. However, an alternative explanation may be also conceptually and statistically justified. For example, both the individual and collective frames may trigger cognitive elaboration of relevant values, which in turn may influence tolerance toward extreme groups (which we refer to as alternative nested model 1). Otherwise, both the individual and collective frames may lead to automatic and simple value activation modes of attitude formation without the elaboration of values (which we refer to as alternative nested model 2).

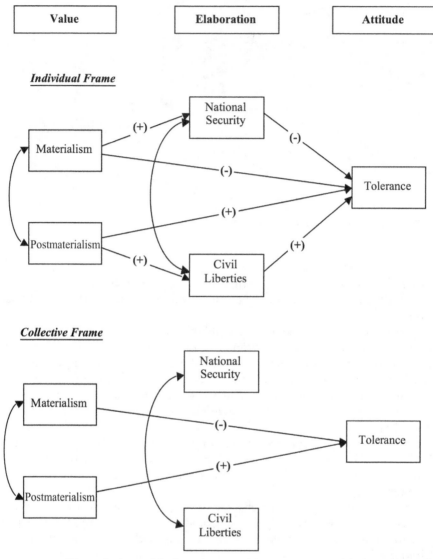

FIGURE 5.5. Theoretical model for the cognitive processes underlying attitude formation.

Before we look at how the cognitive processes underlying attitude formation would differ depending on our frame manipulation, we first test whether these alternate models produced a better fit than our theoretical model by performing a series of multigroup path analyses using LISREL.[1] With our theoretical model

---

[1] This analytical approach was used because it allows us to identify the best-fitting model among a set of nested models by imposing or releasing constraints on the path coefficients (Kline, 1998).

TABLE 5.1. *Multigroup Analysis for Model Comparison*

	CFI	TFI	RMSEA	SRMR	$\chi2$	DF	P
Theoretical Model	.99	.98	.03	.04	8.75	8	.36
Alternative Model 1	1.00	1.00	.00	.04	3.64	4	.46
Alternative Model 2	.79	.65	.79	.11	30.85	12	.00

Note: In the theoretical model, mediating paths in the collective frame condition (paths to and from the elaboration factors) were fixed to zero while those paths in the individual frame condition were set free to be estimated. In alternative model 1, mediating paths in both conditions were set free to be estimated. In alternative model 2, mediating paths in both frame conditions were fixed to zero.

as a baseline model ($df = 8$), we examined the overall model fit of alternative nested model 1 ($df = 4$) and alternative nested model 2 ($df = 12$). As seen in Table 5.1, the results show that the fit of our theoretical model was not worse than the alternative nested model 1, in which mediating paths in the collective frame condition are added to the path structure of the theoretical model ($\chi2$ difference $= 6.65$, $df = 4$, *n.s.*). This analysis revealed that the indirect effects of values on tolerance through elaboration were not statistically meaningful under these conditions. In contrast, the additional constraint of fixing mediating paths to zero in the individual frame condition for alternative nested model 2 significantly reduced the model fit compared with that of the theoretical model ($\chi2$ difference $= 25.47$, $df = 4$, $p < .001$), which suggests that the mediating role of cognitive elaboration in attitude formation is statistically meaningful in the individual frame condition.

Additional path analyses for each frame condition clearly illustrate how the path structures leading to tolerance toward extreme groups differ depending on news framing (Figure 5.6 and Figure 5.7). As expected, materialism and post-materialism had significant direct effects on tolerance in both the individual frame condition (materialism $\rightarrow$ tolerance: $\gamma = -.41$, $p < .001$; postmaterialism $\rightarrow$ tolerance: $\gamma = .30$, $p < .001$) and the collective frame condition (materialism $\rightarrow$ tolerance: $\gamma = -.54$, $p < .001$; postmaterialism $\rightarrow$ tolerance: $\gamma = .39$, $p < .001$). However, there were meaningful differences in the mediating role of cognitive elaboration depending on the news frame manipulation. Specifically, the effects of values on related concept elaborations were statistically significant in the individual frame condition (materialism $\rightarrow$ elaboration of nation security: $\gamma = .22$, $p < .01$; postmaterialism $\rightarrow$ elaboration of civil liberties: $\gamma = .22$, $p < .01$), while such effects of values on elaborations were not significant in the collective frame condition. Similarly, in the collective frame condition, concept elaborations did not influence tolerance, while each concept

A significant $\chi2$ difference between two nested models indicates that the model that constrains specific path coefficients to zero is significantly worse than the unconstrained model, while a nonsignificant $\chi2$ difference between two nested models suggests that the elimination of specific paths produces a parsimonious model without a significant decline in overall fit.

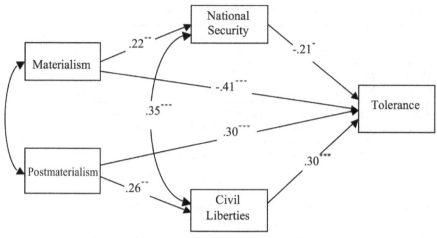

FIGURE 5.6. Framing effects on attitude formation in the individual framing condition. Goodness-of-fit test: $\chi^2(2) = 2.08$, $p = .35$; RMSEA = .02; SRMR = .04; CFI = 1.00; and TLI = .99. Numeric values are standardized coefficients. * $p < .05$, ** $p < .01$, *** $p < .001$

elaboration did significantly affect tolerance in the individual frame condition (elaboration of national security → tolerance: $\beta = -.21$, $p < .05$; elaboration of civil liberty → tolerance: $\beta = .30$, $p < .001$). These finding have clear implications for understanding the power of individual and collective framing on tolerance judgments.

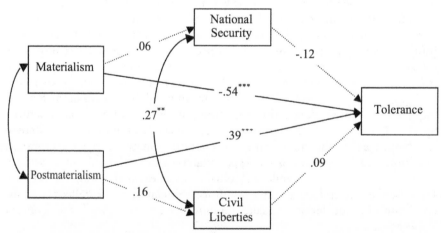

FIGURE 5.7. Framing effects on attitude formation in the collective framing condition. Goodness-of-fit test: $\chi^2(2) = 0.83$, $p = .66$; RMSEA = .00; SRMR = .03; CFI = 1.00; and TLI = 1.00. Numeric values are standardized coefficients. ** $p < .01$, *** $p < .001$

Conclusions

In this chapter, we explored how news frames and cause predispositions influence the complexity of activated thoughts both independently and jointly. The results demonstrate that individual framing generates more complex mental models than collective framing. Although the data did not provide empirical support for direct main effects of cause predisposition, political predisposition did moderate these framing effects. That is, individual frames produced the effects only when the goals of a featured target group conflicted with the readers' political predispositions. Under such conditions, there was a marked increase in thought complexity as measured by respondents' expressions.

The pattern of results, observed across three interrelated measures of cognitive structure (i.e., the number of categories mentioned, the level of elaboration, and integration of these discrete constructs), provides clear evidence of differences in mental processing between individual and collective framing. Stories framed at the individual level promote more extensive and effortful information processing, which in turn affects tolerance toward extreme groups, as suggested by prior research on entitativity (Hamilton and Sherman, 1996), albeit in surprising ways.

The nature of this cognitive activation has implications for judgmental processes. As shown in the structural equation models, the path structures leading to tolerance toward extreme groups differ depending on news framing. While materialism and postmaterialism had direct effects on tolerance in both frame conditions, the mediating role of cognitive elaboration differed considerably depending on the news frame. In the individual frame condition, the effects of materialism and postmaterialism were mediated through the activation of thoughts about national security and civil liberties. These mediating effects were not significant in the collective frame condition. Thus, the effects of individual frames not only produce more effortful information processing and cognitive complexity, but the thoughts activated by these frames mediate the effects of dispositions on tolerance judgments, providing considerable support for the theoretical propositions introduced in Chapter 1.

In this regard, the journalistic tendency to focus on individuals in the construction of news stories appears to encourage audience members to make faster, more confident, and more elaborate inferences (Hamilton and Sherman, 1996; Susskind et al., 1999). This psychological propensity may provide a broader explanation for Iyengar's (1991) provisional findings concerning attributions of responsibility for solving social problems. From our perspective, unfavorable judgments of episodically – that is, individually – framed targets result not from simple attribution processes, but from the perceived entitativity of the target and the nature of mental processing, cognitive responding, and construct activation that results from exposure to these story subjects.

In sum, this chapter develops mental processing models underlying individual and collective framing effects as they interact with cause predisposition.

Further, this chapter provides a broader picture of how individual and collective frames can influence the formation of tolerance attitudes by shaping cognitive processes. This lends a new layer of cognitive processing to our understanding of how media texts may help shape the cognitions, judgments, and actions of individuals.

6

Security Concerns and Tolerance Judgments

"While the FBI possesses no information indicating that violent or terrorist activities are being planned as part of these protests, the possibility exists that elements of the activist community may attempt to engage in violent, destructive, or dangerous acts."

– *New York Times Bulletin*
October 15, 2003

"'Anti-terrorist' legislation has been adopted in a number of western countries which allows for the arrest and detention without charge of alleged terrorists, including leaders of so-called 'domestic radical groups' (meaning antiwar activists), who are now categorized as a threat to Homeland Security."

– Michel Chossudovsky
Professor of Economics, University of Ottawa
December 21, 2005

The above passages illustrate how the focus of the government's antiterrorism activities included political activist groups, who were being considered as a threat to national security. Documented cases of government surveillance and infiltration of nonviolent activist groups, including the Occupy movement, and the dragnet monitoring of Americans revealed by Edward Snowden (as detailed in Chapter 2) substantiate concern that the USA PATRIOT Act is being used to infringe on the privacy and due process rights of citizens, including political activists who may stake out extreme positions on issues but are not suspected of criminal activities.

Public response to this range of government surveillance activities is likely to be shaped by how they are portrayed by the media. We argue that the nature of news coverage about civil liberties controversies has the potential to sway individuals' security concerns and social tolerance judgments. Our theory builds on past research that finds contemporary information works in combination with citizens' political predispositions to shape the level of support for civil liberties (Marcus et al., 1995). However, this past research focused only on how individuals respond when confronted with disliked groups, arguing that it is under these conditions that the limits of tolerance are best understood (Sullivan and Marcus, 1988; Sullivan et al., 1979). An unintended consequence of this focus on disliked groups has been a dearth of research on how individuals make these judgments when they confront efforts to restrict the civil liberties of groups whose causes they support, but whose tactics they may oppose. The decision to defend the civil liberties of radicals, even if only for targets toward which one feels some latent sympathy, is a meaningful test of tolerance in the political climate created after 9/11 and typified by the Snowden revelations.

More important, previous empirical research has studied tolerance toward groups, even though the individual is the traditional center of democratic governance stressing civil liberties (Golebiowska, 1996). Indeed, individual liberties are privileged in the Bill of Rights and other constitutional systems. The need to consider how a focus on individuals rather than groups shapes tolerance judgments is further highlighted by reporters' tendency to personalize press reports through episodic or individual story frames (see Iyengar, 1991). This journalistic propensity to personify the news has been found to condition media effects and shape cognitive processes (Shah et al., 2004). Building on these insights, this study examines framing effects on support for civil liberties relative to national security. We consider whether news framing in *individual* and *collective* terms differentially shapes security concerns and tolerance judgments when people encounter restrictions on fringe activists they are predisposed to support or oppose.

Security Concerns and Tolerance Judgments

In the United States, the preservation of civil liberties and the tolerance of differences have historically been favored over public safety and national security. The ideology of "classic" liberalism encouraged the framers of the Constitution to privilege individual rights, and to guard against the state's potential power to infringe on them. Even with this emphasis on the rights-bearing individual, concerns about safety and the potential for harm have been cited to justify policies that run counter to these guarantees. As discussed in Chapter 2, security concerns periodically overshadow civil liberties, particularly during periods of crisis. Some observers have compared the current "War on Terror" to the Cold War era, noting that concerns about security and liberty once again define citizens' tolerance judgments in the face of growing incursions by government into the private sphere in a prolonged and undefined battle.

Early research on tolerance was developed in response to the intolerance toward leftist groups that characterized threat in the Cold War era. This research defined tolerance as a desirable attitude "that allows people to have freedom of expression even though one may feel their ideas are incorrect or even immoral" (Nunn et al., 1978, p. 12). Education was thought to counter intolerance, since the research showed that individuals with more schooling were more willing to grant speech and other freedoms to radicals and non-conformists. However, Sullivan and colleagues (Sullivan et al., 1979; Sullivan et al., 1981) pointed out that this finding may be an artifact of the fact that previous studies typically measured tolerance in regard to leftist groups, toward which higher educated individuals are more favorably predisposed, and thus more tolerant. When Sullivan et al. (1982) asked respondents to self-select their most disliked group, they found that high-education individuals were not much more tolerant than low-education individuals. The least-liked groups of educated people tended to be on the political right, whereas leftist groups were typically least-liked by the less educated, a finding that explains away previous findings regarding education's apparent relationship to tolerance for the civil liberties of disliked groups.

Beyond education, Marcus et al. (1995) identified how predispositions (such as demographic characteristics), standing decisions (such as support for democratic principles), and contemporary information (such as the threat to norms posed by the target) can shape tolerance judgments when people were exposed to disliked groups in experimental settings. This research has considerably expanded the range of targets examined by scholars interested in public support for civil liberties and the factors underlying tolerance judgments. However, the focus on least-liked groups has also limited understanding of public responses to incursions on the civil liberties of radicals and nonconformists who advocate in behalf of supported causes. As a result, an important question remains unanswered: How do citizens respond to incursions on the civil liberties of radical groups that endorse causes they favor rather than oppose? While research on tolerance has benefited from a focus on disliked groups, when examining the limits of surveillance powers, studies need to consider how citizens respond to government efforts to restrict the freedoms and privacy of more favored, albeit controversial, targets.

This is particularly true in the wake of the 9/11 attacks and ongoing War on Terror, as concern about a realistic, long-term threat to domestic security has repeatedly been made acutely relevant. Given the policy and opinion climate that allowed passage and renewal of the PATRIOT Act, it becomes necessary to consider not only tolerance for disliked radicals, but also the willingness of individuals to defend the civil liberties of political radicals with whom they share a common cause. This orientation toward a broader range of civil liberties targets reflects the belief that the degree to which people are willing to extend civil liberties to disliked social groups is only one point on a continuum of tolerance judgments.

A willingness to restrict the liberties of extremist activists whose ideology one is predisposed to support may reflect a more general orientation toward supporting government efforts to combat terrorism, broadly defined. Conversely, opposition to these efforts suggests that security concerns may be trumped by the desire to protect civil liberties. Tolerance judgments that balance civil liberties and national security concerns are likely to vary according to an individual's orientation toward the targeted group. Therefore, in addition to Sullivan and colleagues' focus on disliked groups, an examination of citizens' security concerns and tolerance judgments in contemporary America necessitates some consideration of how people respond to restrictions on the civic liberties of radicals whose cause they may be predisposed to support, even if they find that group's tactics to be too extreme or distasteful.

The Role of Cause Predisposition

Scholars agree that negative evaluations of a group play a significant role in tolerance judgments (Hurwitz and Mondak, 2002; Kuklinski et al., 1991; Marcus et al., 1995). Groups that an individual dislikes are more likely to be judged as undesirable and threatening, and ultimately less worthy of tolerance (Hurwitz and Mondak, 2002; Marcus et al., 1995). However, if individuals encounter government efforts to infringe the liberties of radicals with whom they share support for a cause, they are more likely to form tolerant attitudes toward the group and its civil liberties. In the current political context, both of these evaluations are important for generating a broader understanding of the processes underlying judgments regarding the trade-off between national security and civil liberties.

Our research manipulated whether respondents were exposed to a news story about a surveillance target that either aligned or did not align with the respondents' political predispositions. We suspected that, even when people encounter an unfamiliar group that advocates for a supported cause, they would identify with the group and feel motivated to support its civil liberties. That is, even when a specific allegiance does not exist, the mere knowledge of a group's political orientation should be enough to produce a sense of affiliation or opposition (Billig and Tajfel, 1973; Tajfel and Billig, 1974; Tajfel et al., 1971; Tajfel and Turner, 1979). This expectation is substantiated by social identity needs (Turner et al., 1987) and reciprocity expectations (Gaertner and Insko, 2001; Ng, 1981; Rabbie et al., 1989). By contrast, support for expressive rights should be reduced and security concerns heightened when people encounter news stories about radical activists who espouse views that stand in opposition to their political predispositions.

The Role of Political Ideology

We also expect political ideology (i.e., liberal vs. conservative) to shape security concerns and tolerance judgments. Many scholars assert that the public's attitude toward these issues stems from fundamental ideological beliefs. Although Marcus et al. (1995) question whether liberals are more tolerant than conservatives when confronted with disliked groups, others have shown that certain features of liberal ideology promote tolerance and openness toward diverse beliefs (Tetlock, 1986; Tetlock et al., 1994). In fact, empirical studies have confirmed a relationship between liberal social ideology and tolerance

(Lipset and Raab, 1970). Thus, we expect that liberals will express greater support for civil liberties and express fewer security concerns compared with conservatives.

The Role of News Framing

Keeping with the central concern of this book, we expect that the main effects of support for or opposition to a cause on tolerance and security judgments will differ depending on the social level at which the news story is framed (i.e., individual vs. collective framing). As noted previously, theory and research associated with the principle of entitativity predicts that audience members will make more extreme judgments about an individual than about a collective. This is attributable to the fact that an individual is viewed as a more coherent and unified psychological unit (Hamilton and Sherman, 1996; Susskind et al., 1999). In making judgments about individuals under government scrutiny, perceivers should assume greater consistency between beliefs and actions and therefore assume the best or the worst about these individuals (Susskind et al., 1999). By contrast, social judgments are less likely to depend on such extreme inferences when the target is a group because evaluations of collectives are tempered (Iyengar, 1991; Shah et al., 2004).

Relying on this entitativity argument, we predict that the individual versus collective framing conditions will amplify or attenuate, respectively, the effects of cause predisposition. Those who encounter the collective framing of the civil liberties/national security controversy are expected to form evaluations that are less extreme – whether favorable or unfavorable – with regard to concerns about public safety and civil liberties. Supporting this view, Susskind et al. (1999) observed that tolerance judgments about individual targets were more extreme than the judgments about group targets. Thus, we expect that the individual story frame will condition the effects of cause predisposition such that security concerns and tolerance judgments are polarized under this condition.

Finally, to further test the interplay of frames with political predispositions known to influence judgments about safety and liberty, we theorize that political ideology interacts with individual and collective framing of this controversy to shape tolerance and security judgments. Just as individual and collective frames are expected to amplify or attenuate the effects of cause predispositions, we believe the same underlying process of entitativity should condition the effects of political ideology on these political evaluations. That is, individual framing is expected to amplify preexisting political leanings such that liberals become less concerned about security issues and more likely to support civil liberties when they encounter individually framed news accounts of government restrictions. Likewise, conservatives are expected to become more concerned about security and less supportive of civil liberties when they encounter news accounts framed in individual terms. In essence, we predict multiple interactions between the news frame and both cause predisposition and political ideology.

Additional Factors: Demographics, Orientations, and Communication Patterns

In addition to cause predisposition, ideology, and news framing, previous research has found that basic demographic variables shape political tolerance (Marcus et al., 1995; Stouffer, 1955; Sullivan et al., 1981). High social status, younger, and female respondents tend to be more tolerant. However, in addition to demographic controls, the analysis presented in this chapter also includes measures tapping maternalism and interpersonal trust, which are expected to increase tolerance. As dispositional factors, such values constitute a basis for political judgments (Ball-Rokeach and Loges, 1994; Kinder and Sears, 1985; Krosnick et al., 1994; Sotirovic and McLeod, 2001). In particular, research has found that maternalism has a substantial influence on social tolerance (McLeod et al., 2001). Sullivan and colleagues (1981) demonstrated that people who trust others displayed higher levels of political tolerance. Given the significance of maternalism and interpersonal trust in past research, it was deemed necessary to account for them in examining tolerance and security judgments.

Three communication variables – newspaper hard news use, television hard news use, and interpersonal discussion of political issues – are also expected to explain political tolerance. Although there has not been much research directly addressing the relationship between communication and tolerance, news consumption and interpersonal discussion promote knowledge and reflection, encouraging acceptance of other viewpoints. Through various communication channels, citizens can be exposed to diverse people and learn the democratic principle that "free exchange of ideas is necessary and that to be different is not necessarily to be dangerous" (Sullivan et al., 1981, p. 94). For these reasons, we include these communication factors in our models predicting security concerns and tolerance toward activists.

Cause Predisposition, Ideology, and News Framing

As described in the previous section and represented in Figure 6.1, two main factors (cause predisposition and ideology), two conditional factors (cause predisposition × frame, and ideology × frame), and three additional factors (demographics, orientations/attitudes, and communication patterns) were expected to affect security concerns and tolerance judgments. We propose that people who are predisposed to support the group's cause and who are liberal are less likely to be concerned about security, but more likely to be tolerant of the targeted group. Individual framing of the surveillance target is expected to amplify the effects of cause predisposition and political ideology on security concerns and tolerance judgments. Analysis of Covariance (ANCOVA) was used to test the main effects of cause predisposition and political ideology and their interactions with news framing, as well as the predicted influence of demographic,

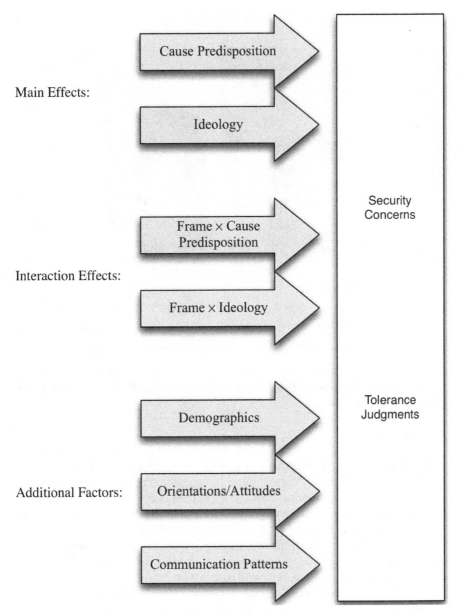

FIGURE 6.1. Conceptual model of factors affecting security concerns and tolerance judgments.

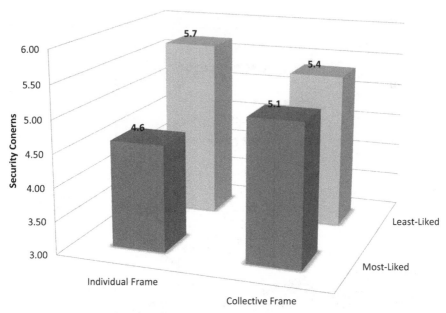

FIGURE 6.2. Security concerns by group/individual frame and cause predisposition.

orientation, and communication variables. For control purposes, two experimental elements (source cue and number of pages visited) were included as covariates in the analyses.

Security Concerns

Testing supported all expected relationships except for the interaction between frame and ideology on security concerns. As expected, main effects of cause predisposition and ideology were found to be significant (cause predisposition: $F[1, 576] = 11.76, p < .001$; ideology: $F[1, 576] = 6.03, p < .05$). Conservatives and respondents who encountered activists whose cause they opposed were more concerned about security. In terms of the interactions, we posited that the individual news frame would amplify the effects of cause predisposition and political ideology on security concerns. As shown in Figure 6.2, cause predisposition interacted with the news frame on security concerns ($F[1, 576] = 5.23, p < .05$). In contrast, as illustrated in Figure 6.3, ideology did not have a significant interactive effect with the news frame on security concerns, counter to expectations.

Tolerance Judgments

A separate ANCOVA tested the effects of cause predisposition, ideology, and news framing on tolerance for the targeted group, all while including security concerns to the list of covariates. The main effects of cause predisposition

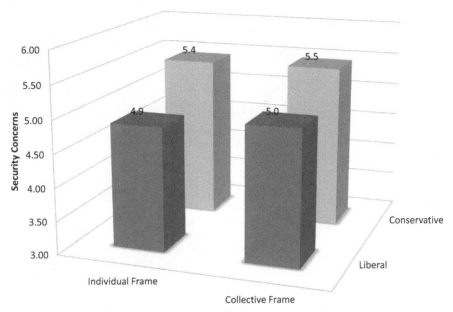

FIGURE 6.3. Security concerns by group/individual frame and ideology.

and ideology were found to be significant predictors of tolerance toward the targeted group. Participants were most likely to be tolerant when they encountered the story about activists for a cause they supported ($F[1, 572] = 22.10$, $p < .001$), and when they were more liberal ($F[1, 572] = 14.28$, $p < .001$).

In terms of the conditional effects, we predicted that the news frame would moderate the effects of cause predisposition and political ideology on tolerance toward the surveillance target, with the individual frame amplifying the effects of these dispositional factors. As shown in Figure 6.4, cause predisposition had a significant interactive effect with the news frames ($F[1, 572] = 8.61$, $p < .01$). Likewise, as illustrated in Figure 6.5, ideology and news frames were found to interact in shaping tolerance toward the targeted group ($F[1, 572] = 3.69$, $p < .05$).

These findings suggest that story frames work jointly with cause predispositions and political ideology to influence public reactions toward political radicals and restrictions of their civil liberties. At the most basic level, the results of this study indicate that when respondents were exposed to a surveillance target that they were predisposed to support, they expressed fewer security concerns and greater support for civil liberties. Similar patterns were observed for political ideology, with liberals more tolerant and conservatives less so. That is, when confronted with news about surveillance and profiling of political radicals, political liberals and cause supporters back Constitutional rights. This is not particularly surprising in light of past research on the factors

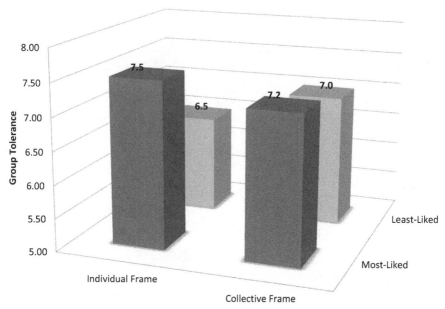

FIGURE 6.4. Group tolerance by group/individual frame and cause predisposition.

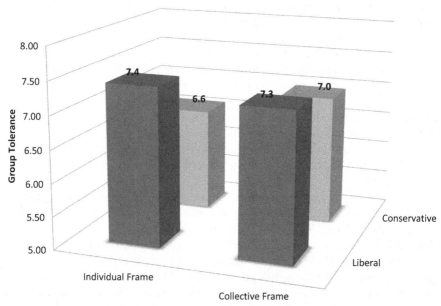

FIGURE 6.5. Group tolerance by group/individual frame and ideology.

that explain support for civil liberties (Lipset and Raab, 1970; Sullivan et al., 1981).

What is new and most intriguing here is that individual framing amplified these effects whereas collective framing attenuated them. As a result, individual framing led to the polarization of opinions about security and civil liberties between cause supporters and cause opponents, with these two groups of respondents making opposing judgments about the same targets of civil liberties restrictions. Likewise, individual story frames made conservatives somewhat intolerant and liberals more tolerant than they would have been had they encountered the collective frame. These findings are particularly noteworthy in light of the dynamic design of our study, which gauged political preferences in advance of presenting respondents with the radical targets they would be inclined to support or oppose. As a result, the groups for which some respondents favored restrictions were the same ones for which others favored protection, potentially exacerbating the conflict that this polarization of attitudes may produce.

This pattern of results highlights inherent biases in the cognitive processing of information about individuals and groups. As social psychologists have noted, the perceived *entitativity* of social units, the degree to which they are understood as being cohesive and consistent, influences the extremity of social judgments (Hamilton and Sherman, 1996). Individuals are thought to have greater consistency between attitudes and behaviors because they are self-contained; thus, they are less likely to be constrained from acting on their beliefs, leading to more extreme judgments about their potential behavior. The opposite is true of groups, mitigating security concerns and social tolerance judgments. It is notable that framing a story in individual or collective terms can change how an activist group is understood, and influence the tolerance judgments and security concerns associated with them. The amplification of these judgments and concerns by the individual frame supports our guiding expectations.

Additional Factors: Demographics, Orientations, and Communication Patterns

Although the results described here confirm the main effects of cause predisposition and political ideology, and their interactive effects with individual news frame, they do not fully explain security concerns or tolerance judgments. To do so, we explore additional factors that are listed in Figure 6.1. These include demographics (gender, age, income, and education), orientations (maternalism and interpersonal trust), and communication variables (newspaper hard news use, television hard news use, and interpersonal discussion). To test the effects of these additional factors, we conducted a series of multivariate regression analyses, controlling for cause predisposition, ideology, news frame, their interactions, and the other design elements.

Security Concerns

Among the additional variables, several were found to be significant in predicting security concerns, while the relationships observed in the ANCOVA
remained robust. Those who were female ($\beta = .10$, $p < .05$), older ($\beta = .10$,
$p < .05$), and more maternalistic ($\beta = .15$, $p < .001$) were more likely to
be concerned about security. Television hard news use was also related to an
increase in security concerns ($\beta = .18$, $p < .001$), while interpersonal trust was
related to a decrease in concerns ($\beta = -.18$, $p < .001$).

Tolerance Judgments

Those who were more maternalistic ($\beta = .08$, $p < .05$) and more trusting
($\beta = .09$, $p < .05$) were more likely to be tolerant of the targeted group, in addition to the the the direct and interactive relationships observed in the ANCOVA.
Interestingly, television hard news use was related to diminished tolerance
($\beta = -.11$, $p < .05$), while other communication variables – newspaper hard
news ($\beta = .14$, $p < .01$) and interpersonal discussion ($\beta = .12$, $p < .01$) –
were related to increased tolerance. Content analytic and survey research conducted in the aftermath of the September 11 attacks found medium differences
between broadcast and print news in the emotional tone of coverage, with TV
news more emotional than print news. In turn, television news consumers had
stronger emotional reactions to the attacks (Cho et al., 2003). These medium
differences might help explain the observed relationships with intolerance.

Conclusions

In this chapter, we investigated the effects of cause predisposition and ideology
and how they intersect with news frames to amplify security concerns and tolerance judgments. From the results, we argue that the journalistic tendency to
focus on individuals in the construction of news stories appears to encourage
audience members to make faster, more confident, and more extreme trait inferences (Hamilton and Sherman, 1996; Susskind et al., 1999). This propensity
may provide a broader explanation for Iyengar's (1991) provisional findings
concerning episodic framing and attributions of responsibility for solving social
problems, as well as the observed role of individual framing in moderating the
effects of gain-loss frames (Shah et al., 2004; Shah et al., 2010). From our perspective, episodically or individually framed content produces more extreme
judgments, which are more and less sympathetic to the subject of the story,
coloring how related information is understood. For civil liberties, individual
framing amplifies the effects of citizens' deeper convictions, both their cause
predispositions and political ideologies, thus contributing to deep divisions
within public opinion around "fighting terrorism."

Given the classic liberal emphasis on the rights-bearing individual, news
stories tend to frame civil liberties controversies around particular subjects that
personify the concerns of a group or organization under government scrutiny,

leading audience members who are so disposed to become even more likely to stand up for activists' free expression, privacy, and autonomy. However, people who oppose the activists' cause should be that much less likely to extend these democratic rights when the group targeted for government surveillance is framed around an individual case. As a result, individual framing of PATRIOT Act investigations and prosecutions may deepen the schism over civil liberties, with those who are predisposed to support the cause least likely to sense security concerns and most steadfast in sustaining Constitutional rights, and those who oppose the cause holding equally strong, yet sharply divergent positions in support of surveillance powers.

This polarizing effect of individual framing may be a salient feature of the current political landscape given the proclivity of journalists to frame stories around individuals. We contend this polarization began to occur as the public responded to reports confirming that the Bush administration used the PATRIOT Act to investigate, infiltrate, and surreptitiously monitor the activities of antiwar protesters (Goldberg, 2004). Similar to the COINTELPRO programs of the 1970s, which empowered the FBI to engage in surveillance and sabotage of political dissidents, these investigations fostered the sentiment that "civil disobedience, seen during peaceful times as the honorable legacy of heroes like Gandhi and Martin Luther King Jr., is being treated as terrorism's cousin" (Goldberg, 2004, p. 2). In spite of these revelations, a majority of Americans continued to support the approach of "restricting civil liberties in order to fight terrorism," albeit less and less so over the course of President Bush's second term (see Figure 2.1). The growing sense that encroachments on civil liberties had "gone too far" began to polarize opinion. Given that stories covering concrete applications of the PATRIOT Act focused on individual surveillance targets rather than broader collectives (see Figure 2.6), the polarization of opinion would be an expected consequence of such reporting.

Also consistent with these findings, public support for the surveillance state has diminished in recent years (see Figures 2.2 and 2.3), especially after the revelations of the FBI's surveillance and monitoring of the Occupy movement (Wolf, 2012), the failure to stop the Boston Marathon Bombing (Savage, 2013), and the Snowden leaks about the massive and unprecedented surveillance program undertaken by the NSA and CIA (Greenwald, 2013b). Much of this coverage shifted the national security/civil liberties frame away from the individual level, despite efforts to focus attention on Tsarnaev brothers, Najibullah Zazi, and Edward Snowden's "traitorous" behavior. This frame shift may have further contributed to the softening of opinion, and the movement toward more support for civil liberties.

If the results of this study are any indication, the framing of domestic surveillance may have conditioned how citizens' political predispositions shaped whether they saw the targets of government surveillance as participants in democracy or threats to it. When journalists favored individual framing of this news, the norm for the coverage during the years first following the passage of the PATRIOT Act, this likely polarized opinion about these targets; evaluations that would have been tempered had the activists been presented as a collective. Given the journalistic tendency to personalize news, the clash of values between those supporting surveillance and those opposing these efforts was probably substantially sharpened, diminishing the likelihood of thoughtful debate and deliberation. When the coverage shifted to the massive expansion of these surveillance activities, with everyone – both liked and disliked groups – included in the government's databases, opinions moderated, allowing for some compromise that balances security with liberty. In more general terms, the polarizing effects of the individual frames may explain why disagreements over values increasingly define our politics, with a shift away from this tendency suggesting an avenue to return to greater deliberation.

In addition to this insight into the polarization of political discourse and the growing sense that things have gone too far in restricting the average person's civil liberties, a theoretical contribution of this study is to advance research on news framing by exploring the moderating influences of frames on other variables. Although we did not find the direct effects of story frames on security concerns and tolerance judgments, the frames produced conditional effects in relation to cause predisposition and political ideology. This study extends recent framing research on the interactions among frame elements and individual predispositions (Chong and Druckman, 2007a,c; Shah et al., 2004; Shah et al., 2010). We advanced this line of inquiry by examining frames as moderators in the influences of core beliefs, namely, cause predispositions and ideology, which would not be apparent without attention to the conditional nature of these news influences.

Given the focus on national security issues since 2001, Americans have experienced heightened concerns about public safety. Like tolerance judgments, these concerns may be exacerbated or downplayed by framing issues in different ways. Many critics of both Bush and Obama administration policies have expressed fears that security concerns are being used to manipulate the public. If one believes that tolerant moderation is desirable in judgments about extending civil liberties to disliked groups, then the press should make an effort to focus less on individuals and more on the collective implications when covering these conflicts. Such a difference in focus could foster a greater recognition of civil liberties consequences and concern about unjust or inappropriate infringements. This seems particularly relevant in light of the disclosure of the classified NSA surveillance program by Edward Snowden. It could also temper the threats people perceive in politically or culturally different groups, as well as increase general tolerance among the American public. While the classic liberal marketplace of ideas may always remain an unattainable ideal in the realities of political power struggles, journalism still plays a key role in determining how close we might get to that ideal.

7

Group Perceptions and Expressive Action

"Since when did feeding the homeless become a terrorist activity? When the FBI and local law enforcement target groups like Food Not Bombs under the guise of fighting terrorism, many Americans who oppose government policies will be discouraged from speaking out and exercising their rights."

– Ann Beeson
ACLU Associate Legal Director

"To treat a reporter as a criminal for doing his job – seeking out information the government doesn't want made public – deprives Americans of the First Amendment freedom on which all other constitutional rights are based. Guns? Privacy? Due process? Equal protection? If you can't speak out, you can't defend those rights, either."

– Dana Milbank
The Washington Post
May 21, 2013

Shortly after the September 11 attacks, television commentator and comedian Bill Maher found his program losing sponsors. Advertisers Sears and FedEx were among those that pulled advertising from Maher's "Politically Incorrect" program after his comments regarding the attacks proved too "incorrect." Maher proposed that while the 9/11 terrorists could be called many things, "cowardly" was not among them. He went on to suggest that the American military, lobbing cruise missiles from afar, was the cowardly group (Bohlen, 2001). Maher was not the only one to make such a suggestion. In fact, his comments echoed those of a conservative commentator from the American Enterprise Institute (AEI), Dinesh D'Souza, a guest on Maher's show that evening. Susan Sontag also argued that whatever the terrorists might have been, they were not cowards. While Sontag was skewered in columns and letters, there was no evidence of a drop in support for the AEI (Bohlen, 2001).

Maher was one of the first individuals to experience the chilling effect of the post-9/11 climate on public expression, but he was certainly not the last.

Even in recent years, it was revealed that the government had also engaged in efforts to muzzle whistleblowers and silence reporters, prosecuting them as criminal codefendants. Journalist Glenn Greenwald (2012) asserted, referring to the case of William Binney, an NSA leaker who preceded Snowden, that the "war on whistleblowing [was] designed to shield from the American public any knowledge of just how invasive this Surveillance State has become." Many observers, both inside and outside of government, noted that this was just one of many instances of how the government "uses technology to silence critics" (Milbank, 2013).

These are just two prominent examples of efforts to restrict the speech – either through social pressure or government investigations – of outspoken critics of the War on Terror. Perhaps more telling, many other writers reported engaging in self-censorship, concerned about reactions to their comments (Kinsley, 2002) as well as the risks of government eavesdropping (PEN American Center, 2013). A survey of PEN American Center members found that 40% had avoided, curtailed, or considered limiting their social media activities for fear of government surveillance and 33% had avoided or seriously considered dodging certain topics over the phone or on e-mail. Clearly, the social climate created by the ongoing War on Terror had a chilling effect on the expression of many prominent voices.

But what about the chilling effect on public expression for average American citizens, who do not host late-night television programs, work for the NSA, or write newspaper columns? We have far less understanding of whether common citizens felt pressured to limit their opinion expression in the face of threats, especially the specter of terrorism. Could messages provided by the media environment contribute to conditions that alter the willingness of citizens to express their views? Does framing the civil liberties/national security issue in individual terms enhance or suppress citizens' willingness to speak out on behalf of groups? In this chapter, we consider experimental evidence about how shifts in the framing of media coverage work with cause predispositions to influence decisions about the willingness to express opinions.

Free expression may contribute to a better-informed, more thoughtful, attentive, and active citizenry. Expression spans a number of dimensions, from private situations such as friendly dinner conversation to contentious debates in public spaces (Scheufele and Eveland, 2001), and from interpersonal talk to online communications (Shah et al., 2005; Cho et al., 2009). Expression matters here for two reasons. First, people's views about the importance of free expression may shape their tolerance for the opinions and activism of extremist groups. In Chapter 6, we considered individual tolerance for the expressive rights of activist groups. Second, individuals may vary in their willingness to share views about these groups, which is the focus of this chapter. For average citizens, witnessing infringements on the civil liberties of an extremist group provides an opportunity to express their opinions, either favorable or unfavorable, toward that action, and tests whether they will speak out for or against such action. The design of the Activist Study allows us to focus on such a context.

Willingness to take expressive action is tied to several social science research traditions. Expressive actions, such as participating in a protest or writing a letter to the editor, are often included as examples of political behavior. As such, the factors that contribute to political action, including ideology, socioeconomic status, media use, and political interest, may also be tied to willingness to take expressive action (McLeod et al., 1999a; Verba et al., 1995). In addition, individual willingness to express opinions is a central component of spiral of silence research. According to this work, individuals who hold what they perceive are minority opinions and who fear social isolation will prove less willing to speak out (Matthes et al., 2010; Noelle-Neumann, 1993; Petric and Pinter, 2002; Scheufele et al., 2001).

The spiral of silence theory emphasizes the conditional nature of expression. Those on one side of an issue may be eager to speak, while those on the other will remain quiet. It is this very dynamic that contributes to the perceptual dynamics underlying the effect, so it is important to consider both expression *supporting* an extremist group as well as expression intended to *oppose* the group. The Activist Study presents participants with a news story about a radical activist group that they should be predisposed to support or oppose. In one set of questions, we asked each participant how likely he or she would be to take expressive action to either support or oppose the targeted activist group in the event that the group announced its intentions to establish a local chapter in the participant's community. To explain what might sway these judgments, we identify three categories of influences on the willingness to take expressive action: (1) personal, (2) societal, and (3) philosophical. Further, we consider how these factors affect expression in support of and opposition to the group. The nature of expressive action (supportive vs. oppositional) along with these three categories produces the six factors identified in Figure 7.1.

Supportive Expression

In this section, we consider what might trigger expression on behalf of the group, presumably when the participant is predisposed to support the group due to agreement about the underlying issue, if not the featured group's tactics. This would be the case in the *most-liked* experimental condition. Of the three types of factors – personal, societal, and philosophical variables – that might encourage supportive expression, we contend that the power of each would be contingent on how the story was framed. Participants who encountered the extremist group in the individual story frame were told primarily about the experiences of one group member, Greg Anderson. For those reading the story with the collective frame, the government efforts were discussed in terms of

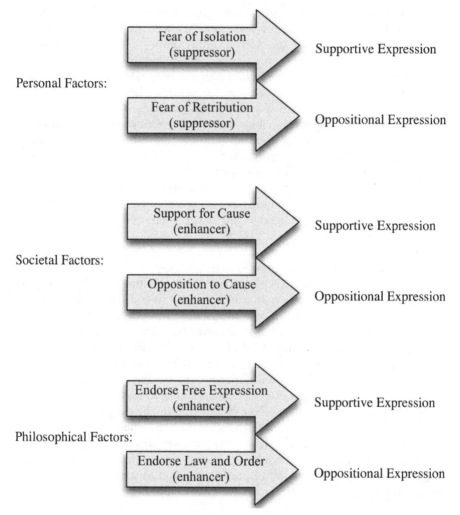

FIGURE 7.1. Conceptual model of factors affecting willingness to take expressive action.

the broader group, without focusing on a particular individual member of the group. Again, we expected the frame manipulation to engage the three different potential motivations behind supportive expression to produce differential outcomes.

Personal Factors
Many participants in the study may be concerned with their own personal well-being and safety. However important expression may be for society as a whole, most people are also concerned about themselves and what personal implications, if any, public expression would have for their freedoms. After all,

the scrutiny of Maher, Sontag, and selected reporters and whistleblowers was directed at them as individuals, and many of the consequences were personal. For those who support the extremist group's cause, the most likely personal consequence would be social isolation, as predicted by spiral of silence theory (Noelle-Neumann, 1993). The group presented in the experimental manipulation for this study is clearly identified as radical and therefore potentially represents an unpopular approach. This impression is only reinforced by the close government scrutiny of the group discussed in the news story. Thus, personal factors, in this case fear of social isolation, may *suppress* supportive expression, as individuals prove reluctant to state unpopular views and opinions.

This suppression would likely be enhanced under the individual frame. In this condition, the isolated group member targeted by the FBI probably evokes thoughts of other lone extremists such as Unabomber Ted Kaczynski or "Shoe Bomber" Richard Reid, making support for such an individual seem even less socially desirable. When the story is framed around a collective, the respondent at least has the comfort of knowing others share in these views, and may fear the broader encroachment of civil liberties onto a wider subset of the population.

Societal Factors

While individual concerns no doubt influence behavior, research into political action tells us that people nonetheless aspire to make a difference in society as well. Expressive action in favor of the group can promote a political cause the respondent already endorsed earlier in the survey. Thus, the social goal of backing the group's cause can *promote* expressive action in favor of that group. For individuals encoutering the collectively framed story, this effect should be strongest. A group has a greater potential to influence policy and might be viewed as possessing a "critical mass" of membership necessary for some legitimate political standing (Chwe, 1999; Macy, 1991). As such, the increased prospects for success make a group seem like a better place to invest personal resources. This is in contrast to the implications of the individually framed stories, which may make the cause seem more hopeless or extreme, leading potential supporters to abandon it as untenable or even undesirable.

Philosophical Factors

As we noted previously, expressive action is important in part because of its role in democratic theory, which values the free exchange of ideas. Many average citizens endorse this concept, supporting free expression through their actions and attitudes. Thus, some people may take expressive action in support of the extremist group as a way to endorse or defend the right to take expressive action (i.e., the Voltairian notion that "I disapprove of what you say, but I will defend to the death your right to say it"). Unlike the other factors identified above, this factor is not necessarily rooted in support for the group's cause, and is exemplified by the 1977 case in which the American Civil Liberties Union

(ACLU) acted in defense of the Ku Klux Klan's right to march in Skokie, Illinois, which is inhabited by thousands of Jewish holocaust survivors (Horowitz and Bramson, 1979; Sullivan et al., 1982). Yet despite the philosophical value some place on free expression for all, the tolerance literature suggests it is far easier to endorse free expression for those we agree with, while support for the expressive rights of opposed groups is far less common (Marcus et al., 1995). Thus, we would expect that a philosophical endorsement of free expression would primarily generate expressive action for groups whose cause the respondent supported. In these cases, the collective frame would likely further increase the likelihood of expression. When the rights of an entire group are threatened, the importance of action should seem greater.

Oppositional Expression

While many people may be willing to speak out in support of a group whose cause they support, others are likely prepared to speak against those they oppose. As with supportive expression, we expected that personal, societal, and philosophical factors all contribute to willingness to take oppositional expressive action. And again, we predict that each factor is moderated by the way in which the story was framed around an individual or collective.

Personal Factors
As with supportive actions, individuals may be motivated by personal concerns. Unlike supportive actions, however, it seems doubtful that participants would be concerned about the popularity of expressing views against the group. After all, the organization is labeled extremist and is already under heavy government scrutiny, presupposing some questionable activity. However, individuals might still have personal fears. In particular, they might be worried about their own safety. If the group is extremist enough to warrant an FBI investigation, it might be extremist enough to lash out against those who speak against it. This could make participants reluctant to express views against the group, thus *suppressing* expressive action. Such a suppressing effect would be heightened under the collective frame, as the danger suggested by opposing an entire group would outweigh that of opposing an isolated individual.

Societal Factors
For participants who are predisposed to oppose the extremist group's cause, expressive action also represents an opportunity to promote a socially desirable outcome, in this case by challenging the group's goals. Thus, the desire to protect society from the influence of the group should *promote* expressive action against the group. The motivation to take such action ought to be greater when the ideas promoted by a group appear particularly radical, such as when the group is labeled as extremist or radical. Perceptions of extremism are likely to be accentuated when participants encounter a news story that is

framed around an individual case. Based on the logic of the *entitativity* principle (Hamilton and Sherman, 1996), we expect participants would perceive an individual extremist to be more likely to engage in volatile behavior than are groups, whose actions are perceived as being moderated by the varied orientations and perspectives of the collective (Susskind et al., 1999). As such, we would expect that individual story framing would be more likely to stimulate oppositional expression than would collective framing.

Philosophical Factors

Despite its Constitutional pedigree, all Americans do not praise free expression equally. Indeed, the ongoing controversy over the PATRIOT Act, large-scale government surveillance, and other post-9/11 policies is widely viewed as a debate between those who place greater emphasis on personal liberties and those who emphasize national security. For individuals who advocate for the security position, the scenario presented in the Activist Study offers a chance to express that view. Individuals who engage in expressive action against the group may be showing support for government efforts to ensure safety. Thus, greater support for security should *promote* expressive action in opposition to the group. Clearly, this depends in part on whether the individual perceives that the extremist group represents a social threat, which is more likely when the group backs a cause disliked by the study participant. In addition, as already noted, we tend to perceive individuals as being more extreme, thereby representing a greater threat. This implies that respondents who value safety and read the individually framed story would be more likely to speak out against the group and, by extension, in favor of the government and its efforts to ensure security.

Effects of Frame and Cause Predisposition

As described in the previous section, and represented in Figure 7.1, six factors likely act to suppress or promote expressive action. For those who would speak out on behalf of the radical activist group, we expect that the collective framing condition should consistently make expressive action more likely. For those who stand against the group, expression should be greater under the individual condition. In this study, however, expressive action is measured as a single variable without differentiating between action for or against the group. This reflects the likelihood that a few individuals may be ambiguous about their reasons for acting or the direction of their action, but nonetheless would be willing to discuss the issue and take other expressive actions. However, this means that testing the expectations of Figure 7.1 requires some proxy measure for the nature of expressive action.

In these data, the best candidate for such a proxy is the most-liked/least-liked manipulation. This manipulation varies the participants' predispositions to support or oppose the cause of the extremist group by matching the cause of that group to the cause of their own most- or least-liked real-world group. Support for a group is largely conditional upon a belief in the cause of that group, as demonstrated in the literature on social movements (Klandermans and Oegama, 1987). Related to this, intolerance is also linked to cause predispositions. Marcus et al. (1995) argue that the concept of tolerance is only meaningful when an individual opposes the cause of a group. That is, an individual displays tolerance by either defending a group's right to express itself or speaking on its behalf even when he or she disagrees with its goals.

Logically, people speak on behalf of groups they support and against those they oppose. Even if cause predispositions, as manipulated by the most-liked/least-liked conditions, are not a perfect proxy for direction of expressive action, they provide an effective test of the factors outlined in Figure 7.1. The relationship between frame and cause predisposition is illustrated in Figure 7.1 and tested using analysis of variance (ANOVA). If the argument presented regarding the factors outlined in Figure 7.1 is correct, this interaction of frame and cause predisposition should be significant. That is, for those participants reading about a group whose cause they support, expressive action should be greater under the collective-frame condition, likely in support of the group. For those who read about a group whose cause they oppose, expressive action should be greater under the individual-frame condition, likely in opposition to it.

Statistical evidence in support of this interaction is marginal. Although shy of standard significance levels, the nature of the relationship conforms to the expectations laid out earlier in this chapter (F [1, 597] = 2.98, $p < .10$). As shown in Figure 7.2, among those who oppose the group's cause, expressive action is higher for those in the individual frame condition. Whereas among those who support the group's cause, expressive action is higher for those in the collective frame condition. Moreover, as illustrated in Figure 7.2 and shown by the significant main effect for cause predisposition (F [1, 597] = 7.65, $p < .01$), expressive action is higher for those who oppose the group's cause, since it is easier to speak in alignment with authority.

Additional Factors

Although the results described here represent a good first look at the expectations outlined in Figure 7.1, they do not fully explain expressive action or necessarily identify which of the factors listed in Figure 7.1 is most important. In the remainder of this chapter, we explore additional variables that might help explain expressive action. These variables include evaluations of the group featured in the story, evaluations of the FBI, support for national security over civil liberties, media use, and ideology. They were included as covariates in an analysis of covariance (ANCOVA) that also tested the main effects and interactions.

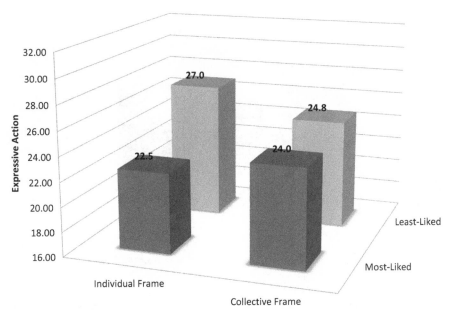

FIGURE 7.2. Willingness to take expressive action by group/individual frame and cause predisposition.

Potentially, some of these variables could mediate the effects of the individual versus collective frame distinction, clarifying the mechanism through which framing influences willingness to take expressive action. Alternatively, these variables might be potential moderators, shifting the way in which framing and expressive action relate. Absent either of those scenarios, the concepts presented can help explain variation in expressive action.

Of these additional variables, the most meaningful is the postmanipulation evaluation of the extremist group by the study participant. Participants were more likely to commit to expressive action when reading about a group whose cause they opposed, as illustrated in Figure 7.2. One possible explanation is that the factors that motivate oppositional expression are stronger than those motivating expression in support of a group. Certainly past research on tolerance suggests people are especially driven – through fear – to suppress those groups with which they disagree more than to aid those groups with which they agree (Marcus et al., 1995). However, another explanation is that because these news stories presented extremist groups as sufficiently worrisome to warrant FBI attention, the organizations described in the manipulation were generally disliked. That is, even under the most-liked predisposition condition, study participants may have had some negative feelings toward the group, while those in the unfavorable condition may have truly loathed the extremist group.

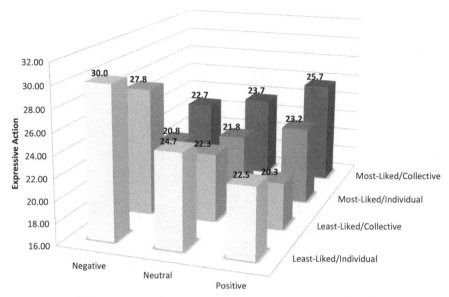

FIGURE 7.3. Willingness to take expressive action by group/individual frame, cause predisposition, and group evaluation.

One way to explore these issues, and to further assess the validity of using cause predisposition as a proxy for direction of expressive action, is to account for group evaluations. Figure 7.3 illustrates the relationship between cause predisposition and frame at different levels of group evaluation. This figure provides telling evidence. First, it shows that cause predisposition and evaluations operate in conjunction. When individuals are predisposed to oppose the group's cause, their levels of expressive action increase as evaluations become more negative, confirming that most of this action is likely oppositional. However, when individuals are predisposed to support the group's cause, expression rises as the group evaluation becomes more positive, indicating this action is largely supportive. Moreover, cause predispositions and group evaluations are highly, though not perfectly, correlated. Participants in the most-liked condition were more likely to express positive evaluations, while those in the least-liked condition more likely to express negative evaluations ($r = .49$, $p <$ .001). Nevertheless, even when evaluations and cause predispositions are both positive, the levels of action are still lower than for those who disliked the group and its cause.

Thus, by themselves, analyses of the variables represented in Figure 7.3 do not preclude the idea that individuals are naturally more inclined to oppose an activist group. However, further exploration of the group evaluation measure suggests that at least some of the difference is due to the strength of feelings regarding the groups. The mean value for evaluation, when expressed as a continuous variable instead of being categorized (as they are in Figure 7.3), is 21.08 (the possible range for this variable was 6 to 42). For the least-liked condition the value is 17.78, whereas group evaluation for the most-liked condition is higher at 24.32. In these data, at least, it is likely that much of the relationship between cause predispositions and expressive action is rooted in differences in evaluations – people who strongly dislike their least-liked group are more vocal than those who weakly favor their most-liked group.

However, group evaluation does not offer a clear explanation for the influence of frames on expressive action. The inclusion of group evaluation as a covariate in statistical analyses does not eliminate the interaction between frame and cause predisposition; rather, it strengthens the relationship to statistical significance (F [1, 597] = 3.94, $p < .05$). Despite strengthening the relationship, group evaluation does not appear to mediate the effects of frames, as there is no significant correlation between frame condition and group evaluation. Also, frames do not appear to alter evaluations of the group, although they might shape beliefs about the importance of the group's cause. Beyond this, the data offer no evidence of a moderating role for group evaluation on frames, as the interaction between the two is not significant (F [1, 597] = 2.34, *n.s.*).

Group evaluation is not the only factor that might mediate the relationship between frames and expressive action or otherwise clarify the relationship of these two variables. In the story presented in the Activist Study, concerns about the group were contrasted with FBI arguments about the value of expanded police powers. It is likely that evaluations of the FBI would influence willingness to take expressive action. If individuals have a favorable impression of the FBI, it could make them less likely to speak out – that is, they assume the FBI already has the situation under control. Those who dislike or mistrust the FBI would be more likely to speak out, especially if they support the group or value civil liberties. Indeed, the data suggest that evaluations of the FBI are a significant predictor of expressive action (F [1, 597] = 7.60, $p < .01$). Further, the data suggest that support for the FBI is negatively related to expressive action ($r = -.17$, $p < .001$). However, this factor does not appear to influence the relationship between framing and expressive action. An additional test found no significant interaction between the frame manipulation and FBI evaluations. Those who support the FBI are not more or less influenced by the way a news story is framed. Moreover, even with FBI evaluations controlled, the interaction of frame and cause predisposition remains the same, indicating evaluations of the FBI do not attenuate or mediate framing effects.

Several other factors might offer insight into which of the six aspects of Figure 7.1 most likely explains the influence of framing. Of particular note is support for national security, which reflects the relative weight individuals place on security over civil liberties. This measure is indicative of the philosophical issues that might underlie expressive action. Those who value security ought to speak against the potentially dangerous group, while those who favor free expression should speak in favor of the group's civil liberties. These data do show a direct relationship between whether study participants valued security or liberty and expressive action; those who were more concerned with safety were *less* expressive (F [1, 597] = 5.15, p < .05). Perhaps one reason some people value free expression is their own willingness to apply it. However, additional analyses using these data do not suggest that the effects of framing operate by altering endorsement of these values (F [1, 597] = .13, *n.s.*). It is likely that beliefs about security and freedom are too deeply held to shift in response to a single news story.

Two other factors offer further insight into expressive action: media use and ideology. Neither could function as mediators of the effects of framing, as both were measured in advance of the framing manipulation. However, the two might function as possible moderators, clarifying how framing functions. This is not the case, as neither the interaction of frame and ideology (F [1, 597] = .616, *n.s.*), nor frame and media use (F [1, 597] = .20, *n.s.*) was significant. That is, the effects of framing are largely constant regardless of the politics or media use of the participant. However, each proves to be related to expressive action, helping to clarify how participants understood expressive action. In particular, willingness to speak out is strongly tied to media use, as is political participation and political talk in other research (McLeod et al., 1999a; Shah et al., 2005; Cho et al., 2009). Thus, expressive action is connected with this broader range of political behaviors, all of which mark engaged and active citizens. In the case of expressive action, media use can, for example, offer resources for action, giving information about protests and inviting comment in the form of letters and commentary. In addition, media use provides information that people can employ in political discussion and even suggest topics for conversation – a function fulfilled by the manipulated story in this study. In these data, media use (F [1, 597] = 46.28, p < .01) remains an important predictor of expressive action even when using statistical models that account for all variables discussed in this chapter.

Expressive action also shares a direct relationship with political ideology (F [1, 597] = 20.36, p < .01) such that liberals in this study were more expressive than were conservatives. Research suggests that partisans are more reactive to political messages than are independents (Kaid, 1997; Kaid and Boydston, 1987), but this work does not suggest that liberals are more expressive than conservatives. However, work by Lemert et al. (1999) identify important differences in how liberals and conservatives react to candidates of their own party. Specifically, this work collectively points toward liberals being more sensitive to ideology than conservatives. Liberals were *more critical* of conservative candidates than conservatives were of liberal candidates, and *more supportive* of liberal candidates than conservatives were of conservative candidates (Scarbrough, 1984). This research is consistent with our finding that liberals were generally more willing to take expressive action.

Finally, the relationship between ideology and expressive action may reflect the time of the study and the community in which it took place. In the period following the September 11 attacks leading up to the collection of data used for these analyses, the House, Senate, and presidency were all Republican-controlled. A result of this conservative-dominated environment may be that liberals *had* to be more expressive out of necessity. Spiral of silence research suggests liberals would find themselves in the minority and remain quiet. However, the ideological makeup of the community from which participants in this study were drawn may counteract the effects of the spiral of silence. Specifically, the Madison, WI area is renowned for not only being liberal leaning, but for being a hotbed of protest and other expressive activities. These external conditions offer liberals both opportunities and social support for expression.

Conclusions

In this chapter, we presented a set of factors likely to influence expressive action both for and against a group, a list outlined in Figure 7.1. Each of these factors suggested that when news coverage was framed around an individual, participants would be more willing to take oppositional expressive action. However, when coverage discussed the topic in collective terms, supportive expressive action would be more likely. Although the data did not provide a direct measure of the direction of expressive action (supportive or oppositional), the cause predisposition manipulation offered a viable proxy, as supported by the relationship between this measure and group evaluation. This prediction received marginal statistical support, even when accounting for other variables such as group evaluations. Although not as influential as ideology or media use, frames appear to shape willingness to take expressive action, an effect that depends on the predisposition of readers to support or oppose the group's cause.

However, efforts to identify potential factors that might mediate this relationship or otherwise clarify it proved unsuccessful. Neither perceptions of the group nor evaluations of the FBI altered the interactive effects of framing, although each was an important predictor on its own. Underlying philosophical beliefs also mattered, but did not mediate the relationship either. In the context of the six potential influences on expressive action, this implies that societal and personal factors are more important than philosophical influences, at least in the population considered in this study. These factors may work together. Beliefs about whether a group represents a personal threat might also reflect a perception that the group's ideas are dangerous for society. Similarly, a perception that a group is unpopular and that supporting it would risk social isolation may be tightly linked to a belief that the group will be unsuccessful and its efforts not worth backing, suggesting a relationship between spiral of silence theory and the notion of critical mass. Ultimately, questions exploring individual motivations for taking expressive action are required, although such questions risk causing people to "overthink" their answers and give inaccurate assessments of likely behaviors.

Still, understanding why people are willing to take expressive action is important and frames appear to play a consistent – if not fully determined – role in this process. Expression is a key element in democratic theory, and is a desirable outcome. At the same time, expressive action designed to stifle the rights of a group to speak out and organize might actually suppress the diversity of opinions in the marketplace of ideas. If stories about unpopular groups are framed at the individual level, this might promote greater expression in the short term, but the long-term effect would be to reduce the diversity of views by stimulating resistance against unpopular groups. Yet such framing techniques are common. Researchers have noted the tendency of media coverage to frame protest groups in terms of particular individuals (Boyle et al., 2004; McLeod and Hertog, 1992), often those whom the press select as figureheads or deem especially interesting or unique. As such, research on media coverage of protest groups would suggest a consistency in the nature of news framing that likely serves to stifle supportive expression and encourage oppositional expression.

This becomes even more important in light of the revelations that it was not just jihadist terrorists, or even radical political groups, that were targeted by government surveillance activities; rather it was virtually all Americans who were included in the NSA's electronic dragnet. While it was known that the PATRIOT Act permitted access to records from doctors, libraries, bookstores, travel agencies, credit card companies, universities, phone companies, and Internet service providers without providing probable cause, public opinion toward these policies shifted when it became clear that programs such as PRISM and XKeyscore allowed analysts to search vast databases containing e-mails, online chats, and the browsing histories of millions of individuals with no prior authorization. Speaking out against this type of intrusive government surveillance became more common when its scope was understood, and that it was not isolated individuals but all citizens who were included in this monitoring.

In sum, this chapter further develops the role that the individual/collective frame distinction can play in either promoting or suppressing expressive action. This chapter also enumerates the important relationship that shifts in frames can have for theories such as spiral of silence that explain how and why people choose to express themselves. Perhaps most importantly, however, this chapter reinforces the key role the media and journalists can play in the democratic process. That is, how journalists choose to represent an issue – including choices about how to frame news stories – can have serious implications for the audience's willingness and interest in taking an active role in either opposing or supporting a group and its cause. More broadly, the freedom of both citizens and journalists to speak out is essential to safeguarding all other Constitutional rights, just as silencing oppositional voices is the first step in eroding freedoms.

PART III

IMPLICATIONS AND CONCLUSIONS

8

Covering "Big Brother"

"The consciousness of being at war, and therefore in danger, makes the handing-
over of all power to a small caste seem the natural, unavoidable condition of
survival."

– George Orwell in *1984*

"There are many other things that are excluded from the official framing of the
'global war on terror,' such as oil, the economy, the deficit, health care, jobs,
education, taxes, and the effects of global trade. The implication is that none of
these things matter if every American is in mortal danger, even those in the swing
states where there's little to no chance of a terrorist strike. But rationality is not
at issue here. People think in terms of frames."

– George Lakoff
Professor of Linguistics at U. of California – Berkeley
August 31, 2004

Framing that enhances a sense of danger and threat is a potent tool in the
hands of powerholders. If the research presented in this book is any indication,
this influence is bestowed by the factors that shape the production of news,
not the least of which are the codes and practices of the journalistic profession.
When covering the tension between national security and civil liberties – that is,
reporting on the government's massive surveillance powers – journalists tended
to construct news reports on that basis of these conventions, emphasizing the
conflict between these contending values while trying to find ways to personify
and personalize the policy debate. Framing coverage around principled conflicts
and individual instances are longstanding news values (Price and Tewksbury,
1997). Although framing news around "rights talk" has been well studied
(Shah et al., 1996; Brewer, 2007), in this book we find it is this personification –
framing stories in individual as opposed to collective terms – that plays such an
important role in shaping the responses of audiences, their thought processes,

their mental sophistication, their social tolerance, and their political expression. Such individual framing is a fixture of news construction, particularly when covering "Big Brother."

For the vast majority of Americans, the mass media are their only window into this policy debate, potentially even the only reason that they are aware of the PATRIOT Act and the erosion of civil liberties, first under the Bush administration and then expanded under the Obama administration. But as has been repeatedly pointed out, the media are not flawless windows any more than they are objective mirrors of reality. Elite sources often get disproportionate weight in defining the reality presented through the media. Political elites play a central role in shaping the boundaries and terms of policy debates as they appear in media coverage and the cues used to label individuals and groups featured in the news (Bennett, 1990). This was certainly true in the debate over national security after 9/11, in which elites tried to shape the national conversation with the very naming of the act that curtailed civil liberties – the USA PATRIOT Act. Even when the debate shifted back to an overt concern with civil liberties in light of disclosures about NSA monitoring of U.S. citizens, journalists continued to frame a considerable amount of coverage around individual successes of the PATRIOT Act or the threats to U.S. security posed by whistleblowers such as Snowden himself. Our studies isolate how the frames and cues favored by journalists to construct this debate actually shaped public responses to the purported danger of domestic terror, the extent of government power, and the reach of policies enacted to protect us.

Key Research Insights

Any research conducted against the backdrop of the domestic War on Terror, the PATRIOT Act, and the tradeoff between national security and civil liberties is sure to produce provocative findings. The insights available from this work certainly do so. Of course, the implications of this research are not limited to understanding the role of the media in public responses toward this debate; they also extend to basic knowledge about the processes underlying framing and cueing effects and the psychology of media influence. Before we turn to these more basic implications, we first reflect on the findings presented in the prior chapters as they relate to the issues of national security, civil liberties, social tolerance, and political action.

Particularly important for these normative insights, the experiments examined how the public reacted to news framing of both Arab and activist groups targeted under the auspices of the PATRIOT Act. These studies recognized that the PATRIOT Act could be extended beyond its professed target of international terrorists to be used against a wider cross-section of Arab-Americans and domestic policy groups (i.e., activists who espoused views that the administration found objectionable, but posed little actual threat to national security). Although the extent of NSA monitoring was almost unimaginable, the scenarios we tested were certainly within the realm of possibility. By studying both Arabs and activists, framing effects were understood within the actual context of the PATRIOT Act and journalistic coverage of its application.

In the Arab Study, the experiment manipulated the story frame (individual vs. collective frame) and two concept frames (immigrant vs. citizen and extremist vs. moderate cues). The Activist Study also used the individual versus collective frame manipulation, and additionally manipulated cause predisposition (whether the story was about a group that shared a cause with the participant's self-designated most-liked or least-liked activist group). Thus, the effects of individual and collective framing were central to both studies, but were crossed either with other cues or predispositions to explore how message effects were conditioned by features of the information environment. In this way, we were able to maintain strict experimental control while exploring the real complexity of how news construction and consumption lead to effects.

As examined in Chapter 4, the convergence of concept frames (i.e., cues) influenced the nature and extent of mental processing as illustrated by the correlation among related response items and patterns of response latency. The findings showed that the extremist and immigrant cues converged to increase the consistency of responses, strengthening correlations among negative group evaluations, intolerance toward extremists, opposition to immigration, and minority disempowerment. Participants were also able to form these evaluations more quickly, which we interpreted as an indicator of an underlying process of spreading activation through interconnected cognitions. Defining Arabs as the "radical other" appears to trigger a host of associations linked to racial xenophobia and intolerance for expression. Notably, it is only when these cues converge that these effects were observed. Thus, it is the co-occurrence of the fundamentalist and outsider markers that trigger these associations, indicating that small shifts in the language used in story construction can have large effects. Notably, individual framing bolstered these effects, amplifying the influences observed for cue convergence.

These findings have several implications. They demonstrate that the layering or convergence of cues can shape fundamental aspects of judgments including evaluations of the group and tolerance, extending the finding of other recent research (Cho et al., 2006; Chong and Druckman, 2007a,c). This reflects how our approach to conceptualizing the influence of message framing and operationalizing the testing of these effects balances a concern with the ecological validity of message complexity with the internal validity of message control and precision. By layering frames and cues, we are able to control the message features, yet at the same time observe the effects of more complex combinations of language. And what we observe is that subtle changes in the construction of news accounts, especially as they present the individual targets of surveillance, has implications for the activation of and connections among cognitions underlying tolerance judgments. This clearly has implications for the political sophistication of news audiences bombarded with such content.

Chapter 5 found that the story frame and predisposition toward the cause advocated by the targeted group interacted to influence the complexity of cognitive responses and formation of attitudes. Specifically, the individual frame led to more elaborate processing when participants encountered a group advocating a cause they opposed, suggesting the threat posed by the specter of a lone radical activist encouraged deeper processing. Indeed, this interaction led to more elaborate responses to open-ended questions about the story and to more structurally detailed attitudes. We observed differences across three interrelated measures of cognitive structure (i.e., the number of categories mentioned, the level of elaboration, and overall integration), providing further evidence of the influence of individual framing of a radical activist threat on mental processing. Thus, when oppositional viewpoints are framed at the individual level, this promotes more extensive and effortful information processing, which in turn affects tolerance toward extreme groups. Notably, the individual frame and the cognitive responses it generated produced less tolerance for these least-liked groups. Thus, more elaborate message processing does not necessarily correspond to greater tolerance, potentially amplifying social cleavages.

In this regard, the journalistic tendency to focus on individuals in the construction of news stories appears to encourage audience members to make faster, more confident, and more elaborate inferences against disliked groups. In turn, these responses contribute to intolerant attitudes. This is generally consistent with the conclusions of past research concerning the biases in attributions of responsibility due to episodic or individual framing (see Iyengar, 1991; Shah et al., 2004; Shah et al., 2010), though the pattern of cognitive responses we observed underlying these unfavorable judgments is much more specific and appears to stem from the perceived entitativity of the target and effects of this on mental responding. These results contribute to the development of mental processing models underlying individual and collective framing effects. This lends a new approach to understanding how cognitive processing of media texts helps shape the judgments and actions of audiences in relation to the civil liberties–national security debate.

In Chapter 6, we further examined the relationship between framing, tolerance, and civil liberties by looking more closely at how political predispositions condition the effects of news frames on security concerns and tolerance judgments. In terms of the frame's interactions with predispositions toward the group featured in the story, we found that exposure to the individual frame not only made people less tolerant of activists they opposed, but also more tolerant of activists whose cause they supported than did exposure to the collective frame. In other words, the individual frame had a polarizing effect on tolerance judgments. Likewise, personification of this target of government surveillance polarized national security concerns. When encountering activists framed in individual terms as opposed to collective terms, disliked causes amplified concerns about violent acts by extremists, whereas liked causes reduced those concerns. Such individual framing had a similar polarizing effect in leading liberals and conservatives to express more divergent opinions on the tradeoff between national security and civil liberties.

The evidence of such polarizing effects of individual framing raises larger questions about the implications of this common journalistic practice. Does framing news stories about "homegrown" threats around individual exemplars contribute to adversarial politics? Does this type of individual framing have similar polarizing effects in the context of other types of stories, and do such effects contribute to a political mentality of "win at all costs," reducing the interest of policymakers and the public in seeking political compromises? Does the shift to collective frames, as the Snowden leaks became public, allow for compromise and some reconsideration of these policies? If so, there is an irony in the journalistic practice of using individual exemplars to personalize stories. While this practice is ostensibly designed to bring stories and issues to life for readers, it may also have antidemocratic effects. When such exemplars are used, audience members may become more engaged in the story, but they may also become more polarized toward the subjects in the story, and, in the process, become less tolerant and less deliberative.

The research presented in Chapter 7 leads to similar, though perhaps more troubling, conclusions. This research examined the influence of framing and cause predisposition on the willingness to speak out for or against the targeted group. Again, we observed an interaction between the frame and cause predisposition in which individual framing made participants less likely to speak out when they encountered a group whose cause they supported, but more likely to speak out against a group whose cause they opposed. It seems that personifying the national security/civil liberties debate indeed stimulates an oppositional politics, though one that favors government surveillance powers. It encourages people to stand up against what they oppose more so than standing behind what they support. The inaction for supported groups is particularly concerning from a normative perspective because it suggests that opponents might be able to "shout down" the expressive rights of supported activists. This is particularly troubling in light of the fact that Bush and Obama administrations applied the PATRIOT Act to debatably "radical" groups such as antiwar protesters and the Occupy movement.

This also provides evidence that a similar process that encouraged intolerance was implicated in expressive participation. We believe that it is likely that perceptions of group entitativity led to more engagement that opposes disliked groups, but lessened engagement when it comes to defending the civil liberties of liked groups. Again, these findings suggest that the practice of framing stories around individual exemplars may simultaneously polarize security concerns and tolerance judgments while at the same time supporting the power of the surveillance state – that is, providing cover for "Big Brother." In combination, these findings raise some serious concerns about news framing of the civil liberties–national security debate in an age of heightened concern about the erosion of civil liberties in the fight against terrorism.

Ultimately, these findings concerning journalistic framing of the war at home have some paradoxical implications for such important democratic goals as enhancing citizen sophistication, encouraging social tolerance, and motivating social action. While these goals are all important to maintaining a functioning democracy, they are complicated by the journalistic practice of personifying issues through individual framing. The practice of individual framing may foster greater political sophistication – in terms of categories mentioned, the level of elaboration, and overall integration – but this complexity is actually linked to greater intolerance, at least among some citizens. In turn, greater intolerance, and the security concerns entwined with this sentiment, may also produce more expressive action, though mainly against disliked groups. Although political participation in certainly laudable, when it is grounded in intolerance, deeper issues are implicated. If intolerance encourages adversarial participation while tolerance encourages demobization, media may contribute to an antidemocratic dynamic by motivating people to speak out against disliked groups when framed in individual terms, yet discouraging supportive speech when liked groups are under threat of government surveillance. From this perspective, tolerance may be associated with complacency and an unwillingness to act, while intolerance spurred by individual framing encourages oppositional action.

In short, our results suggest that sophistication, tolerance, and engagement are bound together in a complex set of interrelationships that are brought into greater tension when the national security/civic liberties conflict is framed at the individual level. Individual story frames produce more elaborate thoughts, but also lower tolerance, and in turn increase the likelihood of actions in opposition to activist groups. This set of findings paints a troubling picture of media's role in reducing tolerance and eroding support for civil liberties in an era of limited domestic terrorist threats and expanded government surveillance.

On the Nature of Framing Effects

This book not only offers new insights on the implications for news framing of the tradeoff between national security and civic liberties, it also contributes to our basic understanding of framing effects by applying and testing the frameworks for research introduced in Chapter 1. The research resulting from these organizing models supports the following generalizations about framing: Framing effects are rarely simple main effects. They are likely to involve interactions among different story elements framed at different levels within the news story. They are also likely to be conditioned by interactions with personal predispositions and processing factors. As such, framing effects are likely to be stronger on some individuals and under some conditions than others. Finally, framing effects on perceptions, attitudes, and behaviors vary according to the topical context in which they are observed, the nature of the framing message, and the characteristics of the audience member.

These generalizations certainly provide important insights on the nature and extent of framing effects. Yet the implications of this research run a bit deeper. In Chapter 1, we introduced a 2 × 2 typology to locate past framing effects research (see Figure 1.1). This typology was based on two dimensions. The first dimension concerns whether the frames explored in effects research are context specific (i.e., relevant only in the particular context at hand) or context transcendent (i.e., relevant to a variety of different contexts). The second dimension deals with the epistemological and methodological assumptions of the framing effects researchers. On one hand, there are the idealists who adopt a strict experimentalist approach by saying that to measure framing effects per se, researchers must strive to manipulate only the frame while holding all other content elements constant. On the other hand, pragmatists argue that isolating frames is impractical, if not undesirable, and take a more lenient approach when it comes to manipulating and measuring frames. The former approach stresses the internal validity of experimental control to isolate what is causing the effect, while the latter approach emphasizes the ecological validity of assessing the true power of media frames.

The idealistic approach raises two related problems. First, how do you isolate the frame? As an abstract characteristic of the story as a whole, it becomes difficult to reduce a frame to a specific content feature. Second, even if one could isolate the frame, holding all of its attendant content elements – elite sources, consonant cues, salient facts, and so on – constant across different frames for the purpose of experimental manipulation would strip the frame of its potential power. Different frames call for different sets of sources and facts. While the pragmatic approach provides more latitude in which to observe the true power of framing, it is still haunted by questions concerning what is causing the framing effect. If shifts in frames also include shifts in sources, cues, and facts, then it could be a particular source (a partisan politician in a strategy frame) or a resonant cue (labeling an Arab as an immigrant in an individual frame) that gives particular frames their power (see Vraga et al., 2010).

Our research offers a compromise between these two approaches by layering message elements such as story frames with shifts in cues and facts to deal with the problems of "framing isolation" and "defanging the frame." That is, when altering between individual and collective framing, we also systematically altered the cues surrounding the featured targets of government surveillance (i.e., the citizenship status and political extremism of targets in the Arab study) and the featured facts (i.e., the specific group being featured from among the six "extremists" in the activist study). In doing so, we were able to systematically control message features (the overall story frame) consistent with the need for internal validity and at the same time write stories that had the potential to amplify the frame's power (through the manipulation of cues and consonant facts and details) as they would in more ecologically valid settings.

This design gives us an opportunity to test elements of our Message Framing Model (MFM) and Message Processing Model (MPM) introduced in Chapter 1 (see Figures 1.2 and 1.3). While these experiments only begin to put these models to the test, their combination does illuminate new paths for future research. Using this approach, we can assess which textual features account for observed effects while capturing more of the true power of frames by looking at interactions between converging framing elements. Our general conclusion is that frames and cues do matter, that they work in concert, and that they work similarly across different factual contexts. Our designs allow for these insights. Of course, one drawback of this approach is that it requires larger and larger sample sizes with each additional layer that is added. Yet without these design features, many of these effects would remain undocumented and misunderstood, limiting the ability to separate framing effects from accompanying shifts.

The Message Framing Model

The recognition that framing can take place at different textual levels led to the MFM represented by Figure 1.2. This model defines a frame as the potential meaning that is embedded in a particular unit of text. In this model, a concept frame is the meaning that is conveyed by the power of a label that is used to represent a particular concept (cue). An assertion frame is contained in a sentence that is used to convey a particular idea. These assertions are assembled into arguments in a way that takes the form of a thematic frame. Finally, the news package as whole may be organized around an abstract narrative pattern that emerges from the structure and composition of the story as a whole. Again, the framing power of a story may not only reflect the main effects of framed story components, but also the interaction of these components.

When we explore these distinctions at the message level, we find considerable support for the general assumption that frames and cues function similarly, that they interact with one another to amplify and attenuate message effects, and that even though they operate at different textual levels, they similarly structure the construction of press accounts. This MFM leads us to an alternative to the "picture frame" and "window" analogies that have been used to illustrate framing. Our framing analogy is one of building a house. The journalist begins by approaching a story with an abstract blueprint of what the ultimate house is going to look like. Like the way in which architectural traditions influence house design, news story blueprints are influenced by journalistic traditions for how to write a particular type of story. For example, journalists sent to cover a protest story may follow a protest paradigm (see McLeod and Hertog, 1999), which is a constellation of common protest story characteristics that guide the journalist as to how a protest story should be constructed. When it comes to writing the specific story, the concepts are the bricks, the assertions are the walls, and the arguments are the rooms that ultimately comprise the structure of the news package. These component parts work together to give the news story meaning. As such, this analogy is consistent with the notion that framing effects take place at different linguistic levels (Entman, 1993;

Pan and Kosicki, 1993), which underscores the importance of looking at frame interactions among concepts, assertions, thematic, and story frames. While our research has only begun to explore some of these linkages, it provides examples of how this kind of research might be done.

The Message Processing Model

While our MFM identifies the structural characteristics of messages that might account for particular types of effects, we also provide a model that synthesizes material from the cognitive processing literature that illustrates how framing effects work – the MPM (see Figure 1.3). According to this model and validated by our findings, media frames interact with predispositions and activate knowledge from the mental network. Then, these schemas are applied when interpreting the message. The effects of the message/schema interactions are a function of the processes of availability, applicability, activation, and usability, as described in Chapter 1. Ultimately, the effects of these processes may be manifested in the form of changes in cognitions, evaluations, and behavior, as we saw in this research. However, the nature of these effects is moderated by a host of other factors such as political predispositions and personal ideology.

Our findings, when interpreted in light of this model, also provide deeper insights into the processes underlying message framing effects. The process is viewed, not only as iterative and constantly reinforcing (see Price and Tewksbury, 1997), but also as highly mediated and conditional. Message frames are understood as existing on multiple textual levels, all of which have similar cognitive effects. The activation of cognitions and the nature of effects are conditioned by orientations such as cause predispositions. We find evidence that resonant frames activate cognitions that result in a spread of activation and judgmental application. Further, these message characteristics, especially when understood in combination, have effects at a range of levels: cognitive, attitudinal, and behavioral. These findings provide considerable support for the general MPM and insight about future research directions.

The Future of Framing Effects Research

In this book, we have advanced a framework for understanding and investigating the framing effects of mediated news coverage. In doing so, we are proposing a sizable agenda for future research. The results reported in this book represent only a small part of that agenda. Future research is needed to illuminate the complex interrelations of the proposed processes and effects. Research should further isolate the factors that govern the processes of the MPM: availability, applicability, activation, and usability. Although not all of these processes were explored directly in our research, several were tested implicitly and found to function as theorized. The possibility of unifying the wide range of framing research under a single model of effects would go a long way toward mending this "fractured paradigm" (Entman, 1993).

Our research also explored the interaction of frames operating at different textual levels, as well as a variety of factors that moderate their effects, but clearly we have only begun to examine these relationships. The largely uncharted research territory (cf. Chong & Druckman, 2007a,c; Shah et al., 2004; Shah et al., 2010) is further expanded when one considers the variety of the potential cognitive, attitudinal, and behavioral outcomes of framing effects that may occur when frames come into contact with one another. These combinations may both amplify and attenuate framing effects, moving us toward more ecologically valid tests of these effects. It is particularly notable that the framing effects and the conditions that produced them do not vary in response to the different contextual situations our online experimental manipulations created across the Activist Study. Of course, only one set of contexts and frames was tested here. When one considers the range of other predispositions, textual frames, moderators, outcomes, and situations, and the potential interactions among them, the possible combinations are virtually infinite. We hope that these mediated and moderated effects will continue to draw the interest of researchers and that the generalizable principles that regulate framing effects will emerge from the collective efforts of multidisciplinary researchers testing and extending the MFM and the MPM.

Final Thoughts on Framing and the War on Terrorism

As we noted at the outset of this chapter, during times of conflict, news frames can play a powerful role in the process of social control. Politicians have long recognized the power of using a personified enemy not only to mobilize public opinion, but also to seize ideological control over media frames. Following the logic of the rally-round-the-flag thesis (Mueller, 1973; Mueller, 2006), we expected that this control over framing during periods of external conflict would be short lived as the threat either dissipated or dragged on. Rather, personification remained a prevalent and powerful framing device throughout the first decade of the War on Terror. The opening paragraphs of two news stories illustrate how quickly this frame was adopted after September 11. The first appeared in the *New York Times* on September 16, 2001:

A day after proclaiming flatly that the nation was "at war," President Bush and his senior advisers took pains to warn Americans today that it would be a war unlike any other, fought in the shadows, testing the patience of the public and leaders alike, but that nations failing to join the crusade would face the "full wrath of the United States," as Vice President Dick Cheney put it.

"This is a new kind of evil," Mr. Bush said at the White House after a weekend war council with senior aides at Camp David, "and we understand, and the American people are beginning to understand, this crusade, this war on terrorism, is going to take a while, and the American people must be patient."

"We will rid the world of the evil-doers," Mr. Bush said, adding a moment later, "They have roused a mighty giant, and make no mistake about it, we're determined." (Purdum, 2001, p. A2)

Not long after this story was published, Osama bin Laden was identified as the leader responsible for the September 11 attacks, allowing stories to be framed around an individual, placing a name and face on the threat to national security. This personification of evil is exemplified in the following article from *USA Today*, published on November 7, 2001:

President Bush upped the rhetorical ante Tuesday against Osama bin Laden and put reluctant allies on notice that he expects more of them.

Eight weeks after the Sept. 11 terrorist attacks, Bush wants to ensure that support and resolve among the American public and U.S. allies don't wilt as the bombing campaign in Afghanistan enters its second month and anthrax fears at home continue.

In a speech via satellite to European leaders discussing terrorism in Warsaw, Poland, Bush said for the first time that bin Laden wants to acquire nuclear, chemical and biological weapons.

Later, at a news conference with French President Jacques Chirac at the White House, Bush said, "This is an evil man we're dealing with, and I wouldn't put it past him to develop evil weapons to try to harm civilization as we know it." (Keen, 2001, p. 8A)

While both of these news stories are essentially framed as explications of the government's proposed responses to terrorism, one key difference between them centers on the framing of the threat. In the first story, evil is framed as a shadowy abstraction. In the second, Osama bin Laden has emerged as the embodiment of our enemy, a lightening rod for the fears and anger of the public. As such, this personification of evil provides a mechanism for social control, spurring the rally-round-the-flag effect, fostering intolerance, mobilizing the public, and shifting the pendulum of public opinion toward national security concerns and away from civil liberties. It is worth noting that when Osama bin Laden eluded capture, the Bush administration set its sights on another "evildoer" in the form of Saddam Hussein.

International terrorist targets such as Khalid Sheikh Mohammed (an al-Qaeda leader, called "the principal architect of the 9/11 attacks"), Abu Musab al-Zarqawi (first leader of Al-Qaeda in Iraq), Abu Ayyub al-Masri (second leader of Al-Qaeda in Iraq), Anwar al-Awlaki (the Yemeni-American Imam linked to the Fort Hood Shooter and Time Square Bomber), Moktar Belmoktar (a commander of Al-Qaeda in the Islamic Maghreb and mastermind of the Tigantourine gas facility attack), and Ayman al-Zawahiri (current leader of al-Qaeda) allowed this personification of evil continue throughout the remainder of the Bush administration and for much of President Obama's first term, even after the death of Osama bin Laden at the hands of U.S. Navy SEALs in Abbottabad, Pakistan. This strategy was certainly effective in drumming up support for the War on Terror and wars in Afghanistan and Iraq.

Examined more closely, these passages may also illustrate our larger point about the nature of framing – that framing takes place, not just at the level of the story as a whole, but in the form of the concepts (cues) and assertions (arguments) that structure those stories. Among the salient concept frames contained in these passages are the framing of the U.S. government's response to terrorism as a "war" and a "crusade" and the representation of the enemy as "evil." The prominent assertion frames contained in these passages include the idea that the named enemy is seeking to employ weapons of mass destruction and that the War on Terror will protect the security of the American public. This would later be extended to include the assertions that protecting security would mandate policies such as the USA PATRIOT Act. As such, story frames are an amalgam of frames operating at smaller textual levels.

Another point of similarity between these two articles is that they largely take cues from high-level political officials (e.g., President Bush and Vice President Cheney). The power of these officials to shape the framing of these news stories is quite evident. Elite sources also worked to keep individual perpetrators of domestic terrorist attacks in the news. There was no shortage of "homegrown" terrorists around which to frame news accounts, including Bruce Ivins (a microbiologist and biodefense researcher falsely suspected in Anthrax attacks), Hesham Mohamed Hadayet (an Egyptian national who committed the Los Angeles International Airport shooting), John Allen Muhammad and Lee Boyd Malvo (the Washington Beltway snipers), Mohammed Reza Taheri-azar (an Iranian-American who perpetrated the SUV attack at UNC-Chapel Hill), Nidal Malik Hasan (the U.S. Army major who committed the Fort Hood mass killing), Faisal Shahzad (a Pakistani-American convicted of the attempted Time Square bombing), Wade Michael Page (the white supremacist Sikh temple shooter), Najibullah Zazi (an Afghan-American convicted of planning suicide bombings on the New York Subway system), and of course, the Tsarnaev brothers (Chechen immigrants who committed the Boston Marathon bombings).

It is notable that the massive domestic surveillance program put into place by the NSA in the aftermath of the September 11 attacks did not identify or stop any of these terrorist attacks. Rather, when pressed during Senate testimony in 2013, NSA Director Keith Alexander admitted that his agency's data dragnet could claim "only one example where collection of bulk data is what stopped a terrorist activity" – Basaaly Moalin, a Somali immigrant who had transferred $8,500 to al-Shabaab, a terrorist organization in Somalia (Benkler, 2013). Yet individual framing was the dominant mode of reporting concrete applications of the PATRIOT Act to the U.S. public (see Figure 2.6), and was used to justify expanded surveillance powers.

Also notable is the fact that as this conflict has persisted, the circle of elite sources that influence story framing has expanded, including advocates for civil liberties, whistleblowers, human rights organizations, and prominent politicians, and along with it, the broader range of story frames. Over time, more opposition sources were used to challenge the official position coming first from the Bush administration and later from the Obama administration. Articles began to address the issue of civil liberties and exhibited less consistency and more competition among framing components within the story. Typical for this new coverage regime of the issue are these paragraphs that appeared in the *Washington Post* on July 16, 2013:

Rights activists, church leaders and drug and gun rights advocates found common ground and filed a lawsuit on Tuesday against the federal government to halt a vast National Security Agency electronic surveillance program.

The lawsuit was filed by the Electronic Frontier Foundation, which represents the unusually broad coalition of plaintiffs, and seeks an injunction against the NSA, Justice Department, FBI and directors of the agencies.

Filed in federal court in San Francisco, it challenges what the plaintiffs describe as an "illegal and unconstitutional program of dragnet electronic surveillance."

In this passage, the issue of civil liberties is framed at the collective level, with a broad coalition of actors working against the authority of the surveillance state. The article presents assertions that contribute to the argument that the PATRIOT Act policies erode civil liberties, which has placed the executive branch of government in the defensive position, presented as overstepping its Constitutional mandate and eroding civil liberties of a broad cross-section of Americans.

Notably, the Snowden leaks, along with the efforts of other whistleblowers such as William Binney, forced the Obama administration to respond to public outcry over the size and scope of the surveillance state. On January 17, 2014, President Obama acknowledged the tradeoff between civil liberties and national security as he proposed modest changes to these programs (Landler and Savage, 2014, January 17):

President Obama, acknowledging that high-tech surveillance poses a threat to civil liberties, announced significant changes on Friday to the way the government collects and uses telephone records, but left in place many other pillars of the nation's intelligence programs.

Responding to the clamor over sensational disclosures about the National Security Agency's spying practices, Mr. Obama said he would restrict the ability of intelligence agencies to gain access to phone records, and would ultimately move that data out of the hands of the government.

But in a speech at the Justice Department that seemed more calculated to reassure audiences at home and abroad than to force radical change, Mr. Obama defended the need for the broad surveillance net assembled by the N.S.A.

This juxtaposition raises an important point about news stories – in mainstream media, the canons of journalistic objectivity often produce news stories that contain competing frames as journalists attempt to balance various perspectives on the news. As such, framing effects – if tested using ecologically valid news reports – are rarely going to be the kind of powerful effects that are assumed by observers who claim that the media have inherent liberal or conservative ideological biases, though news stories produced under conditions of the rally effects in the early stages of external conflicts may be an exception. Instead, framing effects more typically operate through more subtle distinctions, and have conditional effects, such as whether stories are framed around individual exemplars or around larger units such as social groups and intersect with other cues within news content or predispositions within the audience members encountering them.

Another important point to recognize about competing frames is that, not only do they compete in news stories, but these news stories reflect a more general competition of frames within the larger political and social arenas (Chong and Druckman, 2007a,c). These frames are likely to be debated in the halls of government and within other social institutions. In turn, the media may shape the issues, frames, and terms that structure public deliberation about these issues. They shape the issues the public is talking about through the process of agenda setting (McCombs, 2004), as well as the way these issues are perceived and replicated in discussion (Chong and Druckman, 2007b; Iyengar, 1991). In other words, frames operating at various textual levels permeate the interplay of government, media, and the public, competing to influence larger macropolitical outcomes. In this interplay, we are likely to observe ebbs and flows in the relative influence of these competing frames.

In the case of the tension between civil liberties and national security, by 2013, the pendulums of both public policy and public opinion had forcefully swung back in the direction of civil liberties. Congress, the courts, and prominent politicians were critically evaluating the PATRIOT Act. As indicated in Chapter 2, polls showed that public opinion has shifted in regard to the policies of the war on terror (see Figures 2.1–2.3). Though the post-9/11 tension between national security and civil liberties was unique in many respects, the dynamic interplay between the media, public policy, and public opinion is replicating a common pattern. As we look back at the various eras in history that were reviewed in Chapter 2, the pendulum first swung in the direction of national security and the impetus was frequently provided by the onset of an external conflict, which precipitated policy actions sponsored by the executive branch. These actions were predicated on fear and justified in the name of protecting national security. Over time, the policy actions were often eroded by: (1) actions within the judicial branch in the form of court decisions based on preserving civil liberties, in concert with (2) a shift in public opinion responding to either the abatement or protraction of the conflict. The sociopolitical dynamics surrounding the PATRIOT Act largely fit this pattern, although they took much longer to reassert the importance of civil liberties than was typical in past conflicts. This may be partly a function of the amorphous and enduring War on Terror, though the findings in this book indicate that the framing of the War in Terror by journalists likely contributed to this slow response.

Ultimately, the example passages from news stories listed earlier reflect this pattern, albeit over a dozen-year span. But they also illustrate two important principles of the framing of terrorism, and indeed framing in general, that we hope our research has delivered. First, they show that the framing of a news story involves a complex interaction between elements operating at different textual levels. Second, they illustrate that the various frames contained within a single news story may offer competing perspectives and thus have diametrically opposite effects, thereby complicating our ability to observe framing effects on thoughts, attitudes, and behaviors if we do not approach that challenge with sensitivity, since both sides get equal treatment under the norms of journalist balance. This suggests that research seeking to understand the effects of framing must utilize factorial experimental designs that allow for the layering of cues and frames at different levels of the text, and their interaction with the predispositions that individuals bring with them to news consumption. This allows researchers to observe both complimentary and competing characteristics and their effects on cognitive outcomes, social judgments, and participatory behaviors, as we have here.

Such research deconstructing, isolating, and assessing the interactions of frames operating at various levels within a text, and their relation to individual differences, is essential for understanding the impact of messages on the public. By examining the impact of commonly observed frames, researchers can help society mitigate media power as a force of social control. In the case of the War on Terror, or future "threats to the homeland," such knowledge may subdue the amplitude of the pendulum swings between national security and civil liberties. Framing research lifts the veil on how personifying the threat of terrorism can alter thinking, foster intolerance, and even spur unjust political actions. In closing, we are reminded of the words of George Orwell, whose writing inspired us to subtitle this book *Covering "Big Brother."* He offered the following cautionary insights:

> Every war when it comes, or before it comes, is represented not as a war but as an act of self-defense against a homicidal maniac.... The essential job is to get people to recognise war propaganda when they see it, especially when it is disguised as peace propaganda.
>
> – George Orwell
> Review of F. P. Crozier's *The Men I Killed*
> New Statesman, August 1937

> In our time, political speech and writing are largely the defense of the indefensible.... But if thought corrupts language, language can also corrupt thought.
>
> – George Orwell
> *Politics and the English Language*, April 1946

Measurement Details for Arab Study

Dependent Variables

Group Evaluation Index

Respondents evaluated the target group according to four 7-point semantic-differential scales (foolish/wise, unfair/fair, threatening/nonthreatening, and dangerous/harmless). We used the mean of these items to create the group evaluation index (Cronbach's $\alpha = .87$, $M = 5.17$, $SD = 1.63$).

Tolerance for Extremists Index

Two statements, "the media should give extremist groups the opportunity to express their views" and "the media should not encourage extremist groups by providing news coverage" were used. Subjects rated their agreement with each statement using a 10-point scale, ranging from "strongly disagree" to "strongly agree." The second item was reverse-coded and averaged with the first item to create an index where a higher score means a more tolerant attitude (Inter-item $r = .39$, $M = 6.56$, $SD = 1.99$).

Support for Immigration Index

Two statements, "U.S. immigration guidelines should be more restrictive" and "U.S. restrictions on immigration have gone too far" were used. Again, a 10-point scale ranging from "strongly disagree" to "strongly agree" was used to assess participants' agreement with the statements. To create an index for support for immigration, the first item was reverse-coded and averaged with the second item (Inter-item $r = .58$, $M = 5.35$, $SD = 2.13$).

Minority Empowerment Index

Subjects were asked the following question: "How would you feel about these groups gaining more political power in the U.S.?" with reference to five minority categories, including Hispanic Americans, Arab Americans, Asian Americans, African Americans, and Native Americans. A 10-point scale, ranging from "extremely negative" to "extremely positive" was used. Scores were averaged across all five categories (Cronbach's $\alpha = .93$, $M = 7.04$, $SD = 2.02$).

APPENDIX B

Measurement Details for Response Latency

In addition to addressing response-time outliers, we also considered the potential differences in the rate of response as influenced by the individual and technological differences particular to each participant. For example, some people are naturally faster than others in answering questions or have faster Internet connections that may influence baseline response latencies. To control for this, Mulligan et al. (2003) make the following recommendation:

Researchers typically include in their models the latency or average latency on one or more simple, factual, nonpolitical questions considered to be indicative of respondents' baseline rate of response. Controlling for the baseline speed of response allows researchers to isolate between-respondent differences in response latency on particular survey questions from systematic differences in answering survey questions generally. (p. 294)

Accordingly, time scores used for our analyses were normalized by dividing time spent responding to the item battery by overall time spent completing preexperimental questions.

Following accepted practice in response latency measurement (Mulligan et al., 2003), outliers were assumed not to represent the actual time participants spent in answering questions and, instead, were replaced with corresponding sample mean scores. Although seemingly arbitrary, "trimming the tail of the latency distribution in this manner results in the loss of a very small proportion of the latencies and improves analysis by reducing the signal-to-noise ratio, allowing researchers to assess more clearly associations between accessibility and substantive variables of interest" (Mulligan et al., 2003, p. 293).

APPENDIX C

Measurement Details for Activist Study:
Close-Ended Responses

Dependent Variables

Tolerance for Extremists Index

Tolerance toward extreme groups was measured by asking respondents for their level of agreement with the following statements: "I feel sorry for groups that are the targets of FBI surveillance," "the media should give extremist groups the opportunity to express their views," "a group that is targeted by the FBI probably deserves the treatment it gets" (reverse-coded), and "the media should not encourage extremist groups by providing news coverage" (reverse-coded). Tolerance toward extreme groups was constructed by averaging respondents' answers on a 10-point scale (Cronbach's alpha = .75, $M = 6.00$, $SD = 1.77$).

Tolerance for Targeted Group Index

Tolerance for the targeted group was operationalized with an additive index of four statements taken from Marcus et al. (1995), but modified to fit the current social context. Subjects were asked how they felt about a set of statements regarding the treatment of the hypothetical group that had appeared on the manipulation stories: group members should be allowed to work as a teacher in public schools, hold public rallies, broadcast public access cable programs, and share their views over the Internet. Items were measured on 10-point scales from "strongly disagree" to "strongly agree." Responses were used to create an index averaging the scores from these items (Cronbach's $\alpha = .77$, $M = 7.12$, $SD = 1.86$).

National Security Concerns Index

For security concerns, an index was created by averaging the scores from two items asking subjects how concerned they are about their own safety and the safety of other people in the U.S. from violent acts by extremists (see Appendix A). Subjects rated their agreement with the statements using a

10-point scale, ranging from "not at all concerned" to "extremely concerned" (Cronbach's $\alpha = .80$, $M = 5.16$, $SD = 2.42$).

Group Evaluation Index

To construct a group evaluation variable, we asked participants to evaluate the fictional group described in the story (e.g., Arm America Front) using a series of six semantic differential items. Measured on a 7-point scale, the six group favorability items were: honest/dishonest, wise/foolish, good/evil, fair/biased, beneficial/detrimental, harmless/dangerous. For analyses, scores on these items were divided into three distinct groups based on whether the respondent's score was neutral, unfavorable, or favorable toward the group. The initial measures were scored on a 7-point scale, with 1 indicating the most negative evaluation of the group and 7 the most positive evaluation. As scores between three and four are essentially the midpoints, any respondent who scored between 19 and 24 was recoded as neutral ($n = 266$, 42.8%). Respondents who scored below 19 were recoded as unfavorable ($n = 199$, 32.0%). Finally, any respondent who scored higher than 24 was recoded as favorable ($n = 156$, 25.1%). While the most-liked/least-liked manipulation and evaluations of the group featured in the stimulus story were clearly related, they are distinct concepts. Of the respondents in the least-liked condition, 51.5% evaluated the group negatively, 37.4% neutrally, and 11.1% positively. Of the respondents in the most-liked condition, 12.9% evaluated the group negatively, 47.9% neutrally, and 39.2% positively (Cronbach's $\alpha = .89$, $M = 21.08$, $SD = 6.72$).

Willingness to Take Expressive Action

Respondents were asked to indicate how likely they would be to engage in various behaviors if the group portrayed in the stimulus materials attempted to establish a local chapter. This measure was composed of six items, each measured on a 7-point scale. These items included talking to friends and family, expressing their views to other people, sending a letter to an editor, contacting public officials, attending a public meeting, and attending a rally (Cronbach's $\alpha = .88$, $M = 24.64$, $SD = 12.01$).

Pre-Test Control Variables

Materialism Index

Materialism was constructed from three items asking how much importance respondents assigned to maintaining law and order, promoting a high rate of economic growth, and maintaining national security on a 10-point scale (Cronbach's $\alpha = .80$, $M = 7.72$, $SD = 1.74$).

Postmaterialism Index

Postmaterialism was constructed by asking how much importance respondents assigned to providing opportunities for people to express their opinions, preserving personal privacy, and protecting individual freedoms on a 10-point scale (Cronbach's $\alpha = .74$, $M = 8.20$, $SD = 1.43$).

Maternalism Index
Maternalism was developed from two items: "I worry about what happens to other people, even total strangers," and "it bothers me greatly to see other people get hurt." Both were measured on a 10-point scale (Cronbach's alpha $\alpha = .76$; $M = 7.65$; $SD = 1.74$).

Interpersonal Trust Index
Interpersonal trust was also assessed with two items: "if they got the chance, most people would take advantage of you" (reverse-coded), and "most people are honest" (Inter-item $r = .37$, $M = 5.74$, $SD = 1.66$).

Interpersonal Discussion Index
Interpersonal discussion was averaged across four measures of frequency of discussion about politics and current affairs with the following groups: family members, friends, neighbors, and co-workers. Frequency of discussion was measured on a 10-point scale (Cronbach's $\alpha = .77$, $M = 5.72$, $SD = 1.96$).

Newspaper Hard News Use Index
Our measure of newspaper hard news use averaged responses to four items. We assessed exposure (measured on an 11-point scale ranging from "never" to "frequently") and attention (measured on an 11-point scale ranging from "none" to "very close attention") for both international affairs and national politics, and local government and community issues (Cronbach's $\alpha = .86$, $M = 5.67$, $SD = 2.12$).

TV Hard News Use Index
Television hard news use was also constructed by averaging four items using similar scales to assess exposure and attention to international affairs and national politics, and to local government and community issues for television news stories (Cronbach's $\alpha = .79$, $M = 5.79$, $SD = 2.27$).

Post-Test Control Variables

Number of Story Segments Viewed
This measure was constructed based on computerized tracking of Web page views. All respondents were presented with the main fictional news story. After reading that story, respondents were invited to seek more related information by clicking on links to up to nine additional stories. Most respondents bypassed this opportunity. Nonetheless, this variable was included in analyses for control purposes, since it potentially increased the dosage of the manipulations and

added to the cognitive complexity of respondents' activated thoughts on the topic ($M = 1.26$, $SD = 2.22$, Range = 0–9).

Political Ideology Index
Ideology was tapped using a 7-point scale ranging from "very liberal" to "very conservative." Subjects were asked to locate themselves in terms of their position on social issues and economic issues ($M = 4.92$, $SD = 1.60$).

Positive Evaluation of the Target Group Index
Respondents were asked to assess the group targeted by the FBI using six semantic differential items (deceitful/honest, foolish/wise, evil/good, biased/fair, detrimental/beneficial, and dangerous/harmless). An additive index was created by averaging responses to these items (Cronbach's alpha = .90, $M = 3.53$, $SD = 1.09$).

For analyses, scores on the group evaluation index were divided into three distinct groups based on whether the respondent's score was neutral, unfavorable, or favorable toward the group. Values below 3.2 were treated as negative ($n = 199$; 32.0%). Values between 3.2 and 4.0 were classified as neutral ($n = 266$; 42.8%). Scores above 4.0 were considered favorable ($n = 156$; 25.1%). While the most-liked/least-liked manipulation and evaluations of the group featured in the stimulus story were clearly related, they are distinct concepts. Of the respondents in the least-liked condition, 51.5% evaluated the group negatively, 37.4% neutrally, and 11.1% positively. Of the respondents in the most-liked condition, 12.9% evaluated the group negatively, 47.9% neutrally, and 39.2% positively.

Then, this index was recoded into a categorical variable, with one representing "negative evaluation" and the other representing "neutral/positive evaluation." Since 7-point semantic differential scales were initially employed to measure responses, we considered the midpoint as neutral emotional response on the negative-positive continuum, and divided the index into two at the midpoint rather than at the mean score to increase face validity of this measure. A total of 53% of respondents reported negative evaluations of the target and the remaining 47% of respondents expressed either neutral or positive responses. This variable measured the effects of the political predisposition manipulation, while also serving as the predictor of cognitive complexity in our analysis of the direct and interactive effects of news framing.

Positive Evaluations of the FBI Index
Attitudes toward the FBI were assessed using the following six 7-point semantic differential items: honest/deceitful, foolish/wise, good/evil, fair/biased, detrimental/beneficial, dangerous/harmless. Before being averaged into an index (Cronbach's $\alpha = .86$, $M = 4.45$, $SD = .96$), items were recoded so that higher values represented support for the FBI.

Demographic Variables

Several basic demographic variables were used in the analyses including gender (female = 63.1%), age ($M = 27.33$, $SD = 12.69$), household income (assessed on a six-point scale; $Mdn = \$30,000-50,000$), and education (highest year of school completed; $M = 14.80$, $SD = 3.54$).

APPENDIX D

Measurement Details for Activist Study: Open-Ended Responses

According to the coding scheme, coders focused exclusively on manifest content in order to establish a high degree of reliability in coding three factors: the degrees of differentiation (i.e., the number of discrete cognitive categories mentioned), the average elaboration (i.e., the extent of detail provided for each mentioned category), and integration (i.e., the interconnectedness of the various cognitive categories mentioned) in the answers provided by respondents.

The coding instrument asked coders to focus on nine conceptual categories that had been identified from a preliminary examination of the open-ended responses. To establish differentiation, coders were asked to judge which constructs were present in an explicit fashion in each answer. For example, if a respondent mentioned in her answer the "importance of ensuring due process for all," this would have been coded as one construct (category #6: rights/constitution/freedoms). If in addition to mentioning due process, the respondent wrote about the threats posed to national security by the activities of certain groups and the need to ensure public safety, the coder, recognizing the presence of a second construct (category #5: national security/safety), would give this response a value of 2 in terms of construct differentiation.

In addition to the number of constructs present in the answer, coders were asked to rate the degree of elaboration for each concept that was present. Following the example given, just mentioning the importance of due process would have been coded as low in elaboration. A one-sentence explanation of due process would have received a medium elaboration grade, while an extended explanation of due process (two sentences or more on the subject) would have been coded as high on elaboration.

Finally, coders judged the degree of integration among concepts (i.e., the existence of logical connections among the categories used to express their thoughts and feelings). For example, an answer that stated: "I value the freedoms we are guaranteed in this society. It is okay to detain dangerous people without a judicial order," would be classified as low on integration since there is no apparent linkage among the categories in the response. On the other hand, an explanation that says: "Despite the importance of due process as a fundamental right granted by the Constitution, I think that in certain situations, where national security is at stake, those rights have to be limited for the protection of the majority," would have been coded as being high on concept integration.

For purposes of establishing intercoder reliability, the four coders worked as pairs and cross-coded 60 open-ended responses. This exercise yielded a 90% agreement rate among coders. These trained coders evaluated the remaining responses.

Number of Unique Categories
The number of unique categories mentioned by respondents ranged from 0 to 5, with about 21% giving no categories and about 73% giving 1 to 3 categories ($Mdn = 2, M = 1.63, SD = 1.19$). Fewer than 6% mentioned 4 or 5 categories. To adjust the skewed distribution of the variable, we took the square root of the number of unique categories and used this as our dependent measure ($M = 1.11, SD = 0.64$).

Level of Elaboration
The elaboration variable was constructed by summing up the elaboration levels for each category. It ranged from 0 to 15, with about 71% falling between 1 and 5 ($M = 2.51, SD = 2.16$). Again, to adjust for the skewed distribution of the variable, we took the square root of the overall elaboration score ($M = 1.35, SD = 0.83$).

Cognitive Complexity
Cognitive complexity was constructed by multiplying the square root of the unique categories by the square root of the level of elaboration ($Mdn = 2, M = 1.85, SD = 0.78$). The cognitive complexity index ranged from 0 to 6.71 ($M = 2.21, SD = 1.40$). The resulting variable had a relatively normal distribution.

Statements about National Security and Civil Liberties
Among the nine elaboration variables, elaboration of national security ($M = .50, SD = .84$) and elaboration of civil rights ($M = .50, SD = .89$) were used for some analyses. In addition, the elaboration variable was constructed by summing up the elaboration levels for each category. It ranged from 0 to 15, in which about 71% fell between 1 and 5 ($M = 2.51, SD = 2.16$).

Bibliography

9/11 Commission (2004). *The 9/11 Commission report: Final report of the National Commission on Terrorist Attacks upon the United States: Official government edition.* Washington, DC: U.S. Government Printing Office.

ABC News, Washington Post Poll (2001). Conducted by *ABC News/Washington Post* on November 27, 2001.

Ackerman, S., and Ball, J. (2014). Optic Nerve: Millions of Yahoo webcam images intercepted by GCHQ. *The Guardian*, February 27. http://www.theguardian.com/world/2014/feb/27/gchq-nsa-webcam-images-internet-yahoo.

Acton, W. H., Johnson, P. J., and Goldsmith, T. E. (1994). Structural knowledge assessment: Comparison to referent structures. *Journal of Educational Psychology, 86,* 303–311.

Aday, S. (2007). The framesetting effects of news: An experimental test of advocacy versus objectivist frames. *Journalism and Mass Communication Quarterly, 83,* 767–784.

Alien and Sedition Acts of 1798. *Archiving Early America.* Retrieved August 10, 2006, from http://www.earlyamerica.com/earlyamerica/milestones/sedition/.

Allen, M. (2005). House votes to curb Patriot Act: FBI's power to seize library records would be halted. *Washington Post,* June 16, A1.

Altschull, J. H. (1984). *Agents of power: The role of the news media in human affairs.* New York: Longman.

Ambinder, M. (2013). Sources: NSA sucks in data from 50 companies. *The Week,* June 6. http://theweek.com/article/index/245311/sources-nsa-sucks-in-data-from-50-companies.

American Civil Liberties Union (2001). Surveillance under the USA/PATRIOT Act, October 23. https://www.aclu.org/technology-and-liberty/surveillance-under-usapatriot-act.

Anderson, J. R. (1983). A spreading activation theory of memory. *Journal of Verbal Learning and Verbal Behavior, 22,* 261–295.

Anderson, J. R. (1985). *Cognitive psychology and its implications.* New York: Freeman.

Anderson, J. R., and Bower, G. H. (1973). *Human associative memory*. Washington, DC: Winston.

Armony, J. L., and LeDoux, J. E. (1997). How the brain processes emotional information. *Annals of the New York Academy of Sciences, 821,* 259–270.

Asher, H. (1998). *Polling and the public: What every citizen should know* (4th ed.). Washington, DC: CQ Press.

Associated Press. (2011). Senate Considers Patriot Act Despite Concerns. *Foxnews.com,* May 24. http://www.foxnews.com/politics/2011/05/24/senate-considers-patriot-act-despite-concerns-723552392/.

Associated Press. (2013). Broad coalition sues feds to halt electronic surveillance by National Security Agency. *Associated Press,* July 16. http://www.washingtonpost.com/national/broad-coalition-sues-feds-to-halt-electronic-surveillance-by-national-security-agency/2013/07/16/28e467a6-ee3a-11e2-bb32–725c8351a69e_story.html.

Babbie, E. R. (2004). *The Practice of social research* (10th ed.). Belmont, CA: Wadsworth Publishing.

Baker, P. (2010). Inside Obama's war on terror. *New York Times Magazine,* January 10. Retrieved December 17, 2012. http://www.nytimes.com/2010/01/17/magazine/17Terror-t.html.

Ball, J. (2013). NSA monitored calls of 35 world leaders after U.S. official handed over contacts. *Guardian,* October 24. http://www.theguardian.com/world/2013/oct/24/nsa-surveillance-world-leaders-calls/print.

Ball, J. (2014). Angry birds and "leaky" phone apps targeted by NSA and GCHQ for user data. *The Guardian,* January 28. http://www.theguardian.com/world/2014/jan/27/nsa-gchq-smartphone-app-angry-birds-personal-data.

Ball-Rokeach, S. J., and Loges, W. E. (1994). Choosing equality: The correspondence between attitudes about race and the values of equality. *Journal of Social Issues, 50,* 9–18.

Ball-Rokeach, S. J., and Rokeach, M. (1987). Contribution to the future study of public opinion: A symposium. *Public Opinion Quarterly, 51,* 184–185.

Barnett, R. (2013). The NSA's surveillance is unconstitutional: Congress or the courts should put a stop to these unreasonable data seizures. *Wall Street Journal,* July 11. online.wsj.com/article/SB10001424127887323823004578593591276402574.html.

Barry, B. (2001). *Culture and equality.* Cambridge, MA: Harvard University press.

Bateson, G. (1972). *Steps to an ecology of mind.* New York: Ballantine.

Bayley, E. R. (1982). *Joe McCarthy and the press.* New York: Pantheon Books.

Belknap, M. R. (1977). *Cold war political justice: The Smith Act, the Communist Party, and American civil liberties.* Westport, CT: Greenwood Press.

Benkler, Y. (2013). Fact: the NSA gets negligible intel from Americans' metadata. So end collection. *Guardian,* October 8. http://www.theguardian.com/commentisfree/2013/oct/08/nsa-bulk-metadata-surveillance-intelligence?CMP=twt_gu.

Bennett, W. L. (1990). Toward a theory of press-state relations in the United States. *Journal of Communication, 40,* 103–125.

Bennett, W. L. (2001). *News: The politics of illusion* (4th ed.). New York: Longman.

Bennett, W. L., Lawrence, R. G., and Livingston, S. (2006). None dare call it torture: Indexing and the limits of press independence in the Abu Ghraib scandal. *Journal of Communication, 56*(3), 467–485.

Bergman, P., and Sterman, D. (2013). Jihadist terrorism in America since 9/11. *CNN*, September 10. http://www.cnn.com/2013/09/09/opinion/bergen-terrorism-since-9-11/.

Berinsky, A. J. (2007). Assuming the costs of war: Events, elites, and American public support for military conflict. *The Journal of Politics, 69*, 975–997.

Berinsky, A. J. (2009). *In time of war: Understanding American public opinion from World War II to Iraq*. Chicago, IL: University of Chicago Press.

Berkowitz, L., and Rogers, K. H. (1986). A priming effect analysis of media influences. In J. Bryant and D. Zillman (eds.), *Perspectives on media effects* (pp. 57–81). Hillsdale, NJ: Erlbaum.

Billig, M., and Tajfel, H. (1973). Social categorization and similarity in intergroup behavior. *European Journal of Social Psychology, 3*, 27–51.

Bock, K., and Loebell, H. (1990). Framing sentences. *Cognition, 35*, 1–39.

Bohlen, C. (2001). In new war on terrorism, words are weapons too. *New York Times*, September 29, A11.

Bohn, K. (2003). PATRIOT Act report documents civil rights complaints. *CNN*, July 31. Retrieved January 27, 2007. http://www.cnn.com/2003/LAW/07/21/justice.civil.liberties/index.html?eref=sitesearch.

Bowen, G. L. (1989). Presidential action in public opinion about U.S. Nicaraguan policy: Limits to the "Rally Round the Flag" syndrome. *PS: Political Science and Politics, 22*, 793–800.

Boyle M. P., McCluskey, M. R., Devanathan, N., Stein, S. E., and McLeod, D. M. (2004). The influence of level of deviance and protest type on coverage of social protest in Wisconsin from 1960 to 1999. *Mass Communication and Society, 7*(1), 43–60.

Boyle, M. P., Schmierbach, M. P., Armstrong, C. L., Cho, J., McLeod, D. M., and Shah, D. V. (2006). Expressive responses to news stories about extremist groups: A framing experiment. *Journal of Communication, 56*, 271–288.

Brewer, P. R. (2002). Framing, value words, and citizens' explanations of their issue opinions. *Political Communication, 19*, 303–316.

Brewer, P. R. (2007). *Value war: Public opinion and the politics of gay rights*. Lanham, MD: Rowman & Littlefield Publishers.

Brewer, P. R., and Gross, K. (2010). Studying the effects of issue framing on public opinion about policy issues: Does what we see depend on how we look? In P. D'Angelo and J. A. Kuypers (eds.), *Doing news framing analysis: Empirical and theoretical perspectives* (pp. 159–186). New York: Routledge.

Bruner, J. (1957). On perceptual readiness. *Psychological Review, 64*, 123–152.

Cable News Network Poll (2006). Conducted by Opinion Research Corporation, August 30–September 2, 2006.

Cable News Network, USA Today Poll (2001). Conducted by Gallup Organization, September 14–September 15, 2001.

Cable News Network, USA Today Poll (2001–2006). Conducted by the Gallup Organization, November 1, 2001–October 22, 2006.

Campbell, D. T. (1958). Common fate, similarity, and other indices of the status of aggregates of persons as social entities. *Behavioral Science, 3*, 14–25.

Cappella, J. N., and Jamieson, K. H. (1997). *Spiral of cynicism: The press and the public good*. New York: Oxford University Press.

Carley, K. A. (1986). An approach for relating social structure to cognitive structure. *Journal of Mathematical Sociology, 12,* 137–189.

Carley, K. A., and Palmquist, M. (1992). Extracting, representing, and analyzing mental models. *Social Forces, 70,* 601–636.

Chaffee, Z. (1941). *Free speech in the United States.* Cambridge, MA: Harvard University Press.

Chaiken, S. (1980). Heuristic versus systematic information processing and the use of source message cues in persuasion. *Journal of Personality and Social Psychology, 39,* 752–766.

Cho, J., Boyle, M. P., Keum, H., Shevy, M. D., McLeod, D. M., and Shah, D. V. (2003). Media, terrorism, and emotionality: Emotional differences in media content and public reactions to the September 11th terrorist attacks. *Journal of Broadcasting & Electronic Media, 47,* 309–327.

Cho, J., Gil de Zuniga, H., Shah, D. V., and McLeod, D. M. (2006). Cue Convergence: Associative Effects on Social Intolerance. *Communication Research, 33,* 136–154.

Cho, J., Shah, D. V., McLeod, J. M., McLeod, D. M., Scholl, R. M., and Gotlieb, M. R. (2009). Campaigns, Reflection, and Deliberation: Advancing an O-S-R-O-R Model of Communication Effects. *Communication Theory, 19*(1), 66–88.

Chong, D., and Druckman, J. N. (2007a). Framing public opinion in competitive democracies. *American Political Science Review, 101*(04), 637–655.

Chong, D., and Druckman, J. N. (2007b). Framing theory. *Annual Review of Political Science, 10,* 103–126.

Chong, D., and Druckman, J. N. (2007c). A theory of framing and opinion formation in competitive elite environments. *Journal of Communication, 57*(1), 99–118.

Chwe, M. S. Y. (1999). Structure and strategy in collective action. *American Journal of Sociology, 105,* 128–156.

Clemetson, L. (2004). Homeland Security given data on Arab-Americans. *New York Times,* July 30. http://www.nytimes.com/2004/07/30/politics/30census.html.

Cloherty, J., and Thomas, P. (2010). Attorney General's blunt warning on terror attacks: AG Eric Holder says "Terrorists only have to be successful once." *ABC News,* December 21. http://abcnews.go.com/Politics/attorney-general-eric-holders-blunt-warning-terror-attacks/story?id=12444727.

Cohen, R. (2002). Homeland war on terror worries civil libertarians. *Newhouse News Service,* November 25.

Cohen, T. (2013). Snowden claims online Obama expanded "abusive" security programs. *CNN,* June 17. http://www.cnn.com/2013/06/17/politics/nsa-leaks/.

Collins, A. M., and Loftus, E. F. (1975). A spreading activation theory of semantic processing. *Psychological Review, 82,* 407–428.

Conery, B. (2009). Obama seeks Patriot Act extensions, defies liberties groups. *Washington Times,* September 16, p. A1.

D'Angelo, P. (2010). Conclusion: Arriving at the horizons of news framing analysis. In P. D'Angelo and J. A. Kuypers (eds.), *Doing news framing analysis: Empirical and theoretical perspectives* (pp. 356–368). New York: Routledge.

Daniels, R. (1975). *The decision to relocate Japanese Americans.* Philadelphia, PA: Lippincott.

Davis, D. W. and Silver, B. D. (2004). Civil liberties vs. security: Public opinion in the context of the terrorist attacks on America. *American Journal of Political Science, 48,* 28–46.

De Volpi, A., Marsh, G. E., Postol, T. A., and Stanford, G. S. (1981). *Born secret: The H-bomb, the Progressive Case, and national security*. New York: Pergamon Press.

De Vreese, C. H. (2005). News framing: Theory and typology. *Information Design Journal & Document Design, 13*, 48–59.

De Vreese, C. H. (2010). Framing the economy: Effects of journalistic news frames. In P. D'Angelo and J. A. Kuypers (eds.), *Doing news framing analysis: Empirical and theoretical perspectives* (pp. 187–214). New York: Routledge.

De Vreese, C. H. (2012). New avenues for framing research. *American Behavioral Scientist, 56*, 353–364.

Devine, P. G. (1989). Stereotypes and prejudice: Their automatic and controlled components. *Journal of Personality and Social Psychology, 56*, 5–18.

DeYoung, K. (2007). Terror database has quadrupled in four years: U.S. watch lists are drawn from massive clearinghouse. *Washington Post*, March 25, p. A1.

Diamond, J., and Cauley, L. (2006). Pre-9/11 records help flag suspicious calling. *USA Today*, May 22, p. A6.

Dilanian, K. and Lauter, D. (2013). Government is tracking all U.S. phone calls. *Los Angeles Times*, June 6. www.latimes.com/news/nationworld/nation/la-na-secret-surveillance-20130607,0,5263648.story.

Dinan, S. (2013). Patriot Act not a government fishing license, measure's author says. *Washington Times*, June 7, p. 10.

Doctorow, C. (2014). NSA trove shows 9:1 ratio of innocents to suspicious people in "targeted surveillance," July 6. http://boingboing.net/2014/07/06/huge-nsa-surveillance-trove-sh.html.

Domke, D. (2004). *God willing: Political fundamentalism in the White House, the "War on Terror" and the echoing press*. Ann Arbor, MI: Pluto Press.

Domke, D., Shah, D. V., and Wackman, D. (1998). Media priming effects: Accessibility, association, and activation. *International Journal of Public Opinion Research, 10*(1), 51–74.

Donohue, G. A., Olien, C. N., and Tichenor, P. J. (1985). A guard dog perspective on the role of media. *Journal of Communication, 45*, 115–132.

Dr. Gallup's finger on America's pulse. (1997). *The Economist, 344*, September 27, 95–97.

Druckman, J. N. (2001). The implications of framing effects for citizen competence. *Political Behavior, 23*, 225–256.

Druckman, J. N., and Nelson, K. R. (2003). Framing and deliberation: How citizens' conversations limit elite influence. *American Journal of Political Science, 47*, 729–745.

Dwyer, J. (2007). City police spied broadly before G.O.P. convention. *New York Times*, March 25, p. A1.

Eagly, A. H., and Chaiken, S. (1993). *The psychology of attitudes*. Fort Worth, TX: Harcourt Brace Jovanovich.

Edelman, M. (1993). Contestable categories and public opinion. *Political Communication, 10*, 231–242.

Eggen, D., and Solomon, J. (2007). FBI audit prompts calls for reform. *Washington Post*, March 10, p. A1.

Ellsberg, D. (2002). *Secrets: A memoir of Vietnam and the Pentagon papers*. New York: Viking Press.

Entman, R. M. (1991). Framing US coverage of international news: Contrasts in narratives of the KAL and Iran Air incidents. *Journal of Communication*, 41(4), 6–27.

Entman, R. M. (1993). Framing: Toward the clarification of a fractured paradigm. *Journal of Communication*, 43, 51–58.

Entman, R. M. (2003). Cascading activation: Contesting the White House's frame after 9/11. *Political Communication*, 20, 415–432.

Entman, R. M. (2004). *Projections of power: Framing news, public opinion, and U.S. foreign policy*. Chicago, IL: University of Chicago Press.

Entman, R. M., and Rojecki, A. (1993). Freezing out the public: Elite and media framing of the U.S. anti-nuclear movement. *Political Communication*, 10, 151–167.

Entman, R. M., Matthes, J., and Pellicano, L. (2009). Framing politics in the news: Nature, sources and effects. In K. Wahl-Jorgensen, and T. Hanitzsch (eds.), *Handbook of Journalism Studies*. London: Routledge.

Eveland, W. P., Jr. (2001). The cognitive mediation model of learning from the news: Evidence from nonelection, off-year election, and presidential election contexts. *Communication Research*, 28, 571–601.

Eveland, W. P., Jr., Marton, K., and Seo, M. (2004). Moving beyond "just the facts": The influence of online news on the content and structure of public affairs knowledge. *Communication Research*, 31, 82–108.

Favell, A. (1998). *Philosophies of integration: Immigration and the idea of citizenship in France and Britain*. New York: St. Martin's Press.

Fazio, R. H., Sanbonmatsu, D. M., Powell, M. C., and Kardes, F. R. (1986). On the automatic activation of attitudes. *Journal of Personality and Social Psychology*, 50, 229–238.

Feldman, S. (2003). Enforcing social conformity: A theory of authoritarianism. *Political Psychology*, 24, 41–74.

Feldman, S., and Stenner, K. (1997). Perceived threat and authoritarianism. *Political Psychology*, 18, 741–770.

Feuerlicht, R. S. (1971). *America's reign of terror: World War I, the Red Scare, and the Palmer Raids*. New York: Random House.

Field Poll (2001). Conducted by the Field Poll of California #2009. September 17–18. http://field.com/fieldpollonline/subscribers/Rls2009.pdf.

Fishman, M. (1980). *Manufacturing the news*. Austin, TX: University of Texas Press.

Fiske, S. T., and Taylor, S. E. (1991). *Social Cognition* (2nd ed.). New York: McGraw-Hill.

Forgas, J. P. (1992). Affect in social judgments and decisions: A multiprocess model. In M. Zanna (ed.), *Advances in experimental social psychology* (Vol. 25, pp. 227–275). Orlando, NE: Academic Press.

Forgas, J. P. (1995). Mood and judgment: The affect infusion model (AIM). *Psychological Bulletin*, 117, 39–66.

Fox News Poll (2001–2013). Conducted by *Opinion Dynamics*, May 9, 2001–April 16, 2013.

Fried, R. M. (1990). *Nightmare in red: The McCarthy era in perspective*. New York: Oxford University Press.

Frumin, A. (2013). Can the NSA convince Americans to surrender privacy concerns? *MSNBC*, June 14. http://tv.msnbc.com/2013/06/14/can-the-nsa-convince-americans-to-surrender-privacy-concerns/.

Gaertner, L., and Insko, C. A. (2001). On the measurement of social orientations in the minimal group paradigm: Norms as moderators of the expression of intergroup bias. *European Journal of Social Psychology, 31,* 143–154.

Gamson, W. A. (1992). *Talking politics.* New York: Cambridge University Press.

Gans, H. (1980). *Deciding what's news: A study of CBS Evening News, NBC Nightly News, Newsweek, and Time.* New York: Vintage Books.

Garrison, T. A. (2002). *The legal ideology of removal: The southern judiciary and the sovereignty of Native American nations.* Athens, GA: University of Georgia Press.

Garrow, D. J. (1983). *The FBI and Martin Luther King, Jr.* New York: Penguin Books.

Gellman, B. (2005). The FBI's secret scrutiny: In hunt for terrorists, bureau examines records of ordinary Americans. *Washington Post,* November 6, p. A1.

Gellman, B., and Poitras, L. (2013). U.S. mines Internet firms' data, documents show. *Washington Post,* June 6, p.A1.

Gellman, B., and Soltani, A. (2013). NSA tracking cellphone locations worldwide. *Washington Post,* December 27. http://www.washingtonpost.com/world/national-security/nsa-tracking-cellphone-locations-worldwide-snowden-documents-show/2013/12/04/5492873a-5cf2-11e3-bc56-c6ca94801fac_story.html.

Gellman, B., and Soltani, A. (2014). NSA surveillance program reaches "into the past" to retrieve, replay phone calls. *Washington Post,* March 18. http://www.washington post.com/world/national-security/nsa-surveillance-program-reaches-into-the-past-to-retrieve-replay-phone-calls/2014/03/18/226d2646-ade9-11e3-a49e-76adc9210f19_story.html.

Gellman, B., Linzer, D., and Leonnig, C. D. (2006). Surveillance net yields few suspects: NSA's hunt for terrorists scrutinizes thousands of Americans, but most are later cleared. *Washington Post,* February 5, p. A1.

Gellman, B., Blake, A. and Miller, G. (2013). Edward Snowden comes forward as source of NSA leaks. *Washington Post,* June 9. http://www.washingtonpost.com/politics/intelligence-leaders-push-back-on-leakers-media/2013/06/09/fff80160-d122-11e2-a73e-826d299ff459_story.html.

Gellman, B., Tate, J., and Soltani, A. (2014). In NSA-intercepted data, those not targeted far outnumber the foreigners who are. *Washington Post,* July 5. http://www.washingtonpost.com/world/national-security/in-nsa-intercepted-data-those-not-targeted-far-outnumber-the-foreigners-who-are/2014/07/05/8139adf8-045a-11e4-8572-4b1b969b6322_story.html.

Gibson, J. L. (1992). Alternative measures of political tolerance: Must tolerance be 'least-liked'? *American Journal of Political Science, 36,* 560–577.

Gitlin, T. (1980). *The whole world is watching: Mass media in the making and unmaking of the new left.* Berkeley: University of California Press.

Glassner, B. (1999). *The culture of fear.* New York: Basic books.

Glynn, C. J., Herbst, S., O'Keefe, G. J., and Shapiro, R. Y. (1999). *Public opinion.* Boulder, CO: Westview Press.

Goffman, E. (1974). *Frame analysis: An essay on the organization of experience.* Boston: Northeastern University Press.

Goldberg, M. (2004). Outlawing dissent. *Salon,* February 11. Retrieved January 28, 2007. http://www.salon.com/2004/02/11/cointelpro_3/.

Goldstein, R. J. (2001). *Political repression in modern America: 1870 to 1976.* Urbana, IL: University of Illinois Press.

Golebiowska, E. A. (1996). The "pictures in our heads" and individual-targeted tolerance. *The Journal of Politics, 58*(4), 1010–1034.

Gorman, S., and Valentino-DeVries, J. (2013). New details show broader NSA
surveillance reach. *Wall Street Journal,* August 21. http://online.wsj.com/article/
SB10001424127887324108204579022874091732470.html.

Graber, D. A. (1988). *Processing the News: How people tame the information tide*
(2nd ed.). New York: Longman.

Graber, D. (2002). *Mass media and American politics.* Washington, DC: CQ Press.

Gray, J. A. (1990). Brain Systems that mediate both emotion and cognition. *Cognition
and Emotion, 4,* 269–288.

Green, D. P., and Blair, I. V. (1995). Framing and the price elasticity of private and
public goods. *Journal of Consumer Psychology, 4,* 1–32.

Green, M. D. (1982). *The politics of Indian removal: Creek government and society in
crisis.* Lincoln: University of Nebraska Press.

Greenwald, G. (2012). Surveillance state evils: 35 years ago, a leading liberal Senator
issued a grave warning about allowing the NSA to spy domestically. *Salon,* April 21.
http://www.salon.com/2012/04/21/e_2/.

Greenwald, G. (2013a). NSA collecting phone records of millions of Verizon customers daily. *Guardian,* June 5 http://www.theguardian.com/world/2013/jun/06/
nsa-phone-records-verizon-court-order.

Greenwald, G. (2013b). XKeyscore: NSA tool collects nearly everything a user does
on the internet. *Guardian,* July 31. http://www.theguardian.com/world/2013/jul/31/
nsa-top-secret-program-online-data/print.

Greenwald, G. (2014). From Martin Luther King to Anonymous, the state targets
dissenters not just "bad guys." *The Guardian,* May 12. http://www.theguardian.com/
world/2014/may/13/glenn-greenwald-anonymous-mass-surveillance-governments-
nasa-no-place-to-hide.

Gross, K., Aday, S., and Brewer, P. R. (2004). A panel study of media effects on political
and social trust after September 11, 2001. *Press/Politics, 9,* 49–73.

Gurevitch, M., and Blumler, J. G. (1990). Political communication systems and democratic values. In J. Lichtenberg (ed.), *Democracy and the mass media* (pp. 269–289).
Cambridge: Cambridge University Press.

Hall, S., Critcher, C., Jefferson, T., Clarke, J., and Roberts, B. (1978). *Policing the crisis:
Mugging, the state, and law and order.* New York: Holmes and Meier.

Hallin, D. C. (1986). *The "uncensored war": The media and Vietnam.* Oxford: Oxford
University Press.

Hamilton, D. L. and Sherman, S. J. (1996). Perceiving persons and groups. *Psychological
Review, 103,* 336–355.

Hamilton, R. (1989). The effects of learner-generated elaborations on concept-learning
from prose. *Journal of Experimental Education, 57,* 205–217.

Hamud, R. (2003). We are fighting terror but killing freedom. *Newsweek,* September
21, p. 11.

Hanggli, R. (2012). Key factors in frame building: How strategic political actors shape
news media coverage. *American Behavioral Scientist, 56,* 300–317.

Harvey, R. (2003). *Amache: The story of Japanese internment in Colorado during
World War II.* Dallas, TX: Taylor Trade Publishing.

Hayashi, B. M. (2004). *Democratizing the enemy: The Japanese American internment.*
Princeton, NJ: Princeton University Press.

Hebdige, D. (1979). *Subculture, the Meaning of Style*. London: Methuen.
Heider, F. (1946). Attitudes and cognitive organization. *Journal of Psychology*, 21, 107–112.
Herman, E. S., and Chomsky, N. (1988). *Manufacturing consent: The political economy of the mass media*. New York: Pantheon.
Higgins, E. T. (1989). Knowledge accessibility and activation: Subjectivity and suffering from unconscious sources. In J. S. Uleman and J. A. Bargh (eds.), *Unintended thought* (pp. 75–123). New York: Guildford.
Higgins, E. T. (1996). Knowledge activation: Accessibility, applicability, and salience. In E. T. Higgins and A. W. Kruglanski (eds.), *Social psychology: Handbook of basic principles* (pp. 133–168). New York: Guilford.
Higgins, E. T., and Brendl, C. M. (1995). Accessibility and applicability: Some "activation rules" influencing judgment. *Journal of Experimental Social Psychology*, 31, 218–243.
Higgins, E. T., and King, G. (1981). Accessibility of social constructs: Information-processing consequences of individual and contextual variability. In N. Cantor and J. Kihlstrom (eds.), *Personality, cognition, and social interaction*. Hillsdale, NJ: Erlbaum.
Hines, A. (2012). FBI investigated "Occupy" as possible "terrorism" threat, internal documents show. *Huffington Post*, December 23. http://www.huffingtonpost.com/2012/12/23/fbi-occupy-wall-street_n_2355883.html.
Horowitz, I. L., and Bramson, V. C. (1979). Skokie, the ACLU and the endurance of democratic theory. *Law and Contemporary Problems*, 43, 328–349.
Horwitz, S. (2013). NSA collection of phone data is lawful, federal judge rules. *The Washington Post*, December 27. http://www.washingtonpost.com/world/national-security/nsa-collection-of-phone-data-is-lawful-federal-judge-rules/2013/12/27/4b99d96a-6f19-11e3-a523-fe73f0ff6b8d_story.html.
Hosenball, M., and Heavey, S. (2013). Obama administration defends Verizon phone record collection. *Reuters*, June 6. http://www.reuters.com/assets/print?aid=USBRE95502920130606.
Hoyt, E. P. (1969). *Palmer raids, 1919–1920: An attempt to suppress dissent*. New York: Seabury Press.
Huddy, L., Feldman, S., Taber, C., and Lahav, G. (2005). Threat, anxiety, and support of antiterrorism policies. *American Journal of Political Science*, 49, 593–608.
Huddy, L., Khatib, N., and Capelos, T. (2002). The polls-trends: Reactions to the terrorist attacks of September 11, 2001. *Public Opinion Quarterly*, 66, 418–450.
Hurwitz, J., and Mondak, J. J. (2002). Democratic principles, discrimination and political intolerance. *British Journal of Political Science*, 32, 93–118.
Hwang, H., Schmierbach, M., Paek, H., Gil de Zuniga, H., and Shah, D. V. (2006). Media dissociation, Internet use, and anti-war political participation: A case study of political dissent and action against the war in Iraq. *Mass Communication & Society*, 9, 461–483.
Hwang, H., Gotlieb, M. R., Nah, S., and McLeod, D. M. (2007). Applying a Cognitive Processing Model to Presidential Debate Effects: Post-Debate News Analysis and Primed Reflection. *Journal of Communication*, 57, 40–59.
Inglehart, R. (1971). The silent revolution in Europe: Intergenerational change in post-industrial societies. *American Political Science Review*, 65, 991–1017.

Inglehart, R. (1977). *The silent revolution: Changing values and political styles among Western Publics*. Princeton, NJ: Princeton University Press.

Isikoff, M. (2004). Intelligence: The Pentagon spying in America? *Newsweek*, June 21, p. 6.

Isikoff, M. (2005). Profiling: How the FBI tracks eco-terror suspects. *Newsweek*, November 21, p. 6.

Isikoff, M. (2006). The other big brother: The Pentagon has its own domestic spying program: Even its leaders say the outfit may have gone too far. *Newsweek*, January 30, p. 32.

Iyengar, S. (1991). *Is anyone responsible? How television frames political issues*. Chicago, IL: University of Chicago Press.

Iyengar, S., and Kinder, D. (1987). *News that matters*. Chicago: University of Chicago Press.

Iyengar, S., and Simon, A. (1994). News coverage of the Gulf crisis and public opinion: A study of agenda-setting, priming, and framing. In W. L. Bennett and D. Paletz (eds.), *Taken by storm* (pp. 167–185). Chicago, IL: University of Chicago Press.

Iyengar, S., Peters, M. D., Kinder, D. R., and Krosnick, J. A. (1984). The evening news and presidential evaluations. *Journal of Personality and Social Psychology, 46*, 778–787.

Jasperson, A. E., Shah, D. V., Watts, M., Faber, R. J., and Fan, D. P. (1998). Framing the public agenda: Media effects on the importance of the federal budget deficit. *Political Communication, 15*, 205–224.

Johnsey, A., Morrison, G. R., and Ross, S. M. (1992). Using elaboration strategies training in computer-based instruction to promote generative learning. *Contemporary Educational Psychology, 17*, 125–135.

Johnson, B. (2007). Alabama terror web site angers activists. *Huffington Post*, May 28. Retrieved January 28, 2007. http://www.huffingtonpost.com/huff-wires/20070528/web-site-terror/.

Judd, C. M., and Krosnick, J. A. (1989). The structural bases of consistency among political attitudes: Effects of political expertise and attitude importance. In A. Pratkanis, S. Beckler, and A. Greenwald (eds.), *Attitude structure and function* (pp. 99–128). Hillsdale, NJ: Erlbaum.

Kaid, L. L. (1997). Effects of the television spots on images of Dole and Clinton. *American Behavioral Scientist, 40*(8), 1085–1094.

Kaid, L. L., and Boydston, J. (1987). An experimental study of the effectiveness of negative political advertisements. *Communication Quarterly, 35*(2), 193–201.

Kam, C. D., and Kinder, D. R. (2007). Terrorism and ethnocentrism: Foundations of American support for the War on Terrorism. *The Journal of Politics, 69*, 320–338.

Kaplan, R. (2013). Eight months later, Edward Snowden defies labels. *CBS News*, December 29. http://www.cbsnews.com/news/eight-months-later-edward-snowden-defies-labels/.

Keen, J. (2001). Bush tells U.S. allies that it's "time for action." *USA Today*, November 7, p. 8A.

Keum, H., Hillback, E., Rojas, H., Hove, T., de Zuniga, H. G., Heather, M., Hawkins, J., Shah, D. V., and McLeod, D. M. (2003). *News framing of civic liberties restrictions: Conditional effects on security and tolerance judgments*. Paper presented at the meeting of the Association for Education in Journalism and Mass Communication, Kansas City, MO.

Keum, H., Hillback, E., Rojas, H., Gil de Zuniga, H., Shah, D. V., and McLeod, D. M. (2005). Personifying the radical: How news framing polarizes concerns and tolerance judgments. *Human Communication Research*, 31, 337–364.

Kinder, D. R., and Sanders, L. M. (1990). Mimicking political debate with survey questions. *Social Cognition*, 8, 73–103.

Kinder, D. R., and Sanders, L. M. (1996). *Divided by Color: Racial politics and democratic ideals*. Chicago, IL: University of Chicago Press.

Kinder, D. R., and Sears, D. O. (1985). Public opinion and political action. In G. Lindzey and E. Aronson (eds.), *Handbook of social psychology* (3rd ed., pp. 659–741). New York: Random House.

Kinsley, M. (2002). Many Americans tune in to their "inner Ashcroft." *Milwaukee Journal Sentinel*, January 6, 4J.

Klandermans, B., and Oegema, D. (1987). Potential networks, motivations, and barriers: Steps towards participation in social movements. *American Sociology Review*, 52, 519–531.

Klein, E. (2013). Edward Snowden: Patriot. *Washington Post*, August 9. http://www.washingtonpost.com/blogs/wonkblog/wp/2013/08/09/edward-snowden-patriot/.

Kline, R. B. (1998). *Principles and practice of structural equation modeling*. New York: Guilford Press.

Kosicki, G. M., and McLeod, J. M. (1990). Learning from political news: Effects of media images and information-processing strategies. In S. Kraus (ed.), *Mass communication and political information processing* (pp. 69–83). Hillsdale, NJ: Lawrence Erlbaum.

Krosnick, J. A., and Brannon, L. A. (1993). The impact of the Gulf War on the ingredients of presidential evaluations. *American Political Science Review*, 87, 963–975.

Krosnick, J. A., and Kinder, D. R. (1990). Altering the foundations of support for the president through priming. *American Political Science Review*, 84, 497–512.

Krosnick, J. A., Berent, M. K., and Boninger, D. S. (1994). Pockets of responsibility in the American electorate: Findings of a research program on attitude importance. *Political Communication*, 11, 391–411.

Kuklinski, J. H., and Hurley, N. L. (1994). On hearing and interpreting political messages: A cautionary tale of citizen cue-taking. *Journal of Politics*, 56, 729–751.

Kuklinski, J. H., Riggle, E., Ottati, V. Schwarz, N., and Wyer, R. S., Jr. (1991). The cognitive and affective bases of political tolerance judgments. *American Journal of Political Science*, 35(1), 1–27.

Lakoff, G. (2004). *Don't think of an elephant!: Know your values and frame the debate*. White River Junction, VT: Chelsea Green Publishing.

Landler, M. and Savage, C. (2014). Obama outlines calibrated curbs on phone spying. *New York Times*, January 17. http://www.nytimes.com/2014/01/18/us/politics/obama-nsa.html?_r=0.

Landay, J. S. (2006). FBI monitored anti-war group, may have infiltrated it, documents reveal: Concerns over surveillance raised – Efforts are legal, federal officials. *Seattle Times*, March 15, p. A1.

Lane, C. (2004). Secrecy allowed on 9/11 detention: High court declines to hear appeal. *Washington Post*, January 13, p. A1.

Langston, W., and Kramer, D. C. (1998). The representation of space in mental models derived from text. *Memory & Cognition*, 26, 247–262.

Lavine, H., Lodge, M., and Freitas, K. (2005). Threat, authoritarianism and selective exposure to information. *Political Psychology*, 26, 219–244.

Lawrence, J. M. (2001). War on terrorism: Anti-terror laws in place: Feds urgently implement crackdown. *Boston Globe*, October 27, 5.

Lawrence, R. G. (2000). Game-framing the issues: Tracking the strategy frame in public policy news. *Political Communication*, 17, 93–114.

Lawrence, R. G. (2010). Researching political news framing: Established ground and new horizons. In P. D'Angelo and J. A. Kuypers (eds.), *Doing news framing analysis: Empirical and theoretical perspectives* (pp. 265–286). New York: Routledge.

Lazo, J. K., Kinnel, J., Bussa, T., Fisher, A., and Collamer, N. (1999). Expert and lay mental models of ecosystems: Inferences for risk communication. *Risk: Health, Safety, and the Environment*, 10(1), 45–64.

LeDoux, J. E. (2000). Emotion circuits in the brain. *Annual Review of Neuroscience*, 23, 155–184.

Lemert, J. B., Wanta, W., and Lee, T. T. (1999). Party identification and negative advertising in a US Senate election. *Journal of Communication*, 49(2), 123–134.

Lichtblau, E. (2003a). Ashcroft's tour rallies supporters and detractors. *New York Times*, September 8, p. A1.

Lichtblau, E. (2003b). Bureau wants anti-terror units to review suspicious activities. *New York Times*, November 23, p. A12.

Lichtblau, E. (2004). F.B.I. goes knocking for political troublemakers. *New York Times*, August 16, p. A1.

Lichtblau, E. (2005). Large volume of F.B.I. files alarms U.S. activist groups. *New York Times*, July 18, p. A12.

Lichtblau, E. (2008). *Bush's war: The remaking of American justice*. New York: Pantheon.

Lieberman, J. I., and Collins, S. M. (2011). A "ticking time bomb": Counterterrorism lessons from the U.S. government's failure to prevent the Ft. Hood attack. A special report of the U.S. Senate Committee on Homeland Security and Government Affairs. February 3.

Lipset, S. M., and Raab, E. (1970). *The politics of unreason: Right-wing extremism in America, 1790–1970*. New York: Harper and Row.

Liptak, A., and Lichtblau, E. (2006). U.S. judge finds wiretap actions violate the law. *New York Times*, August 18, p. A1.

Liptak, A., and Schmidt, M. S. (2013). Judge upholds N.S.A.'s bulk collection of data on calls. *New York Times*, December 27. http://www.nytimes.com/2013/12/28/us/nsa-phone-surveillance-is-lawful-federal-judge-rules.html?hpw&rref=technology&_r=0.

Lochhead, C. (2003). Democrats seek rollback of Patriot Act: Meanwhile, Bush administration pushes for added anti-terrorist tools. *San Francisco Chronicle*, September 25, p. A4.

Lodge, M., and Stroh, P. (1993). Inside the mental voting booth: An impression-driven process model of candidate evaluation. In S. Iyengar and W. McGuire (eds.), *Explorations in political psychology* (pp. 225–263). London: Duke University Press.

Luskin, R. C. (1987). Measuring political sophistication. *American Journal of Political Science*, 31(4), 856–899.

Macy, M. W. (1991). Chains of cooperation: Threshold effects in collective action. *American Sociological Review*, 56, 730–747.

Maio, G. R., and Esses, V. M. (2001). The need for affect: Individual differences in the motivation to approach or avoid emotions. *Journal of Personality, 69*, 583–615.

Marcus, G. E. (2000). Emotions in politics. *Annual Review of Political Science, 3*, 221–50.

Marcus, G. E., Sullivan, J. L., Theiss-Morse, E., and Wood, S. L. (1995). *With malice toward some: How people make civil liberties judgments*. New York: Cambridge University Press.

Marcus, G. E., Neuman, W. R., and Mackuen, M. (2000). *Affective intelligence: The role of emotion in the making of political judgments*. Chicago, IL: University of Chicago Press.

Marcus, G. E., Sullivan, J. L., Theiss-Morse, E., and Stevens, D. (2005). The emotional foundation of political cognition: The impact of extrinsic anxiety on the formation of political tolerance judgments. *Political Psychology, 26*, 949–963.

Markus, H., and Zajonc, R. B. (1985). The cognitive perspective in social psychology. In G. Lindzey and E. Aronson (eds.), *The handbook of social psychology* (3rd ed., pp. 137–230). New York: Random House.

Mascaro, L. (2011). Patriot Act provisions extended just in time. *Los Angeles Times*, May 27, 649.

Matthes, J. (2007). Beyond accessibility?: Toward an on-line and memory-based model of framing effects.*Communications, 32*, 51–78.

Matthes, J. (2009). What's in a frame?: A content analysis of media framing studies in the world's leading communication journals, 1990–2005. *Journalism & Mass Communication Quarterly, 86*, 349–367.

Matthes, J. (2012). Framing politics: An integrative approach. *American Behavioral Scientist, 56*, 247–259.

Matthes, J., Morrison, K. R., and Schemer, C. (2010). A spiral of silence for some: Attitude certainty and the expression of political minority opinions. *Communication Research, 37*(6), 774–800.

Mayer, R. E. (1980). Elaboration techniques that increase the meaningfulness of technical text: An experimental test of the learning strategy hypothesis. *Journal of Educational Psychology, 72*, 770–784.

McClosky, H. (1964). Consensus and ideology in American politics. *American Political Science Review, 58*, 361–382.

McClosky, H., and Brill, A. (1983). *Dimensions of Tolerance: What Americans Believe About Civil Liberties*. New York: Russell Sage.

McCombs, M. E. (2004). *Setting the agenda: The mass media and public opinion*. Cambridge, MA: Polity Press.

McCombs, M. E. and Valenzuela, S. (2007). The Agenda-Setting Theory. *Cuadernos de Información, 20*, 44–50.

McConnell, A. R., Sherman, S. J., and Hamilton, D. L. (1994). On-line and memory-based aspects of individual and group target judgments. *Journal of Personality and Social Psychology, 67*, 173–185.

McGraw, K. M., and Ling, C. (2003). Media priming of presidential and group evaluations. *Political Communication, 20*, 23–40.

McLeod, D. M. (1995). Communicating deviance: The effects of television news coverage of social protest. *Journal of Broadcasting and Electronic Media, 39*, 4–19.

McLeod, D. M., and Detenber, B. H. (1999). Framing effects of television news coverage of social protest. *Journal of Communication, 49*, 3–23.

McLeod, D. M., and Hertog, J. K. (1992). The manufacture of "public opinion" by reporters: informal cues for public perceptions of protest groups. *Discourse & Society*, 3, 259–275.

McLeod, D. M., and Hertog, J. K. (1999). Social control and the mass media's role in the regulation of protest groups: The communicative acts perspective. In D. Demers and K. Viswanath (eds.), *Mass media, social control and social change*. Ames, IA: Iowa State University Press.

McLeod, D. M., Eveland, W. P. Jr., and Signorielli, N. (1994). Conflict and public opinion: Rallying effects of the Persian Gulf War. *Journalism Quarterly*, 71, 20–31.

McLeod, D. M., Detenber, B. H., and Eveland, W. P., Jr. (2001). Behind the third-person effect: Differentiating perceptual processes for self and other. *Journal of Communication*, 51(4), 678–695.

McLeod, J. M., Scheufele, D. A., and Moy, P. (1999a). Community, communication, and participation: The role of mass media and interpersonal discussion in local political participation in a public forum. *Political Communication*, 16, 315–336.

McLeod, J. M., Scheufele, D. A., Moy, P., Horowitz, E. M., Holbert, R. L., Zhang, W. W., Zubric, S., and Zubric, J. (1999b). Understanding deliberation: The effects of discussion networks on participation in a public forum. *Communication Research*, 26, 743–774.

McQuail, D. (1987). *Mass communication theory: An introduction*. Beverly Hills, CA: Sage.

Milbank, D. (2013). In AP, Rosen investigations, government makes criminals of reporters. *Washington Post*, May 21. http://www.washingtonpost.com/opinions/dana-milbank-in-ap-rosen-investigations-government-makes-criminals-of-reporters/2013/05/21/377af392-c24e-11e2-914f-a7aba60512a7_print.html.

Miller, J. M., and Krosnick, J. A. (1996). News media impact on the ingredients of presidential evaluations: A program of research on the priming hypothesis. In D. Mutz and P. Sniderman (eds.), *Political persuasion and attitude change* (pp. 79–100). Ann Arbor, MI: University of Michigan Press.

Mondak, J. (1993). Source cues and policy approval: The cognitive dynamics of public support for the Reagan agenda. *American Journal of Political Science*, 37, 186–212.

Morland, H. (1981). *The secret that exploded*. New York: Random House.

Mowat, F. (1985). *My discovery of America*. Boston: Atlantic Monthly Press.

Mueller, J. E. (1970). Presidential popularity from Truman to Johnson. *American Political Science Review*, 64, 18–34.

Mueller, J. E. (1973). *War, presidents and public opinion*. New York: John Wiley and Sons.

Mueller, J. E. (2006). *Overblown: How politicians and the terrorism industry inflate national security threats, and why we believe them*. Simon and Schuster.

Mulligan, K., Grant, J. T., Mockabee, S. T., and Monson, J. Q. (2003). Response latency methodology for survey research: Measurement and modeling strategies. *Political Analysis*, 11(3), 289–301.

Murdock, D. (2004). Guerilla in our midst. *National Review Online*, October 25. Retrieved January 7, 2007. http://www.nationalreview.com/articles/212651/guerilla-our-midst/deroy-murdock.

Nabi, R. L. (2003). Exploring the framing effects of emotion. Do discrete emotions differentially influence information accessibility, information seeking, and policy preference? *Communication Research*, 30, 224–247.

Neely, M. E. (1991). *The fate of liberty: Abraham Lincoln and civil liberties*. New York: Oxford University Press.

Nelson, T. E., and Kinder, D. R. (1996). Issue frames and group-centrism in American public opinion. *The Journal of Politics, 58*, 1055–1078.

Nelson, T. E., and Willey, E. A. (2001). Issue frames that strike a value balance: A political psychology perspective. In S. D. Reese, O. H. Gandy, and A. Grant (eds.), *Framing public life: Perspectives on media and our understanding of the social world* (pp. 245–266). Hillsdale, NJ: Erlbaum.

Nelson, T. E., Clawson, R. A., and Oxley, Z. M. (1997). Media framing of a civil liberties conflict and its effect on tolerance. *American Political Science Review, 91*, 567–583.

Nelson, T. E., Oxley, Z. M., and Clawson, R. A. (1997). Toward a psychology of framing effects. *Political Behavior, 19*, 221–246.

Neuman, W. R. (1981). Differentiation and integration: Two dimensions of political thinking. *American Journal of Sociology, 86*, 1236–1267.

Neuman, W. R., Just, M. R., and Crigler, A. N. (1992). *Common knowledge: News and the construction of political meaning*. Chicago: University of Chicago Press.

New York Times. (2013). Turn off the data vaccuum. *New York Times*, December 18. http://www.nytimes.com/2013/12/19/opinion/turn-off-the-data-vacuum.html.

New York Times. (2014). Edward Snowden: Whistleblower. *New York Times*, January 1. http://www.nytimes.com/2014/01/02/opinion/edward-snowden-whistle-blower.html?_r=0.

Ng, S. H. (1981). Equity theory and the allocation of rewards between groups. *European Journal of Social Psychology, 11*, 439–444.

Nichols, J. (2006). Feingold on Patriot Act: "The fight is not over." *Nation*, March 2. Retrieved August 22, 2012. http://www.thenation.com/blog/feingold-patriot-act-fight-not-over.

Noelle-Neumann, E. (1993). *The spiral of silence: Public opinion, our social skin* (2nd ed.). Chicago, IL: University of Chicago Press.

Novak, J. D., and Gowin, D. B. (1984). *Learning how to learn*. Cambridge: Cambridge University Press.

NPR, Harvard University, Henry J. Kaiser Family Foundation (2001). Conducted by ICR–International Communications Research, October 31–November 12.

NSA has your phone records: "Trust us" isn't good enough. (2006, May 12). *USA Today*, p. A14.

Nunn, C. Z., Crockett, H. J., and Williams, J. A. (1978). Tolerance for nonconformity: A national survey of Americans' changing commitment to civil liberties. San Francisco, CA: Jossey-Bass Publishers.

O'Connor, P. (2003). FBI questioning stuns Muslim arrested at his home: St. Louis man says his views aren't mainstream, but adds he's no terrorist. *St. Louis Post-Dispatch*, February 11, p. B1.

O'Reilly, K. (1983). *Hoover and the un-Americans: The FBI, HUAC, and the red menace*. Philadelphia: The Temple University Press.

O'Rourke, L. M. (2005). Congress to consider Patriot Act revisions: Some groups have criticized the post-Sept. 11 law as trampling on individual rights. *Sacramento Bee*, July 11, p. A6.

Paletz, D. L., and Entman, R. M. (1981). *Media power and politics*. New York: The Free Press.

Pan, Z., and Kosicki, G. M. (1993). Framing analysis: An approach to news discourse. *Political Communication*, 10, 55–75.

Parekh, B. (2000). *Rethinking multiculturism: Cultural diversity and political theory.* Cambridge, MA: Harvard University Press.

Parker, S. L. (1995). Toward an understanding of "rally" effects: Public opinion in the Persian Gulf War. *Public Opinion Quarterly*, 59, 526–546.

Parkinson, J. R. (2013). NSA: "Over 50" terror plots foiled by data dragnets full list of foiled plots will be provided to lawmakers, but not publicly. *ABCNews*, June 19. http://abcnews.go.com/Politics/nsa-director-50-potential-terrorist-attacks-thwarted-controversial/print?id=19428148.

Peffley, M., Hurwitz, J., and Knigge. P. (2001). A multiple values model of political tolerance. *Political Research Quarterly*, 54, 379–406.

Pember, D. R. (1969). The Smith Act as a restraint on the press. *Journalism Monographs*, 10, 1–32.

PEN American Center (2013). *Chilling Effects: NSA Survaillance Drives U.S. Writers to Self-Censor*, November 12. http://www.pen.org/sites/default/files/Chilling%20Effects_PEN%20American.pdf.

Petric, G., and Pinter, A. (2002). From social perception to public expression of opinion: A structural equation modeling approach to the spiral of silence. *International Journal of Public Opinion Research*, 14, 37–53.

Petty, R. E., and Cacioppo, J. T. (1986). *Communication and persuasion: Central and peripheral routes to attitude change.* New York: Springer-Verlag.

Petty, R. E., Unnava, R. H., and Strathman, A. J. (1991). Theories of attitude change. In T. S. Robertson and H. H. Kassarjian (eds.), *Handbook of consumer behavior* (pp. 241–280). Englewood Cliffs, NJ: Prentice-Hall.

Pew Research Center for the People & the Press Poll (2004–2013). Conducted by Pew Research Center, July 8, 2004–November 6, 2013.

Pincus, W. (2005a). Pentagon expanding its domestic surveillance activity: Fears of 9/11 terrorism spur proposals for new powers. *Washington Post*, November 27, p. A6.

Pincus, W. (2005b). Pentagon will review database on U.S. citizens. *Washington Post*, December 15, p. A1.

Posner, E. (2013). The NSA's metadata program is perfectly constitutional: Judge William Pauley, not Judge Richard Leon, got it right. *Slate*, December 30. http://www.slate.com/articles/news_and_politics/view_from_chicago/2013/...ot_it_right_the_nsa_s_metadata_program_is_perfectly_constitutional.html.

Price, V., and Tewksbury, D. (1997). News values and public opinion: A theoretical account of media priming and framing. In G. A. Barnett and F. J. Boster (eds.), *Progress in communication sciences: Advances in persuasion* (Vol. 13, pp. 173–212). Greenwich, CT: Ablex.

Price, V., Tewksbury, D., and Powers, E. (1997). Switching trains of thought: The impact of news frames on readers' cognitive responses. *Communication Research*, 24, 481–506.

Priest, D., and Arkin, W. M. (2010a). A hidden world, growing beyond control. *Washington Post*, July 19. http://projects.washingtonpost.com/top-secret-america/articles/a-hidden-world-growing-beyond-control/print/.

Priest, D., and Arkin, W. M. (2010b). Monitoring America. *Washington Post*, December 20. http://projects.washingtonpost.com/top-secret-america/articles/monitoring-america/print/.

Priest, D., and Arkin, W. M. (2011). *Top secret America: The rise of the new American security state*. New York: Little, Brown and Company.

Prothro, J. W., and Grigg, G. M. (1960). Fundamental principles of democracy: Bases of agreement and disagreement. *Journal of Politics*, 22, 276–294.

Purdum, T. S. (2001). After the attacks: The White House; Bush warns of a wrathful, shadowy and inventive war. *New York Times*, September 16, p. A2.

Putman, R. D. (2000). *Bowling alone: The collapse and revival of American community*. New York: Simon and Schuster.

Quattrone, G. A., and Tversky, A. (1988). Contrasting rational and psychological analyses of political choice. *The American Political Science Review*, 82, 719–737.

Quinnipiac University Poll (2013). Conducted by Polling Institute July 28–July 31.

Rabbie, J. M., Schot, J. C., and Visser, L. (1989). Social identity theory: A conceptual and empirical critique from the perspective of a behavioral interaction model. *European Journal of Social Psychology*, 19, 171–202.

Rachlin, A. (1988). *News as hegemonic reality: American political culture and the framing of news accounts*. New York: Praeger Publishers.

Rasinski, K. A., Berktold, J., Smith, T. W., and Albertson, B. L. (2002). America recovers: A Follow-up to a national study of public response to the September 11 terrorist attacks. *NORC Report*. Retrieved August 8, 2003. http://www.norc.uchicago.edu/projects/reaction/pubresp2.pdf.

Rayman, N. (2013). Top 10 international news stories. *Time*, December 4. http://world.time.com/2013/12/04/world/slide/top-10-international-news-stories/.

Redish, M. H. (2005). *The logic of persecution: Free expression and the McCarthy era*. Stanford, CA: Stanford University Press.

Reese, S. D. (2001). Prologue – Framing public life: A bridging model for media research. In S. D. Reese, O. H. Gandy, and A. Grant (eds.), *Framing public life: Perspectives on media and our understanding of the social world* (pp. 7–31). Hillsdale, NJ: Erlbaum.

Regan, T. (2004). Pentagon seeks OK to spy on Americans. *The Christian Science Monitor Online*, June 17. http://www.csmonitor.com/2004/0617/dailUpdate.html.

Rhee, J. W. (1997). Strategy and issue frames in election campaign coverage: A social cognitive account of framing effects. *Journal of Communication*, 47, 26–48.

Richardson, J. D. (2005). Switching social identities: The influence of editorial framing on reader attitudes toward affirmative action and African Americans. *Communication Research*, 32, 503–528.

Richey, W., and Feldmann, L. (2003). Has post-9/11 dragnet gone too far? *Christian Science Monitor*, September 12, p. 1.

Risen, J., and Lichtblau, E. (2005). Bush lets U.S. spy on callers without courts. *New York Times*, December 16, p. A1.

Risen, J., and Poitras, L. (2014). N.S.A. collecting millions of faces from Web images. *The New York Times*, May 31. http://www.nytimes.com/2014/06/01/us/nsa-collecting-millions-of-faces-from-web-images.html?_r=0.

Roberts, D., and Ackerman, S. (2013). America's surveillance state: Anger swells after data revelations – senior politicians reveal that US counter-terrorism efforts have swept up personal data from American citizens for years. *Guardian*, June 6. http://www.theguardian.com/world/2013/jun/06/obama-administration-nsa-verizon-records.

Rokeach, M. (1968). *Beliefs, attitudes, and values*. San Francisco: Jossey-Bass.

Roskos-Ewoldsen, D. R. (1997). Attitude accessibility and persuasion: Review and a transactive model. In B. Burleson (ed.), *Communication yearbook 20* (pp. 185–225). Beverly Hills, CA: Sage.

Rudenstine, D. (1996). *The day the presses stopped: A history of the Pentagon papers case*. Berkeley, CA: University of California Press.

Rumold, M. (2011). EFF uncovers widespread FBI intelligence violations. *EFF*, January 30. https://www.eff.org/deeplinks/2011/01/eff-releases-report-detailing-fbi-intelligence.

Rye, J. A., and Rubba, P. A. (1998). An exploration of the concept map as an interview tool to facilitate the externalization of students' understandings about global atmospheric change. *Journal of Research in Science Teaching*, 35, 521–546.

Said, E. (2003). *Orientalism*. New York: Vintage Books.

Sanger, D. E., and Savage, C. (2013). Obama is urged to sharply curb N.S.A. data mining. *New York Times*, December 18. www.nytimes.com/2013/12/19/us/politics/report-on-nsa-surveillance-tactics.html?_r=0.

Sanger, D. E. and Shanker, T. (2014). N.S.A. devises radio pathway into computers. *The New York Times*, January 14. http://www.nytimes.com/2014/01/15/us/nsa-effort-pries-open-computers-not-connected-to-internet.html.

Savage, C. (2009). Battle looms over the Patriot Act. *New York Times*, September 20, p. A21.

Savage, C. (2011). Senators say Patriot Act is being misinterpreted. *New York Times*, May 26. http://www.nytimes.com/2011/05/27/us/27patriot.html.

Savage, C. (2013). U.S. weighing wide overhaul of surveillance. *New York Times*, May 8, p. A1.

Savage, C., and Shane, S. (2013). Top-secret court castigated N.S.A. on surveillance. *New York Times*, August 21. http://www.nytimes.com/2013/08/22/us/2011-ruling-found-an-nsa-program-unconstitutional.html?_r=0&pagewanted=print.

Scarbrough, E. (1984). *Political ideology and voting: An exploratory study*. New York: Oxford University Press.

Scheufele, D. A. (1999). Framing as a theory of media effects. *Journal of Communication*, 49, 103–122.

Scheufele, D. A. (2000). Agenda-setting, priming, and framing revisited: Another look at cognitive effects of political communication. *Mass Communication & Society*, 3, 297–316.

Scheufele, D. A., and Eveland, W. P. (2001). Perceptions of "public opinion" and "public" opinion expression. *International Journal of Public Opinion Research*, 13, 25–44.

Scheufele, D. A., and Tewksbury, D. (2007). Framing, agenda setting, and priming: the evolution of three media effects models. *Journal of Communication*, 57, 9–20.

Scheufele, D. A., Shanahan, J., and Lee, E. (2001). Real talk: Manipulating the dependent variable in spiral of silence research. *Communication Research*, 28, 304–324.

Schleuder, J., McCombs, M., and Wanta, W. (1991). Inside the agenda-setting process: How political advertising and TV news prime viewers to think about issues and candidates. In F. Biocca (ed.), *Television and political advertising, Vol. 1: Psychological processes* (pp. 265–309). Hillsdale, NJ: Erlbaum.

Schneier, B. (2013). Mission creep: When everything is terrorism. *Atlantic*, July 16. http://www.theatlantic.com/politics/print/2013/07/mission-creep-when-everything-is-terrorism/277844/.

Shah, D. V. (2001). The collision of convictions: Values framing and value judgments. In R. P. Hart and D. Shaw (eds.), *Communication and U.S. elections: New agendas*. Lanham, MD: Rowman and Littlefield Publishers.

Shah, D. V., Domke, D., and Wackman, D. B. (1996). To thine own self be true: Values, framing and voter decision-making strategies. *Communication Research*, 23, 509–560.

Shah, D. V., McLeod, J. M., and Yoon, S. H. (2001). Communication, context, and community – An exploration of print, broadcast, and Internet influences. *Communication Research*, 28(4), 464–506.

Shah, D. V., Domke, D., and Wackman, D. B. (2001). The effects of value framing on political judgment and reasoning. In S. D. Reese, O. H. Gandy, and A. Grant (eds.), *Framing public life: Perspectives on media and our understanding of the social world* (pp. 227–244). Hillsdale, NJ: Erlbaum.

Shah, D. V., Zubric, J., Keum, H., Armstrong, C. L., Boyle, M. P., and Guggenheim, L. D. (2001). *The interplay of news frames and elite cues: Conditional influence on the activation of mental models*. Paper presented to the Association for Education in Journalism and Mass Communication, Washington, DC.

Shah, D. V., Watts, M. D., Domke, D., and Fan, D. P. (2002). News framing and cueing of issue regimes: Explaining Clinton's public approval in spite of scandal. *Public Opinion Quarterly*, 66, 339–370.

Shah, D. V., Kwak, N., Schmierbach, M., and Zubric, J. (2004). The interplay of news frames on cognitive complexity. *Human Communication Research*, 30, 102–120.

Shah, D. V., Cho, J., Eveland, W. P., Jr., and Kwak, N. (2005). Information and expression in a digital age modeling Internet effects on civic participation. *Communication Research*, 32, 531–565.

Shah, D. V., McLeod, D. M., Gotlieb, M. R., and Lee, N. J. (2009). Framing and Agenda Setting. In R. L. Nabi and M. B. Oliver (eds.), The Sage handbook of media processes and effects (pp. 83–98). Thousand Oaks, CA: Sage.

Shah, D. V. Boyle, M. P., Schmierbach, M. G., Keum, H., and Armstrong, C. L. (2010). Specificity, complexity, and validity: Rescuing experimental research on framing effects. In P. D'Angelo and J. A. Kuypers (eds.), *Doing news framing analysis: Empirical and theoretical perspectives* (pp. 215–232). New York: Routledge.

Shanks, C. (2001). *Immigration and the politics of American sovereignty*. Ann Arbor: The University of Michigan Press.

Sheatsley, P. B., and Feldman, J. J. (1965). A national survey of public reactions and behavior. In B. S. Greenberg and E. B. Parker (eds.), *The Kennedy assassination and the American public* (pp. 149–177). Stanford, CA: Stanford University Press.

Shen, F. (2004a). Chronic accessibility and individual cognitions: Examining the effects of message frames in political advertisements. *Journal of Communication*, 54, 123–137.

Shen, F. (2004b). Effects of news frames and schemas on individuals' issue interpretations and attitudes. *Journalism and Mass Communication Quarterly, 81*, 400–416.

Shen, F., and Edwards, H. H. (2006). Economic individualism, humanitarianism, and welfare reform: A value-based account of framing effects. *Journal of Communication, 55*, 795–809.

Sheridan, M. B. (2004). Interviews of Muslims to broaden. *Washington Post*, July 17, p. A1.

Sherman, M. (2005). FBI says it has files on rights groups. *Associated Press*, July 18.

Sherman, M. (2013). Gov't obtains wide AP phone records in probe. *Associated Press*, May 13.

Shoemaker, P. J. (1982). The perceived legitimacy of deviant political groups: Two experiments on media effects. *Communication Research, 9*, 249–286.

Shoemaker, P. J., and Reese, S. D. (1996). *Mediating the message: Theories of influence on mass media content* (2nd ed.). New York: Longman.

Sigal, L. V. (1973). *Reporters and officials: The organization and politics of newsmaking*. Lexington, MA: D. C. Heath.

Smith, J. A. (1999). *War and press freedom: The problem of prerogative power*. Oxford: Oxford University Press.

Smith, T. W., Rasinski, K. A., and Toce, M. (2001). America rebounds: A national study of public response to the September 11 terrorist attacks. *NORC Report*. Retrieved August 8, 2003. http://www.norc.uchicago.edu/projects/reaction/pubresp.pdf.

Sniderman, P. M., Fletcher, J. F., Russell, P. H., and Tetlock, P. E. (1996). *The Clash of Rights: Liberty, Equality,and Legitimacy in Pluralist Democracy*. New Haven, CT: Yale University Press.

Sniderman, P., Hagenjdoorn, L., and Prior, M. (2004). Predisposing factors and situational triggers: Exclusionary reactions to immigrant minorities. *American Political Science Review, 98*, 35–49.

Sniffen, M. J. (2006). U.S. government terror ratings draw outrage. *Associated Press*, December 2.

Snow, D. A., and Benford, R. D. (1988). Ideology, frame resonance, and participation mobilization. *International Social Movement Research, 1*, 197–217.

Soley, L. C. (1992). *The news shapers: The sources who explain the news*. New York: Praeger.

Solomon, J. (2007). FBI finds it frequently overstepped in collecting data. *Washington Post*, June 14, p. A1.

Soltani, A., Peterson, A., and Gellman, B. (2013). NSA uses Google cookies to pinpoint targets for hacking. *The Washington Post*, December 10. http://www.washingtonpost .com/blogs/the-switch/wp/2013/12/10/nsa-uses-google-cookies-to-pinpoint-targets-for-hacking/.

Sotirovic, M., and McLeod, J. M. (2001). Values, communication behavior, and political participation. *Political Communication, 18*, 273–300.

Sotirovic, M., and McLeod, J. M. (2004). Knowledge as understanding: The information processing approach to political learning. In L. L. Kaid (ed.), *Handbook of political communications research* (pp. 357–394). Mahwah, NJ: Erlbaum.

Stelter, B., and Shear, M. D. (2013). Justice Dept. investigated Fox reporter over leak. *New York Times*, May 21, p. A16.

Stolberg, S. G. (2006a). Patriot Act revisions pass house, sending measure to President. *New York Times*, March 7, p. A20.

Stolberg, S. G. (2006b). Senate passes legislation to renew Patriot Act. *New York Times*, March 3, p. A14.

Stone, G. R. (2004). *Perilous times: Free speech in wartime from the Sedition Act of 1798 to the War on Terrorism*. New York: W. W. Norton and Company, Inc.

Stouffer, S. A. (1955/1963). *Communism, conformity and civil liberties: A cross-section of the nation speaks its mind*. Gloucester, MA: Peter Smith.

Stout, D. (2007). White House says judiciary will monitor spy program. *The New York Times*, January 17, p. A1.

Straight, M. (1954). *Trial by television*. Boston: Beacon Press.

Sullivan, J. L., and Marcus, G. E. (1988). A note on "trends in political tolerance." *Public Opinion Quarterly*, 52, 26–32.

Sullivan, J. L., Piereson J., and Marcus, G. E. (1979). An alternative conceptualization of political tolerance: Illusory increases 1950s–1970s. *American Political Science Review*, 73, 781–794.

Sullivan, J., Marcus, G. E., Feldman, S., and Piereson, J. (1981). The sources of political tolerance: A multivariate analysis. *American Political Science Review*, 75, 92–106.

Sullivan, J. L., Piereson, J., and Marcus, G. E. (1982). *Political tolerance and American democracy*. Chicago, IL: University of Chicago Press.

Susskind, J., Maurer, K., Thakkar, V., Hamilton, D. L., and Sherman, J. W. (1999). Perceiving individuals and groups: Expectancies, dispositional inferences, and causal attributions. *Journal of Personality and Social Psychology*, 76, 181–191.

Tajfel, H., and Billig, M. (1974). Familiarity and categorization in intergroup behavior. *Journal of Experimental Social Psychology*, 10, 159–170.

Tajfel, H., and Turner, J. C. (1979). An integrative theory of intergroup conflict. In W. G. Austin and S. Worchel (eds.), *The social psychology of intergroup relations* (pp. 33–47). Chicago, IL: Nelson-Hall.

Tajfel, H., Billig, M., Bundy, R. P., and Flarnent, C. (1971). Social categorization and intergroup behavior. *European Journal of Social Psychology*, 1, 149–178.

Terkildsen, N., and Schnell, F. (1997). How media frames move public opinion: An analysis of the women's movement. *Political Research Quarterly*, 4, 879–900.

Tetlock, P. E. (1986). A value pluralism model of ideological reasoning. *Journal of Personality and Social Psychology*, 50, 819–827.

Tetlock, P. E., Armor, D., and Peterson, R. S. (1994). The slavery debate in antebellum America: Cognitive style, value conflict, and the limits of compromise. *Journal of Personality and Social Psychology*, 66, 115–126.

Tuchman, G. (1978). *Making news: A study in the construction of reality*. New York: The Free Press.

Turner, J. C., Hogg, M. A., Oakes, P. J., Reicher, S. D., and Wetherell, M. S. (1987). *Rediscovering the social group: A self-categorization theory*. New York: Basil Blackwell.

Tversky, A., and Kahneman, D. (1973). Availability: A heuristic for judging frequency and probability. *Cognitive Psychology*, 5, 207–222.

Tversky, A., and Kahneman, D. (1981). The framing of decisions and the psychology of choice. *Science*, 211, 453–458.

Ungar, S. J. (1989). *The papers and the papers: An account of the legal and political battle over the Pentagon Papers*. New York: Columbia University Press.

Valentino, N. A., Beckmann, M. N., and Burh, T. A. (2001). A spiral of cynicism for some: The contingent effects of campaign news frames on participation and confidence in government. *Political Communication, 18,* 347–367.

Valkenberg, P. M., Semetko, H. A., and de Vreese, C. H. (1999). The effects of news frames and readers' thoughts and recall. *Communication Research, 26,* 550–569.

Verba, S., Schlozman, K. L., and Brady, H. E. (1995). *Voice and equality: Civic volunteerism in American politics.* Cambridge, MA: Harvard University Press.

Vraga, E. K., Carr, D. J., Nytes, J. P., and Shah, D. V. (2010). Precision vs. realism on the framing continuum: Understanding the underpinnings of media effects. *Political Communication, 27,* 1–19.

Wallace, J. D., and Mintzes, J. (1990). The concept map as a research tool: Exploring conceptual change in biology. *Journal of Research in Science Teaching, 27,* 1033–1052.

Wallace-Wells, B. (2011). Patriot Act: The kitchen-sink approach to national security. *New York Times Magazine,* September 7. http://nymag.com/news/9–11/10th-anniversary/patriot-act/.

Wanta, W., Golan, G., and Lee, C. (2004). Agenda setting and international news: Media influence on public perceptions of foreign nations. *Journalism & Mass Communication Quarterly, 81,* 364–377.

Waterman, S. (2013). NSA chief's admission of misleading numbers adds to Obama administration blunders. *Washington Times,* October 2. http://www.washingtontimes.com/news/2013/oct/2/nsa-chief-figures-foiled-terror-plots-mis leading/?page=all.

Weisman, J. (2007). Democrats to widen conflict with Bush. *Washington Post,* April 2, p. A1.

Wolf, N. (2012). Revealed: how the FBI coordinated the crackdown on Occupy: New documents prove what was once dismissed as paranoid fantasy: totally integrated corporate-state repression of dissent. *Guardian,* December 29. http://www.theguardian.com/commentisfree/2012/dec/29/fbi-coordinated-crackdown-occupy.

Woloshyn, V. E., Willoughby, T., Wood, E., and Pressley, M. (1990). Elaborative interrogation facilitates adult learning of factual paragraphs. *Journal of Educational Psychology, 82,* 513–524.

Wyer, R., and Srull, T. (1986). Human cognition in its social context. *Psychological Review, 93,* 322–359.

Wyer, R., and Srull, T. (1989). *Memory and cognition in its social context.* Hillsdale, NJ: Erlbaum.

Yancey, D. (1998). *Life in a Japanese American internment camp.* San Diego, CA: Lucent Books.

Zaller, J. R. (1992). *The nature and origins of mass opinion.* New York: Cambridge University Press.

Index

Other Books in the Series (*continued from page iii*)